85-
BMW
2013

Franklin D. Roosevelt's Rhetorical Presidency

President Franklin D. Roosevelt, First Inaugural Address, March 4, 1933
(UPI/Bettmann Newsphotos: The Bettmann Archive)

Franklin D. Roosevelt's Rhetorical Presidency

HALFORD R. RYAN

CONTRIBUTIONS IN POLITICAL SCIENCE, NUMBER 206

GREENWOOD PRESS
New York • Westport, Connecticut • London

Library of Congress Cataloging-in-Publication Data

Ryan, Halford Ross.
  Franklin D. Roosevelt's rhetorical presidency / Halford R. Ryan.
    p. cm.—(Contributions in political science, ISSN 0147–1066
  ; no. 206)
  Bibliography: p.
  Includes index.
  ISBN 0–313–25567–9 (lib. bdg. : alk. paper)
  1. Roosevelt, Franklin D. (Franklin Delano), 1882–1945—Oratory.
2. Roosevelt, Franklin D. (Franklin Delano), 1882–1945—Literary
art.   3. Political oratory—United States—History—20th century.
4. Rhetoric—Political aspects—United States—History—20th
century.   5. United States—Politics and government—1933–1945.
I. Title. II. Series.
E807.R93   1988
973.917'092'4—dc19   87–31778

British Library Cataloguing in Publication Data is available.

Library of Congress Catalog Card Number: 87–31778
ISBN: 0–313–25567–9
ISSN: 0147–1066

First published in 1988

Greenwood Press, Inc.
88 Post Road West, Westport, Connecticut 06881

Printed in the United States of America

∞™

The paper used in this book complies with the
Permanent Paper Standard issued by the National
Information Standards Organization (Z39.48–1984).

10 9 8 7 6 5 4 3 2 1

Copyright Acknowledgments

The author and publisher are grateful to the following for permission to reprint the following material:

Homer S. Cummings Papers (#9973), Manuscripts Department, University of Virginia Library.

The Reminiscences of Samuel I. Rosenman, (1959), in the Oral History Collection of Columbia University. The copyright is held by The Trustees of Columbia University in the City of New York.

Halford Ross Ryan, "Roosevelt's First Inaugural: A Study of Technique," *Quarterly Journal of Speech* 65 (1979): 137–49. Courtesy of William Work, Speech Communication Association.

Halford Ross Ryan, "Roosevelt's Fourth Inaugural Address: A Study of Its Composition," *Quarterly Journal of Speech* 67 (1981): 157–66. Courtesy of William Work, Speech Communication Association.

The frontispiece photograph of Roosevelt's First Inaugural Address is by permission of UPI/Bettmann Newsphotos: The Bettmann Archive.

Contents

Tables

Preface

This book is not about President Franklin Delano Roosevelt's life, nor is it a history of his New Deal. However, these matters are within the scope of the book as it discusses how FDR addressed the American people in order to persuade them to accept him and his political agenda from 1933 to 1945. The focus is on the rhetorical relationship between Roosevelt and the national audience.

The progression of chapters in this book is probably not what one usually expects in a work on Roosevelt, but they were ordered purposefully. Chapter 1 argues that FDR was a prototypical rhetorical president. That is, he delivered programmatic speeches and Fireside Chats to move the people to elect and support him, and to persuade the public to move the Congress to adopt his legislative agenda. He practiced the tenets of the rhetorical presidency and usually excelled in all of them. However, there were occasions when he did not succeed as he would have wished, as in the purge and Court fight. These instances, too, are worth investigating for their own intrinsic merit and for the purposes of demonstrating how certain tenets should not have been abused and how they could have been practiced better.

Chapter 2 treats his speech delivery. Roosevelt's delivery has not been given the credit it deserves in his persuasive practices. The fact is that his audiences saw him speaking in person, heard him on the radio, watched him on the newsreels, and read his speeches in the newspapers. Except for in the print media, FDR communicated his thoughts to audiences by combining the artistry of his words with the artifice of his skills in speech delivery. This chapter makes the focused argument that his delivery was a potent factor in his rhetorical presidency.

Naturally flowing from a treatment of delivery, chapter 3 details how Roosevelt used the media to convey his oratorical skills. The Fireside Chats were exemplars of his technique with radio. The chats served wider purposes than have been accorded them, and the canon of chats should be expanded from twenty-eight to thirty. As for the movie newsreels, scholars have neglected to consider their role in promoting the president's rhetorical image. The press conferences, technically not public speeches, suggest that FDR occasionally used the press for his persuasive purposes.

Chapter 4 explicates the similarities and differences in FDR's four campaigns to the people. Although he faced different rhetorical situations with increasingly difficult adversaries, from Hoover to Landon to Willkie to Dewey, he responded in similar patterns from 1932 to 1944. Except for the strategy of attack in 1932, Roosevelt relied on an aggressive- or offensive-defense to stir Democrats, woo the independents, entice moderate Republicans, and infuriate the Old Guard. In addition to his other clever devices, Roosevelt spared no Republican presidential candidate from his turning of the tables on a recurring Republican campaign posture: "me too, me better."

Chapter 5 investigates Roosevelt's four inaugural addresses. None were pedestrian; they intrinsically merit recognition for inaugural artistry. In explaining the rhetorical function of the investiture speech, his inaugurals can indicate the strengths and limitations of a theory on inaugural addresses. One of his speeches confirms the theory; three confound it. A genre theory can help illuminate some facets of FDR's inaugural gems, but the theory's strictures cannot confine the critic's treating each speech *in situ*.

President Roosevelt's greatest rhetorical defeat, his attack on the Supreme Court in 1937, is examined in chapter 6. The Court fight was important politically and rhetorically because FDR's perception of it in part motivated his ill-fated purge. By employing my theory of accusation and apology, I discuss the degree to which his failure to pack the Court may be attributed to his rhetoric, and I offer how the attack could have been mounted better. Viewed in light of his campaign techniques, especially those he had used in 1936, his posture in the Court fight was characteristic of his speaking.

Chapter 7 examines the purge of 1938 and the war rhetoric. FDR began the purge on the offensive but ended on the defensive, and he initiated his preparation-for-war rhetoric on the defensive but triumphed in 1941 only by a dastardly deed. Regarding the purge, the theses are that Roosevelt repeated the rhetorical errors he committed in the Court attack and, unlike the Court battle that produced two eloquent speeches, failed to deliver any memorable addresses in the process. As for his words of war, the focus is on the techniques, artifices, and strategies he used to ready the nation for action. It was more a commentary on the American people, or at least those with isolationist and noninterventionist beliefs, than on Roosevelt that he was constrained to employ such methods.

Eschewing a listing of stylistic devices on the grounds that these have been illustrated throughout the book, I propose to reveal some of the tenets of Roosevelt's persuasive presidency in chapter 8. FDR might have had a rhetorical theory, but it is too ambitious to discern, and one imagines there was not such a theory. Nevertheless, some broad findings can be advanced concerning why he, and his speech staff, composed addresses and Fireside Chats in a decidedly Rooseveltian style.

On the assumption that a bibliography should be helpful to readers and researchers, a topical bibliography, which correlates with the subject matter of the eight chapters, follows the endnotes. Since this book is about Roosevelt's rhetoric, his speeches, radio addresses, Fireside Chats, and press conferences have been separated in a Speech Index; the General Index includes traditional listings.

Acknowledgments

I wish to record the help I have received along the way. My scholarly interest in Franklin D. Roosevelt's presidential rhetoric was first supported by a grant from the Eleanor Roosevelt Institute for research in the Franklin D. Roosevelt Library in Hyde Park, New York. There, I examined FDR's First Inaugural Address and Fourth Inaugural Address. My findings, originally published in the *Quarterly Journal of Speech* in 1979 and 1981, appear in a slightly altered state in the chapter on inaugural addresses. The editors, Robert Friedman and Hermann Stelzner, respectively, and nameless referees helped me to focus my thoughts.

The chapter on FDR vs. the Supreme Court was begun as a writing project for a National Endowment for the Humanities Summer Seminar on "Rhetoric and Public Discourse," directed by Edward P. J. Corbett, Ohio State University, 1981. Corbett and the other participants, especially Lawrence Rosenfield, helped to clarify my thoughts on speeches of accusation and apology. I presented a version of the chapter on a panel I organized, "Presidential Libraries: Researching the Rhetorical Presidency," at the national convention of the Speech Communication Association, Washington, D.C., 1983. As a respondent to the panel, I wish to thank Jeffrey Auer for his suggestions on how to refine my treatment of FDR's Second Inaugural Address with respect to the Court fight.

A substantial Washington and Lee University Glenn Grant enabled me to conduct extensive research in the Roosevelt Library in 1982. The product of that research forms the core materials for this book. Under the guidance of John Elrod, dean of the College, I was granted a leave in 1987 to finish the manuscript.

My ideas on rhetorical revisionism were presented for a panel on "Studies on FDR: In Memory of Leroy W. Copperthwaite," Central States Speech Com-

munication Association, Cincinnati, Ohio, 1986. I thank Ray Heisey for inviting
me to participate on the panel, and Wil Linkugel for sharing his paper on FDR's
Commonwealth Club address.

My thoughts on the genre of inaugurals were presented on a panel I assembled
at the national convention of the Speech Communication Association, Chicago,
1986. I thank Karlyn Campbell for her responses to my paper on FDR's Third
Inaugural Address, not to mention the hallway conversations that invariably
ensue at the close of a panel.

Certain individuals kindly consented to read portions of the manuscript. Bernard Duffy, my colleague and coeditor for two Greenwood Press books, criticized
the chapter on the Supreme Court fight. Waldo Braden carefully read the chapter
on delivery and the media and gave many suggestions on style that polished
these two chapters. Braden also sent materials relating to FDR's presidency, the
most important and useful of which was the *FDR Collector*.

Librarians aided extensively in the research for this book. The staff of the
FDR Library, under the direction of William Emerson, director, made my stay
in Hyde Park most productive. Richard Grefe and Peggy Hays of the Washington
and Lee University Library helped in countless and thoughtful ways. Mark
Renovitch helped me with the photographic files at the FDR Library.

Copyright for The Reminiscences of Samuel I. Rosenman, (1959), in the Oral
History Collection of Columbia University is held by The Trustees of Columbia
University in the City of New York.

I thank the professionals at Greenwood Press who shepherded the manuscript.
Mildred Vasan, politics and law editor, has guided two previous books and
vestiges of her help remain. Alicia Merritt was production editor, and Maureen
Melino helped with permissions.

Finally, I thank my wife for her encouragement.

1

Franklin D. Roosevelt as a Rhetorical President

Franklin Delano Roosevelt was a pre-eminent presidential persuader. FDR's spoken record reveals his rhetorical eloquence during four terms in office. The First Inaugural Address, the acceptance speech at Franklin Field in Philadelphia in 1936, the 1937 Victory Dinner Address on the Supreme Court fight, the War Message to Congress on December 8, 1941, and the 1944 Teamsters' Union speech are orations of the first order, and they stand secure as paramount examples of their oratorical genre. In rhetoric of the second rank are the 1932 speech to the Commonwealth Club in San Francisco, the Second Inaugural Address, the 1937 "Quarantine" speech at Chicago, the "Four Freedoms" speech in 1941, and perhaps the Fourth Inaugural Address. His phrases, which coaxed the consciousness of his contemporaries and still caress our collective memories, evoked Roosevelt, the Depression and his New Deal, and World War II: the "forgotten man"; "the only thing we have to fear is fear itself"; the "economic royalists"; "This generation of Americans has a rendezvous with destiny"; "I see one-third of a nation ill-housed, ill-clad, ill-nourished"; "the hand that held the dagger has struck it into the back of its neighbor"; and "Yesterday, December 7, 1941—a date which will live in infamy."

As a rhetorical president, Roosevelt exploited the technology of his time to its fullest potential. By radio, he spoke to the entire nation in his major addresses and in the prototypic Fireside Chats. By means of the motion picture newsreels, selected segments of his major addresses or staged retakes of important Fireside Chats and radio addresses portrayed his ebullient, confident delivery and infectious Rooseveltian grin; thus, the sound of his superb voice was reinforced by the visual dynamism of his delivery. FDR also used the press conference in an unprecedented manner to guide, as best he could, reporters' perceptions—and hence to some extent the nation's perceptions—of him and his administration. Although not the first president to use speech writers, FDR unabashedly assembled a talented staff of thinkers and writers who, in tandem with him, produced his oratorical gems. Thus, in many significant respects, Franklin Roosevelt was an archetypal rhetorical president. But what is a rhetorical president, or for that matter, what is presidential rhetoric?

THE RHETORICAL PRESIDENCY

The rhetorical presidency is an institutional practice that has arisen within the presidency in the twentieth century. James Ceaser, Glen Thurow, Jeffrey Tulis, and Joseph Bessette wrote that the rhetorical presidency is a kind of institutionalized popular rhetoric: "Popular or mass rhetoric, which Presidents once employed only rarely, now serves as one of their principal tools in attempting to govern the nation." They also observed that the rhetorical presidency is based on the mistaken assumption that presidential speaking equals presidential governing. Moreover, they noted that the rise of the rhetorical presidency was due to three factors: a modern doctrine of presidential leadership, the mass media, and modern presidential campaigns.[1]

The present-day problems of the rhetorical presidency in terms of its possibilities and limitations were faced by President Roosevelt in the 1930s and 1940s. FDR had a modern conceptualization of the presidency as "pre-eminently a place of moral leadership," and his stress on this doctrine was evident in his speeches throughout his tenure in office. With regard to the modern mass media, some allowances have to be made. FDR was without the mixed blessings of television, which has exacerbated the speaking-is-governing misconception. But if one grants that the basic structure of modern mass media was in place— newspapers, radio, and the now defunct motion picture newsreels (whose format and fast-paced reporting is highly suggestive of today's television news, without the visible anchorperson)—then one will admit that Roosevelt interacted with the mass media of his time. Although the technology of the media has advanced since the 1930s, one still finds in FDR's day similar inherent tensions concerning the diverging self-interests of the president and the media in performing their respective responsibilities. The chapter on Roosevelt and the media explains how and why FDR exploited the media as well as he did. The rise of the modern campaign probably applies least to FDR's case. The change from train to airplane, the waning of the political machines and their bosses, the general weakening of the political parties as power brokers, the rise of the public relations people, the ascendancy of primaries and the almost interminable posturing for them, the advent of the so-called presidential debates, the change in which campaigns are financed, and so on, make FDR's campaigns look dated. Although FDR made different rhetorical choices in his four campaigns than those today's candidates make, he still had to be nominated, to campaign, and to be elected. The rhetoric he used to capture the conventions' and the nation's confidence for four presidential terms is examined in the chapter on campaign oratory.[2]

When one discusses the rhetorical presidency, some caveats are in order. First, what one alleges about the rhetorical presidency in general may not necessarily apply to one of its speakers in particular. The differentiations that the critic must make in FDR's situation have already been indicated. Different presidents contribute idiosyncratically to the rhetorical presidency; therefore, it would seem that substantial case studies should be attempted to offer findings that may be later utilized to codify the practices of the rhetorical presidency. Second, when one attends the rhetorical presidency, one may slight the audience the president addresses. One of the implicit but questionable claims of the rhetorical presidency is that presidential persuasions that are addressed to audiences other than the Congress have an effect on the Congress. This study demonstrates that FDR's attempts to go over the Congress to the people in the Court fight and the "purge" were not successful.

PRESIDENTIAL RHETORIC

Presidential rhetoric refers not to a construct like the rhetorical presidency but to the persuasive speeches the president of the United States delivers. Actually, presidential rhetoric had a more humble beginning than is ascribed to it today.

The only presidential rhetoric enjoined by the Constitution is Article II, Section 3, wherein the president is instructed to "give to the Congress Information of the State of the Union." In Roosevelt's era, this speech was called the Annual Message. Nowadays, it is called the State of the Union Address. Section 3 also allowed the president to "recommend to their Consideration such Measures as he shall judge necessary and expedient." The practice of delivering an inaugural address began with George Washington, whose Second Inaugural endures as the shortest on record at 134 words in comparison to the longest, William Henry Harrison's, at 8,578 words. Holding the record, Roosevelt delivered four annual messages and four inaugural addresses. Inaugurals and annual messages have become a part of the rhetorical presidency, but they both preceded its rise. And when discussing presidential rhetoric, certain caveats are also in order.[3]

First, in order to assure the aura of academic acceptability for the study of presidential rhetoric, a critic could be advised to cite Richard Neustadt's enshrined dictum: "Presidential power is the power to persuade." Perhaps because Neustadt's definition of presidential power contained the word *persuasion* in it, rhetorical critics have felt comfortable in claiming the dictum as a raison d'etre for the study of presidential rhetoric. Theodore Windt used Neustadt's dictum in the introductions of two pioneer books he edited on presidential speaking. But to apply Neustadt's definition to presidential rhetoric is to apply it in a manner not necessarily intended or warranted. Neustadt did not write that presidential power is presidential rhetoric; neither is it the case that presidential rhetoric is presidential power. Neustadt's findings were concerned more with a president's persuasive powers with the federal bureaucracy and the Congress than with public speeches to the nation. Harry Bailey has observed that Neustadt's time frame was really the 1960s and that many constraints operate to check the bargaining chips with which the president can persuade the bureaucracy and the Congress. Additionally, several critics have noted that some presidential powers flow from the prerogatives of the office. Nevertheless, Windt has extended Neustadt's dictum to argue that presidential rhetoric is a study of presidential power based on public opinion: "Presidential rhetoric is a study of how Presidents gain, maintain, or lose support of the public. It is not a study of literary or rhetorical style. It is not an academic study of rhetorical techniques intended to refine rhetorical theory. It is a study of power, of the fundamental power in a democracy: public opinion and public support."[4]

One objects to defining presidential rhetoric in terms of public support while concomitantly eschewing traditional rhetorical concerns for a study of public opinion. The assertion that rhetorical style and techniques—and by implication, other rhetorical factors, too—do not perform to gain, maintain, or lose public support will not stand. Rhetorical style and techniques do affect public opinion, as well as congressional opinion for that matter, as is demonstrated throughout this book. Franklin D. Roosevelt's First Inaugural Address stands as proof enough that rhetorical style and technique persuade people. Moreover, by focusing on public opinion and public support, one may lose sight of the Congress.

The Congress, too, is an important audience to whom presidential rhetoric is addressed. Roosevelt communicated with the Congress through written messages, directly in the annual messages, and indirectly through his inaugurals, speeches, and Fireside Chats. His practice reinforced the premise that the president moves public opinion to move the Congress. Yet, this assumption has not been verified by studies in presidential rhetoric. Given that the legislative power of the United States resides in the Congress, how does presidential rhetoric function to move the public to move the Congress? One might also seek to ascertain whether a president's losing public support means the loss of congressional action, and whether the loss of public support is attributable to the president's rhetoric or to the nature of his audience. In answer to the last question, Aristotle convincingly argued that the speaker may practice exemplary rhetoric, but fail because of circumstances beyond the speaker's control: "It is clear, further, that its [rhetoric's] function is not simply to succeed in persuading, but rather to discover the means of coming as near such success as the circumstances of each particular case allows. For example, it is not the function of medicine simply to make a man quite healthy, but to put him as far as may be on the road to health; it is possible to give excellent treatment even to those who can never enjoy sound health." This study attempts to address the above questions in relationship to Roosevelt's rhetorical practices. Yet, one is cognizant of the lack of a guiding hand in proceeding to answer those queries.[5]

What one asserts about presidential rhetoric in general may not necessarily apply to a particular president. Pioneering the way, Robert Underhill investigated

President Harry S Truman's rhetoric in *The Truman Persuasions*, which reinforces the wisdom of conducting a case study on an individual president's persuasions. Underhill's findings, and those offered here for Roosevelt, can contribute to an ongoing explication and understanding of president's rhetoric. For instance, Roosevelt and Truman had different approaches to the delivery of their speeches, to editing them, and to using public profanity. One wonders if FDR's substantial attention to the niceties of speech delivery and the editorial care with which he processed his speech drafts made his presidential rhetoric more persuasive than Truman's, or were there other factors, and so on. The point is that descriptive and analytical treatments of presidents' rhetoric may lay the groundwork for later studies that can then take an aggregate view of modern presidential rhetoric. The same can be said for the rhetorical presidency. Following Underhill's work on Truman, this study lays claim to offering a complete case study on Roosevelt's speechmaking.[6]

A RHETORICAL PRESIDENT

This concept denotes a president who employs persuasive techniques. For the purposes of this study, rhetoric may be defined as the art of persuasive speaking. Some may prefer Aristotle's enduring definition: "Rhetoric may be defined as the faculty of observing in any given situation the available means of persuasion." The Greek word for art, *techne*, suggests that in speechmaking there are certain techniques that can be conceived, practiced, and criticized.[7]

To conceive of Roosevelt as a rhetorical president is to affirm certain axioms of the art of rhetoric. These axioms are particularly important to the study of his speaking. First, he practiced the art to get a response from his audiences. Second, his application of the art's techniques contributed to the effects of his speeches. Just as the techniques of carpentry enable the carpenter to craft a comfortable chair, so do the techniques of rhetoric enable the speaker to fashion a functional persuasive message. Third, the effects of his speeches can be ascertained. Although FDR practiced the art of rhetoric for success, he sometimes failed to obtain the desired responses from his audiences. In order to gauge the outcome of FDR's speeches, the critic may rely upon other critics' opinions, upon contemporary commentators' evaluations, upon polls, and upon his own close and careful reading of the speech.

But there is also a corollary that flows from the confluence of these three axioms. Given that the art of rhetoric is purposeful, the critic must not only explain successes but also explicate failures. If he described only the successes, then very few original findings would be claimed as additions to the scholarship on FDR and his speaking. If, however, the rhetorical critic takes the next logical step, as admonished by the art, and evaluates the failures of its practice, then he can claim new insights into Roosevelt and his rhetoric. Nor is it sufficient for the critic to note that a speech failed for such and such reasons; rather, the critic completes the evaluation by offering some reasonable revision of how the art might have been better or more effectively practiced.

The application of oratorical revisionism is critical to the claims advanced in this study. Rhetorical revisionism is not an exercise in "what if": what if Abraham Lincoln had not been assassinated, or what if FDR had fulfilled his fourth term, and so forth. Juxtaposed to instances in which a president had little or no control over events, the practice of rhetoric provides a president with some measure of choice and control: when and where to speak, to whom to speak, on what to speak, and how to speak. Indeed, according to James Andrews, the critic can engage legitimately in revisionism: "The critic who is trained in rhetoric knows what *is* persuasive; when that critic enters a controversy, it is to argue the question of what should be persuasive." In treating the Supreme Court fight in 1937, with the aid of an accepted rhetorical theory, the aim will be to suggest how and why President Roosevelt could have mounted a better and more effective rhetorical attack on the Court.[8]

Roosevelt's presidential rhetoric was generally successful because he demonstrated an awareness of the five arts or classical canons of rhetoric, even if he did not know them by name. First, he was intimately involved in the speech invention process, *inventio*. By choice, he usually played a seminal role in the building of his addresses by suggesting ideas, themes, and guidelines for the speech staff to use, and he even dictated or wrote emendations on the speech drafts. He also attended to the arrangement, *dispositio*, of his messages by purposefully organizing and rearranging materials for persuasive effect. President Roosevelt paid considerable attention to the third canon of rhetorical style, *elocutio*. Evidence from his speech drafts indicates that he developed an effective personal style in the selection and management of his language. His ability to coin memorable phrases and to speak in eloquent diction was an important factor in the overall favorable impact of his presidential rhetoric. Fourth, FDR paid particular attention to the delivery, *actio*, of his addresses and radio talks. Given his physical handicap, his *actio* at the podium was remarkable for its vitality, liveliness, and dynamism. Unlike the ancients who considered *memoria* important, FDR perceived no need to memorize his speeches. He was, though, so thoroughly involved in the speech preparation process that he was able to deliver them, almost flawlessly, from ordinary double- or triple-spaced typewritten pages. Happily, Roosevelt managed without presidential pica and the teleprompter. His attention to the five classical canons of rhetoric may account for John Wilson and Carroll Arnold's assessment of Roosevelt as "perhaps the most expert public speaker to hold the presidency in this century."[9]

ON ROOSEVELT AND HIS RHETORICAL PRESIDENCY

FDR's life and thirteen-year presidency have been the focus of numerous and substantial articles, books, and even multivolume sets, which have treated the man, his era, and his tenure in the White House. The present study does not pretend to add significantly to the general literature on the thirty-second president of the United States. Indeed, a basic knowledge of Roosevelt and the important issues in his New Deal are assumed as departure points for this book. However, one notices the lack of any careful and systematic treatment of FDR's rhetorical practices as a presidential persuader. True enough, the Rooseveltian literature ranges the gamut from fulsome praise for famous phrases to critical explication of important speeches. Granted, there are a number of insightful but unrelated case studies in scholarly journals on his Fireside Chats, press conferences, and speeches. But none of these, taken either separately or together, constitute a comprehensive conception of FDR's presidential persuasions.

By viewing Franklin D. Roosevelt as a practitioner of the rhetorical presidency, one obtains a synergism that has not been realized before, not even by Samuel Rosenman's influential *Working with Roosevelt*. The delicate task of distinguishing this book from Rosenman's, which is based on his first-hand experiences as an equal among equals on Roosevelt's speech staff, is to differentiate the present work without deprecating Rosenman's. Whereas Rosenman organized his chapters on a chronological basis, the various chapters in this book are arranged in a topical fashion. For instance, the four inaugurals are discussed as examples of that rhetorical genre without eschewing their political and historical contexts; likewise, the Second Inaugural will be separated, along with some other speeches, for consideration in the chapter on the Supreme Court fight. Whereas Rosenman discussed a number of speeches, sometimes only in passing, the present plan is to select some twenty significant speeches with the hope that the reduction in numbers will be recompensed by a more penetrating analysis of the addresses examined. Other differences are less obvious.

Certain findings that are not revealed in Rosenman will be advanced in the appropriate chapters here. Roosevelt's delivery deserves systematic attention. First, the critic can take a cue from Roosevelt himself. As a diligent persuader, he devoted substantial time and attention to the initial preparatory stages of his messages with an eye toward their eventual delivery; after he settled on a speech draft, he considered how he might effectively deliver it; and at the moment of utterance, he expertly executed the planned delivery of his remarks. He knew and practiced what most critics tend to downplay and overlook: that speech delivery is a powerful persuasive asset in convincing people. Second, one avoids an egregious error of relegating the techniques of delivery to an inferior position, usually toward the back of a book, when discussing the rhetorical presidency. Given that presidential exhortations and appeals to the people are a function of the construct, the manner in which those appeals are delivered is important. President Ronald Reagan's professional delivery skills attest to the salience of delivery as a contributing factor to his successes in the rhetorical presidency. The insight one gains from studying FDR's delivery techniques is an appreciation of how and why he formulated his political images through them. The explication

of his delivery is based on motion picture newsreels and sound recordings from
the Franklin D. Roosevelt Library's extensive holdings.

It can be a mistake to treat the president differently from other speakers. To
be sure, the president addresses audiences not generally available to most Americans, and his words are usually more significant. But still, the president is a
human being. Notwithstanding how he may be guided and advised, the president,
like other speakers, eventually makes rhetorical choices. In FDR's case, these
choices can be illustrated and criticized because he gave personal attention to
his addresses. In order to gain new insights into Roosevelt's rhetorical presidency,
it is as important to understand the production and evolution of his speeches as
it is to understand what he actually said. This part of the study is based on a
close examination of the progression of the speech drafts that were researched
in the Library. The speech drafts reveal Franklin Roosevelt's political acumen
at critical junctures in his administrations.

The public opinion reaction files at Hyde Park are valuable resources. They
contain a storehouse of information on how FDR's audiences received his com-
munications. A careful perusal of the files produced some particularly insightful,
caustic, and humorous observations from Americans who experienced Roosevelt's rhetoric firsthand. Although these letters and telegrams are idiosyncratic,
they are nevertheless unparalleled in their ability to evoke the efficacy of the
president's persuasions on his listeners, and they often evince this quality much
better than do other standard resource materials. The following poem and New
Deal statistics mailed to FDR in the mid–1930s demonstrate that not everyone
was beguiled by Roosevelt's silver tongue:

I'M SO TIRED OF IT ALL

I'm so tired—Oh so tired—of the whole New Deal;
   Of the juggler's smile; the barker's spiel;
Of mushy speech; and loud bassoon;
   And tiredest all of the leader's croon.

Tired of taxes on my ham and eggs;
   Tired of "Payoffs" to political yeggs;
Tired of Jim Farley's stamps on my mail;
   Tired of my shirt with its tax-shortened tail.

I'm tired of farmer's goose-stepping to laws;
   Of millions of itching job-holder's paws;
Of "Fireside Talks" over commandeered mikes;
   Of passing more laws to stimulate strikes.

I'm tired of the hourly-increasing debt;
   I'm tired of promises still to be met;
Of eating and sleeping by Government plan;
   Of calmly forgetting the "Forgotten Man."

I'm tired of every new brain-trust thought;
   Of the ship-of-state—now a pleasure yacht.
I'm tired of cheating the courts by stealth;
   And terribly tired of sharing my wealth.

I'm tired of "Eleanor" on page one;
   Of each royal "in-law" and favorite son;
I'm tired of "Sistie" and "Buzzie" Dall;
   I'm simply—completely—fed up with it all.

I'm tired and bored, with the whole New Deal;
   With its juggler's smile and barker's spiel.
Dear Lord! Out of all Thy available men,
   Please grant us a Cleveland or Coolidge again.

SOME NEW DEAL FIGURES

U.S. Population		120,000,000
Eligible for Old Age Pension	46,000,000	
Children prohibited from working	30,000,000	
Government employees	30,000,000	
Unemployed	13,999,998	
		119,999,998
Left to produce U.S. wealth		2

Just you and I—and I'm all worn out![10]

When one reviews Roosevelt's thirteen years of presidential rhetoric, two central issues seemed to concern his presidency. First, the political and philosophical theses of FDR's New Deal rhetoric were that the president and the Congress had the legal power and the political obligation to address a national Depression at the national level with national legislation. The people of the United States generally supported those premises, but the Supreme Court did not. President Roosevelt's attack on the Supreme Court of the United States with his judicial reorganization bill of 1937 was a rhetorical effort to bully the Court. Most critics accept, to use the hackneyed metaphor, that the president lost both the battle and the war. Given that agreement, rhetorical revisionism submits (1) why he failed from a persuasive perspective (other political variables played their parts too) and (2) how he could have selected a different argumentative approach to make his persuasive task easier. Since the controversy occurred *in situ*, some attention is given to the possible shifts in argumentative grounds the opposition might have made; but, given even these hypothetical shifts, the critical position still is that these possible lines of attack, as well as the ones that actually occurred, could have been deflected easier than those occasioned by Roosevelt's actual approach. The Court battle is also a classic case of the rhetorical presidency. When it became apparent that the Congress would need prodding to pass the legislation, FDR took to the airwaves in order to exhort the people to move the Congress. But it did not work. For when the chief executive chooses inappropriate persuasive strategies, the efficacy of the message is seriously weakened or lost. In the same vein, the 1938 purge is seen as a rhetorical mistake in conception and execution because the president evidently violated a tenet of the rhetorical presidency. The president can campaign for candidates in his own party and against his party's opponents because the role of president and head of the party are in accord. But when FDR entered the local level to influence voter's choices against candidates in his own party, even for the best of reasons, the voters apparently resented his unwarranted intrusion as unseemly and inappropriate to the office. The high role of president does not seem to include dividing the party over picayune partisan politics.

The other salient issue was the preparation-for-war rhetoric. In his second term and into the third, FDR increasingly attempted to resolve the tension between isolationism and interventionism. He had to identify his image as anti-war in the 1936 campaign out of political necessity, but when he wanted to disengage from that isolationist stance in order to assume an interventionist posture, he found that it was difficult to urge the country to follow him. Part of this difficulty stemmed from the fact that he was so successful in identifying his anti-war image that he could not shed it without appearing to break political faith, and part was due to Americans' instinctive isolationist ideas (that he had helped reinforce).

Lastly, what are the characteristics of a great Rooseveltian speech? For the purposes of this study, there are three: (1) a notable persuasive success or failure, such as the First Inaugural Address or the series of Court speeches; (2) an outstanding example of the oratorical genre, such as the 1936 acceptance speech at Philadelphia and the War Message; and (3) a speech significant in terms of its eloquence, delivery, rhetorical techniques, and so on. About twenty of Roosevelt's presidential persuasions fit these descriptions, and they represent the core materials for this study.

SUMMARY

The persuasive practices that President Roosevelt developed in his rhetorical presidency are still exercised in the Oval Office, and he remains a kind of benchmark by which to measure the office's successive incumbents.

As a presidential orator, FDR was of the highest caliber. Of eight subsequent chief executives, only Ronald Reagan's manifest delivery skills can compare. FDR institutionalized the symbiotic relationship between the White House and the media, and what was generally his boon with the media was often other presidents' bane. He waged four political campaigns in which he took his case directly to the people with some of the greatest campaign oratory of the modern presidency. Two or three of his inaugural addresses stand at the apex of the presidential inaugural pyramid.

And yet, as one attempts to portray Franklin D. Roosevelt's impressive rhetorical presidency one might be guided wisely by Oliver Cromwell's admonition in 1650 to Peter Leley, his portrait artist who had painted a comely portrait of a homely Lord Protector: "I desire you will use all your skill to paint my picture truly like me, and not to flatter me at all; but remark all those roughnesses, pimples, and warts, and everything as you see me; otherwise I will never pay one farthing for it."

2

Roosevelt's Persuasive Delivery

To forget that words on a printed page were once spoken by FDR to his fellow Americans is to miss the point of why he delivered addresses and Fireside Chats. He communicated the subtle range of his feelings in a manner that imparted directness and sincerity to his listeners. FDR talked to, not at, the American people. Yet, except for Earnest Brandenburg and Waldo Braden's essay on Roosevelt's voice and pronunciation, little has been written about FDR's platform presence, voice management, gestures, use of speech manuscripts, eye contact, or the effect of his physical handicap. Indeed, Gail Compton noted the need to investigate FDR's delivery: ''Studies of Roosevelt's speaking during his twelve years as President tend to center more on issues and less on the other rhetorical elements of speech preparation, style, persuasive techniques and delivery.'' These elements, particularly delivery, impelled FDR's rhetorical presidency.[1]

The materials for a study of FDR's delivery are the audio-visual archives in the Franklin D. Roosevelt Library. Surprisingly, there are only enough film materials to criticize sixteen speeches, and these films are really excerpts of varying lengths from motion-picture newsreels. The audio recordings for Roosevelt's voice are more numerous. These sources are the foundation for an analysis and criticism of President Roosevelt's delivery.[2]

ON THE PLATFORM

The primary point to remember about Roosevelt's standing to deliver a speech is that he was in discomfort due to his handicap of paralyzed legs from an attack of poliomyelitis in 1921. Donald Richberg, a collaborator with Roosevelt's speech staff in the mid–1930s, believed that Roosevelt spoke in "actual pain." During World War II, FDR infrequently utilized his leg braces. He did determine to deliver his Fourth Inaugural Address standing, but he delivered his famous 1944 Teamsters' Union speech seated, and he sat down to address Congress on Yalta, March 1, 1945. In the introduction to the latter speech, he alluded to his handicap with a sympathy appeal: "I hope that you will pardon me for the unusual posture of sitting down during the presentation of what I want to say, but I know that you will realize it makes it a lot easier for me not having to carry about ten pounds of steel around on the bottom of my legs." Actually, by this time FDR had aluminum braces that were considerably lighter than the steel ones, but his point is well taken. Also, this was the first time he ever publicly referred to his handicap in a speech.[3]

The leg braces the president wore are in the Library. When he stood in them, he was in effect sitting in a padded leather saddle-like seat that depended from a circular frame about his waist. His body weight was thus supported by the braces, which hinged at the knee and could be unlocked by a catch. The braces bore his weight to the floor through his shoes, which were firmly attached to the braces. As furniture craftsmen long ago realized, a three-legged table will stand well on uneven surfaces; hence, FDR needed a triad to stand to deliver an address. The braces supplied two-thirds of the triad; the other one-third came from his grasping the podium or holding on to a railing. An interesting portable podium–like device was observable at the 1936 Chautauqua, New York, speech and on the rear platform of a railroad observation car. Because photographic lighting was then often poor, one cannot say with certainty that these devices were identical, nor have such devices apparently survived, but they too looked like the same portable speaking podium. The portability of such a podium would have insured for FDR the predictability of the speaking situation. (Incidentally, observers of the modern rhetorical presidency will note that FDR delivered his speeches without the ever present stage prop of the presidential seal on the podium: he was quite able to communicate a presidential presence without it.) At Chautauqua, the device seemed to be attached to a speaker's stand already on the stage. This portable podium had a slanted surface for the manuscript and protruding rails on both sides that Roosevelt could grasp. The railroad car apparatus appeared to be the same podium, bolted to the brass observation rail. As Roosevelt was still in the era when politicians, movie stars, and presidents were fashionably photographed on the rear platforms of elegant Pullman observation cars and when politicians including the president of the United States addressed whistle-stop crowds from the rear platform, this portable podium would have enabled Roosevelt to speak to crowds while standing.[4]

The above technical discussion illuminates the physical problems FDR faced when he delivered a public speech. His Fireside Chats and other radio messages were delivered from the relative comfort of his chair. Before a live audience, he was not at liberty to move around behind the podium for variety or emphasis, and he was a virtual prisoner of the podium while speaking. Moreover, he had to have help to the podium and away from it. In the one extant film, a home movie, of FDR walking to a podium—the Secret Service confiscated such home movies whenever possible, and the movie newsreel people evidently had an unspoken agreement not to film his walking—he actually walked by swinging his hips and body, while concomitantly shifting his weight so that each leg sort of swung around in front of him in a twisting fashion. This was, of course, with help at both arms for support. The impediments of just getting to the podium and then of standing there in discomfort to deliver a speech made FDR a remarkable orator. His handicap forced him to learn to compensate with other means to obtain a dynamic delivery.[5]

WHAT AMERICANS SAW

After viewing the newsreels that portrayed FDR giving a speech, one could accurately conclude that he enjoyed speaking. Incredulous as it may seem to persons who would rather not address an audience, such as President Harry Truman who did not enjoy giving speeches, Roosevelt reveled in his rhetoric.[6]

If one aspect summarizes Roosevelt's delivery, it would be his famous Rooseveltian smile. It was especially evident in his speaking throughout his first two terms in office. That smile communicated a feeling of warmth and sincerity, of calmness and control in his communication, and of plain fun in addressing his fellow Americans. Whether his grin was heartfelt or cultivated (one imagines it was a little of both), the important rhetorical effect was that his audiences could plainly perceive his goodwill toward them. Doubtless, FDR realized the persuasive impact that a buoyant appearance would have during dreary Depression days. Yet, enough of the man himself comes through on the newsreels, in the recurring image of his friendly face and smile, to suggest that he enjoyed speaking and that the grin was genuine. For instance, Roosevelt flashed his smile at Chautauqua during the beginning of his speech; he was of course without a smile and was deadly serious when telling his audience about how he knew war; but he dispelled the serious mood toward the end of the speech by jauntily smiling again. In fact, one might opine that FDR's jauntiness at the end of the speech belied the seriousness of his anti-war sentiments. At Syracuse, New York, September 29, 1936, Roosevelt was in good form. In the film clip, he started out seriously while feigning sarcasm about Republican campaign promises, but he was soon laughing with the audience, and he had a Cheshire cat smile when he said, mocking the Republicans:

Of course we believe all these things; we believe in social security; we believe in work for the unemployed; we believe in saving homes. Cross our hearts and hope to die, we believe in all these things; but we do not like the way the present Administration is doing them. Just turn them over to us. We will do all of them—we will do more of them—we will do them better; and, most important of all, the doing of them will not cost anybody anything.

He was delightful to watch at Syracuse, and Roosevelt obviously relished every moment of it. Another virtuoso performance was at the University of North Carolina at Chapel Hill, where he delivered his famous "Grilled Millionaire" speech on December 5, 1938. He took great delight in delivering the following lines:

You undergraduates who see me for the first time have read your newspapers and heard on the air that I am, at the very least, an ogre—a consorter with Communists, a destroyer of the rich, a breaker of our ancient traditions. Some of you think of me perhaps as the inventor of the economic royalist, of the wicked utilities, of the money changers of the Temple. You have heard for six years that I was about to plunge the Nation into war; that you and your little brothers would be sent to the bloody fields of battle in Europe; that I was driving the Nation into bankruptcy; and that I breakfasted every morning on a dish of 'grilled millionaire.' [Laughter] Actually, I am an exceedingly mild mannered person—a practitioner of peace, both domestic and foreign, a believer in the capitalistic system, and for my breakfast a devotee of scrambled eggs. [Laughter]

On the world *ogre*, Roosevelt jutted out his chin and screwed up his face to look like one, and he smiled in keen appreciation of the gales of laughter from a very responsive college audience. In these instances, FDR used his smile, his friendly face, and at times his hearty laugh to poke fun at his adversaries at their political expense.[7]

On the other hand, the president was equally at home in evincing a serious visage as appropriate for the rhetorical situation. The First Inaugural Address, the Second Inaugural, the 1937 "Quarantine" speech at Chicago, the "hand that held the dagger" speech at Charlottesville in 1940, the War Message, and the Fourth Inaugural were delivered with somber facial features. The 1944 Teamsters' Union Speech bears special consideration. Although FDR had the audience in gales of laughter throughout the speech and was especially effective when he narrated the story of his little dog Fala, he was not laughing with them as he did at Syracuse and at Chapel Hill. His tone and face suggested a very serious and angry president. He was not feigning sarcasm, but was genuinely peeved at the Republicans. The audience reacted appropriately enough to the levity of the lines, but the words belied the true cynicism that Roosevelt felt, and communicated in his face, toward his political rivals. In the following passage on Fala, information in the brackets indicates FDR's facial gestures and the audience applause:

These Republican leaders have not been content with attacks on me, or my wife, or on my sons. No, not content with that, they now include my little dog, Fala [FDR looked up from reading his manuscript and the audience laughed and applauded for some twenty seconds]. Well, of course, I don't resent attacks, and my family don't [*sic*] resent attacks, *but Fala does resent them* [FDR emphasized every word in the italicized phrase, let his jaw drop in indignation, and the audience laughed for fifteen seconds]. You know, Fala is Scotch [laughter], and being a Scottie, as soon as he learned that the Republican fiction writers in Congress and out had concocted a story that I had left him behind on the Aleutian Islands and had sent a destroyer back to find him—at a cost to the taxpayers of two or three, or eight or twenty million dollars— *his Scotch soul was furious* [FDR again emphasized each word in the italicized phrase, let his jaw drop again, and the audience laughed for ten seconds]. He has not been the same dog since [laughter].[8]

Roosevelt also gestured actively with his head. In addition to emphasizing vocally the italicized words in the Fala passage above, he also punctuated each word with a forceful head chop. It may be that the limitations of his handicap "perhaps account for the vigorous head movements," but pictures taken before his 1921 attack of poliomyelitis suggest that he had already developed similar head gestures because he had some understanding of how to deliver a speech. Roosevelt's head gestures effectively emphasized and reinforced the words he spoke. In his First Fireside Chat on the banking crisis in 1933, he tilted his head back and forth, in an almost good-natured wagging fashion that disarmed fear about the banks, when he said: "It is my belief that hoarding during the past week has become an exceedingly unfashionable pastime . . . I can assure you that it is safer to keep you money in a reopened bank than under the mattress." He used the tilted-head gesture to bring attention to his points in his 1934 Annual Message, and he tilted his head in Chicago for the "Quarantine" speech to emphasize why Americans should support his proposal: "When an epidemic of physical disease starts to spread, the community approves and joins in a quarantine of the patients in order to protect the health of the community against the spread of the disease." One of Roosevelt's star performances was at Syracuse, New York, in 1936. In addition to using the facial features discussed above, FDR shook his head in a mock "no" as he told his audience what the Republicans said they would do, and he communicated with his shaking-the-head-no gesture that they really meant none of it. He obviously loved delivering those lines, and so did the audience as gauged by the laughs and applause. The president also had a very effective head gesture in his War Message to Congress in 1941. When he spoke the anaphora of "our people, our territory and our interest," he swept his head in an inclusive gesture that embraced the entire congressional audience and, symbolically, all of America.[9]

Although the president was constrained in bodily movement at the podium, he did gesture with his hand and arm in order to emphasize his persuasive points. By holding to a railing or to the podium, he could gesture with one arm, usually his right one. Although FDR could not be called an overly active gesturer, neither would the opinion that "he used gestures sparingly" paint an accurate picture. When compared to Mussolini's imperious gestures or Hitler's frenetic motions, or to the frantic gesticulations of a Huey Long or a Father Coughlin, Roosevelt appeared restrained. Neither did he have the vigorous platform presence of his cousin President Theodore Roosevelt. FDR broke with the style of gesturing used by his political contemporaries by adopting a more constrained style of gesturing. Yet, gesture he did.[10]

His most typical gesture was a downward hand-and-arm chop that stressed and punctuated his words. Occasionally, he outstretched his entire arm in a sweeping movement, which seemed to implore his audience to give assent to his rhetoric. For instance, in the 1932 acceptance speech at Chicago, he swept his entire arm to intensify his words: "This convention wants repeal. Your candidate wants repeal. And I am confident that the United States of America wants repeal." At Chautauqua, he used his arm to emphasize the fact that he abhorred war. The following scheme, from his acceptance speech at Philadelphia in 1936, hopefully conveys something of FDR's effectively joining gestures to words. For most of the passage, he had his entire arm extended, and though there was some up-and-down arm movement, most of the actual gesture came from an upward or downward chopping wrist motion. The slashes in the passage denote vocal phrasing, where he stopped speaking, and information in the brackets indicates the kind of gesture he made for the phrase: "We are fighting [hand down] / fighting to save [hand down] / a great [hand down] / and precious [hand down] / form of government [hand down] for ourselves and for the world [hand and arm swept up] / And so / I accept / the commission you have tendered me / I join with you [hand swept up] / I am enlisted [sharp hand-and-arm chop down] / for the duration [hand down] / of the war [hand-and-arm swept down]." His gestures were timed and executed well, and they visually reinforced his rhetoric.[11]

Next, an evaluation of FDR's eye contact with his live audiences and with the camera is needed. Direct eye contact with an audience or the camera's lens is a critical factor in enhancing a speaker's image of competency and trustworthiness, hence a factor in the speaker's power to persuade. Since the age of television and the advent of the teleprompter, presidents have been able to give their live and television audiences the illusion of superb eye contact. When compared to presidents' eye contact in the television age, FDR's appears weak, but on the other hand it does not give a misleading impression. Today's television performances make FDR's eye contact look realistic and natural.

Roosevelt read his speeches from an ordinary triple-spaced typewritten manuscript. But he did not read his speeches as weak or untrained speakers do. FDR knew that a speech is not an essay on its hind legs. He tried to look at the camera or the audience as much as he could. His *modus operandi* was to look down to catch a phrase or sentence and then look up to deliver it, and so he repeated the process.

Another reason for his establishing good eye contact was that he had been so intensely involved in preparing his speeches. He had practiced them, as it were, by going over the various drafts. A case in point was his 1936 acceptance address in Philadelphia. Backstage, with the curtains about to be parted, FDR reached out to shake hands with poet Edwin Markham. Instead, he lost his balance, fell, and dropped his speech. He was picked up, the curtains parted, and he had to rearrange the pages of his text as he began to speak. Yet, this was carried off with aplomb because he knew the speech so well that he could begin it without notes while he got his pages in order.[12]

Whether in person or on the newsreels, Americans saw an unaffected speaker in FDR. At the podium, he enjoyed looking out at his audiences, talking and laughing as if he were one of them. He delivered his Second Inaugural Address in the rain, without an aide holding an umbrella over him, and he campaigned in New York City in 1944 in the freezing rain for some fifty miles in an open automobile. When he needed a drink of water at the congressional rostrum on December 8, 1941, he took it. On a hot day in June at Charlottesville, where he delivered his verbal attack against Mussolini in 1940, he thought nothing of mopping his brow three times during the brief film excerpt. He turned his own manuscript pages, and he made no effort to hide the fact that he used a speech text. FDR was an ordinary speaker; he made no pretensions to appearing, to use the modern term, "presidential."

WHAT AMERICANS HEARD

Americans listened to the Chief Executive in person and on the radio. Since radio had the greater impact, it is the medium under investigation. FDR was not the first president to speak over the radio, but he was the first one to realize its potential for persuading the mass audience by extending his voice into the living rooms of the nation. One recognizes that what is seen is difficult to isolate entirely from what is heard, because platform bearing, gestures, vocal production and pacing, and so forth are so interrelated in speaking; nevertheless, Roosevelt's technical production of speaking, his rate, volume, pitch, and voice quality, can be separated for study.

FDR's speaking rate often surprises the modern student of presidential rhetoric because he spoke slowly whether he addressed live audiences or used the radio. Most orators talk at about 125–175 words per minute (wpm), and the term *hesitant* has been applied to 90–100 wpm. In the sound environment of radio, a rate of 175–200 wpm is deemed suitable, and only at the 250–275 wpm range does comprehension begin to decline significantly.[13]

President Roosevelt's rate for the Fireside Chats was about 30 percent slower than the optimum wpm for a radio broadcast. His first two chats were also his fastest, at 130 wpm and 126 wpm respectively. For the duration of his administrations, he settled in around 120 wpm. The two interesting deviations were his chats after the Nazis invaded Poland, 98 wpm, and after the Japanese bombed Pearl Harbor, 88 wpm. For these, he probably slowed his normal radio rate to communicate the gravity of the two situations, and doubtless these momentous events moved him to address the people in a more measured rate. Table 1 summarizes FDR's rate for significant Fireside Chats.[14] When one compares FDR's rate in wpm for his Fireside Chats to the standard radio broadcast rate, one must conclude that his rate was significantly less than optimal; in other

Table 1
Speaking Rates for Fireside Chats

Date		Name	WPM
March 12,	1933	On the Bank Crisis	130
May 7,	1933	On the New Deal	126
March 9,	1937	On the Judiciary	118
September 3,	1939	On the European War	98
May 26,	1940	On National Defense	119
December 29,	1940	On National Security	121
December 9,	1941	On War with Japan	88
February 3,	1942	On Progress of the War	118

words, one must look for other factors, which will be addressed presently, to explain the persuasiveness of his speaking voice.

The data for the significant speeches FDR delivered to live audiences, which were simultaneously broadcast to the nation, show a correspondingly slow rate. One would naturally expect Roosevelt to speak slower to a live audience, an adjustment FDR appropriately made, but his slow radio rate translated into an even slower live speaking rate. Grace Tully and Robert Sherwood noted that FDR's average rate was 100 wpm. A close examination of his important speeches suggests that an average rate of 95 wpm is more accurate, but the difference is hardly significant. Rather, the important question is, given that FDR's rate was slow, even hesitant by raw data standards, what made his rate effective?[15]

President Roosevelt mastered vocal pacing. He tended to elongate, to prolong, his vowels and consonants. He was quite effective at this, as in the Teamsters' Union speech when he sardonically communicated the Republican Party's professed pledge "that they really love labor." In pronouncing these words to oneself, by stretching the sounds of *l*, *o*, *v*, *l*, and *a* in a sarcastic manner, one will approximate FDR's rendition.[16]

FDR could superbly phrase important thoughts, and he mastered the rhetorical pause effectively. For instance, in the 1937 "Quarantine" speech at Chicago, he used his phrasing and pausing to build suspense and to emphasize his salient language (slashes indicate a pause at the end of a phrase): "It seems to be unfortunately true / that the epidemic of world lawlessness is spreading / *And mark this well* / When an epidemic of physical disease starts to spread / the community approves and joins in / a quarantine / of the patients / in order to protect the health of the community / against the spread of the disease." At the University of Virginia in 1940, he even delivered his phrasing in almost classical iambic rhythm (italicized words indicate the iambic vocal stress FDR gave): "the *hand* that *held* the *dagger* / has *struck* it / into the *back* / of its *neighbor*."

And in the 1937 Victory Dinner Address he phrased the anaphora, or parallel structure, so well that he evoked great applause from the audience: "a Nation intact / a Nation at peace / a Nation prosperous, a Nation clear in its knowledge / of what powers it has / to serve its own citizens / a Nation that is in a position to use those powers to the full / in order to move forward steadily / to meet the modern needs of humanity / a Nation which has thus proved / that the democratic form / and methods of national government / can / and will succeed [sustained audience applause]." These superb examples, and one could cite numerous others, explain why his rate, although slow, was so effective.[17]

A blind reliance on the raw data of mere words per minute for Roosevelt's rate would also obscure some valuable insights into why he spoke so slowly. This question has never been fully addressed and it deserves an answer. Although one cannot say with absolute certainty that FDR purposefully controlled his speaking rate in order to communicate a certain political image, there is evidence to support a thesis that his measured rate was calculated to communicate trust, competency, and tranquillity at the helm of state.

Certain insightful critics described FDR's rate management as cultivated. John Sharon believed it was purposeful: "Roosevelt's cultivated voice, deep and resonant, well knew how to strike upon every chord of human emotion. Possessing the timing of a great actor, he spoke slowly, reassuringly and meaningfully." Thomas Greer believed that Roosevelt was "conscious of the power of his voice." FDR rarely sounded or looked anxious or hurried. He evidently wanted to evince the political image of a deliberate, authoritative, and calm leader. These attributes were requisite political images for a Depression era Chief Executive and a war era Commander-in-Chief.[18]

The president did not use extremes in loudness to convey his spoken thoughts to the country. When compared in terms of voice volume to the dictators and demagogues of his period, FDR controlled his voice within reasonable limits and conversational ranges. Americans never heard their president shout or scream at them. Indeed, FDR's measured volume differentiated and distinguished him from his political contemporaries.

To his credit, Roosevelt broke with the stereotypes of old-time political oratory. Radio technicians who handled the radio control dials noted that Roosevelt did not reach extremes in either loudness or softness for his Fireside Chats and radio addresses. Consequently, there are precious few speeches that one can mention as examples of egregious or tasteless excesses in volume. To be sure, FDR varied his volume, as any conversational orator would do, but these fluctuations were normal and to be expected. If one speech is the exception to the rule, it is surely his Victory Dinner Address of 1937, and even that speech is only a minor exception. This was one of the president's best fighting speeches; it was against the Supreme Court, and he emotionally used intensities in volume that were not characteristic of him. For instance, in that speech's famous peroration of seven lines of anaphora beginning with "Here are . . . ," FDR alternately used a loud and soft voice to deliver each line. The usual oratorical *modus operandi* would be to increase the vocal intensity on each succeeding line in order to end with an extreme loudness to mark the high point of the speech. Martin Luther King, Jr., did just that in the peroration of his famous and memorable "I Have a Dream" speech at the Lincoln Memorial in 1963. But Roosevelt evidently did not want to communicate too strong a vocal attack against the Court, lest it backfire, so he moderated his peroration.

In sum, Roosevelt managed the volume of his voice so that his listeners could adequately hear him, and so that he would not be perceived as a president who spoke in extremes. Some of this was doubtless a part of his personal habit of ordinary conversational speaking. But even in situations, such as the Victory Dinner Address and the Teamster's Union speech, where he could have been easily carried away with favorable feedback from highly partisan audiences, Roosevelt checked himself and maintained control over his speaking voice. His political instincts evidently told him to constrain the volume of his voice because, given that some of his political enemies accused him of being a demagogue or a dictator, he did not need to validate their charges by speaking as such.

Roosevelt also varied his speaking pitch, in its musical sense, in order to communicate effectively his thoughts to audiences. Again, he eschewed the extremes in pitch often associated with older political oratory. In comparison to his contemporary orators for whom there are voice recordings, such as Huey Long, Father Coughlin, Al Smith, and Hitler, all of whom used wide, extreme, and often abrupt pitch changes, FDR's management of pitch was more measured and restrained.

Roosevelt characteristically spoke at a musical pitch ranging from E-flat to F below middle C. Thus, he had a tenor voice. Within this tenor range, FDR's pitch did not go to either extreme. There appear to be no instances on the recordings where his voice broke, from going too high, or became husky, from speaking too low. Like most orators, he had a tendency to begin sentences or phrases at a slightly lower than normal pitch and progressively raise his voice in order to cue a climax. As a matter of fact, he practiced a technique for responding to applause: if the orator waits until the applause has died completely before continuing to speak, the result is flat and the effect is lost. FDR wisely waited until most clapping had died down, and then he spoke over the last few plaudits, thus keeping the momentum of the address moving.

FDR knew how and when to manage the pitch of his voice for effect. He often underlined words and phrases on his preliminary speech drafts and on his final reading copies. Even in these preliminary stages of rhetorical preparation, he considered how he could best deliver his thoughts to audiences. For example, he not only underlined the following words for vocal emphasis at Madison Square Garden in 1936, but he also spoke the lines as intended: "*I hate war*, and *I* know that the *Nation hates war*" and "*I welcome their hatred.*"[19]

The quality of Roosevelt's voice was widely known to his listeners. Of the four characteristics of the human voice, quality is the most difficult to describe, yet its impact on the human ear is considerable. Rate, pitch, and volume can be delineated after a fashion, but quality is that ineffable element that invites yet stubbornly defies description.

Some critics have tried to determine the effect of Roosevelt's dialect on his audiences. FDR had what may be loosely described as an eastern dialect. Audiences could quickly spot some of his famous trademarks, such as "Again and again," pronounced "a-gain" rather than "agen," and "I hate war," pronounced with a broad "a" and a dropped "r." But did his patrician pronunciation have a favorable or unfavorable impact on his persuasiveness? A point many critics fail to make on this question is that there were few presidential role models for comparison. Before the advent of national radio in the late 1920s, unless Americans had heard a president in person, they had no idea what a president was supposed to sound like. Some might have heard Calvin Coolidge, who had a nasal New England accent and unexpressive voice, or Herbert Hoover, who spoke in a standard American dialect but whose voice was cold and dull. A thorough search of the public reaction files did not reveal any favorable responses to FDR's dialect. On the other hand, two writers did caricature the president's snobby eastern pronunciation. One complained that he was "tired of 'Sistie' and 'Buzzie' Dall," and another reacted negatively to the 1937 Victory Dinner Address: "He makes himself sound so omniscient, and omnipotent with his cathedra voice . . . NOW while they are doped with relief, I shall have them in my POW'A. NOW, NOW! I must be the DICTATA. Yours for less poi'sonal pow'a, and more sincere democratic government."[20]

In comparison with his predecessors, Roosevelt was blessed with a vibrant voice, and he made the most of it. One will remember that the "talkies" ended many silent screen stars' acting careers because they did not have the gift of a good voice, but FDR had "a superb newsreel voice."[21]

THE EFFECTS OF FDR'S DELIVERY

Individual Americans reacted favorably to their president's speech delivery. Letters and telegrams from the public reaction files indicate that listeners appreciated FDR's delivery. Although the critic cannot establish a link between their positive letters and telegrams and support for him at the ballot box, it is not unreasonable to infer from these sources that his delivery impressed his audiences. Two speech professors opined that "the cues in Franklin D. Roosevelt's voice—the voice alone—inspired confidence" in his First Inaugural Address and that "if Herbert Hoover had spoken the same words into the microphone . . . the stock market would have fallen another notch and public confidence with it." But ordinary Americans also appreciated FDR's polished delivery of his addresses and Fireside Chats. To the First Fireside Chat, a man responded: "The calm confident voice everyone heard or should have heard seemed to be another step toward prosperity." Joe the Tailor, from Indianapolis, Indiana, commented on the 1936 Annual Message: "It certainly was a masterpiece of rhetoric, which was delivered with perfect pronunciation, enunciation, articulation, and so distinctly given in ordinary language that even the most illiterate could not help but comprehend every word of it.'' FDR's delivery of his acceptance speech in Franklin Field in 1936 prompted positive responses: a man from Pennsylvania wrote that ''I have heard from my father the Cross of Gold speech of Bryan, and have read the speech at Gettysburg, but if you humbly permit me to say, you reached greater heights of logic and oratory than either of those,'' and a Kentucky newspaperman was moved to write that ''your voice carried more conviction, more strength, more confidence than at any time since the spring of 1933.'' In the trying times after the Nazis invaded Poland, an Omaha, Nebraska, person wrote the president after his Fireside Chat: ''The calm tone of the address in the face of great world emotion, as well as the logic of the speech, were truly remarkable.'' And of the Third Inaugural, a man from New York City wrote of ''the delivery so crystal clear, so deliberate, so straight from the heart.''[22]

SUMMARY

FDR spoke to Americans in their homes on the radio, and it must not be overlooked that his voice was a powerful asset in persuading his radio audiences. Of course, Americans also experienced the complete Roosevelt when he addressed live audiences or, to a truncated degree, when they watched him on the newsreels. In these instances, his gestures and physical dynamism added to the positive impact his voice made on his hearers. The examples from the public reaction files indicate that Americans appreciated his effective speech delivery. In a treatment of Roosevelt's rhetorical presidency, one should always remember that FDR delivered the addresses and Fireside Chats to Americans and that they reacted to his words as he delivered them.

3

FDR and the Media:
Radio, Newsreels, and
Press

"Without motor-cars, sound films and wireless," said Fuehrer Adolf Hitler, "no victory for National Socialism."[1] President Franklin Roosevelt could have said the same thing about his New Deal. He was not the first president to address the nation by radio, or to be seen on the movie newsreels, or to hold press conferences. Yet, he developed a symbiotic relationship between the media and himself, and he institutionalized that uneasy alliance in the rhetorical presidency.

Radio's and Roosevelt's rise were inextricably linked. Based on his success with addressing the people of New York from Albany as governor, FDR wisely realized the greater impact he could achieve in speaking to the entire nation by radio as president. When he took to the airwaves, his political foes feared his persuasive mastery over that intimate medium because he could communicate entire speeches and Fireside Chats directly, without editorial comment from an intervening press.

FDR also recognized that no matter how much effort and planning went into the production of a speech or chat, the press often filtered or distorted his discourse. Unlike President Richard Nixon, who used his vice-president, Spiro Agnew, to attack the television news media in 1969, Roosevelt tried to co-opt reporters by flattering, cajoling, and orchestrating them in his press conferences. In a way, FDR tried to have it both ways and often succeeded. He built expectations by hinting what he would say in a speech, the press would report it, and FDR, given valuable pre-speech publicity, was relatively assured of having a large audience. Hence, the prior anticipation of an address, its actual delivery, and its subsequent reporting by the newspapers were three news events, or three persuasive messages, that FDR directed to the American people.

The third member of FDR's persuasive troika was the movie newsreels. The larger-than-life image on the silver screen allowed "Americans in the thirties and forties . . . to witness firsthand President Roosevelt battling the Depression." The newsreels, somewhat akin to contemporary television news broadcasts, tended to highlight appearance over substance, delivery over argument, or, according to Margaret Thorp, "how the man of the hour smiles and speaks." The newsreel editors generally selected for their movie patrons those speaking situations that pictured FDR at his best: his anger at the patricians who could still purchase their Packards and Pierce Arrows; his buoyant optimism that the New Deal would mitigate the nation's economic problems; his compassion in impromptu talks in the Dust Bowl; his steely contempt for Mussolini and Hitler; and when the war finally came, his certainty that "the American people in their righteous might will win through to absolute victory."[2]

Following the reasoning in the chapter on delivery, one should realize that it is as important to appreciate how Roosevelt used the media to communicate his messages as it is to understand the content of the speeches themselves. This was especially true in FDR's case because he carefully tuned his delivery to satisfy the technology of his era. On the radio, Roosevelt knew his listeners would receive his words and the vocal cues to which he gave considerable attention. On the newsreels, where image was paramount, he appeared equally presidential when "explaining some function of the New Deal" or "looking square into the eye of the nation across a desk and reading from a manuscript," because he was "a superb newsreel voice and figure."[3]

THE MOVIE NEWSREELS

From the palatial Paramount on Times Square in New York City to the baroque Fox in San Francisco, not to mention the approximately sixteen thousand other picture houses located across the country, Americans went to the movies in the Thirties. In any given week, approximately twenty million patrons passed through a lobby. As the mighty Wurlitzer pipe organ rose from its orchestra pit singing with its thousand throated voices the popular songs of the day, maybe even "Happy Days Are Here Again," patrons settled back in their seats for a lift from the daily drudgery of the Depression. They came to watch a movie, but also saw a newsreel.[4]

Pathe, Paramount, Fox Movietone, Universal, and Hearst News of the Day produced the newsreels that were distributed to theatres. The rhetorical impact of the newsreels reinforced the speaking-is-governing tenet of the rhetorical presidency. When one saw FDR enacting speeches, one saw his functioning as the president. Leif Furhammar and Folke Isaksson observed that film had the potential to be persuasive: "By manipulating the cinematic image of reality one can also manipulate the spectator's *concepts* of reality—i.e. the concepts on which they base their attitudes and actions." FDR demonstrated this principle in his First Fireside Chat on the banking crisis, Sunday, March 12, 1933, portions of which were staged for retake before the newsreel cameras. The jocularity with which he poked fun about keeping one's money under the mattress rather than in a reopened bank was as disarming as were his words. By the time of his Second Inaugural, evidence documents that the newsreel cameras were not accidental to, but were an integral part of, the rhetorical presidency: "At the last inauguration, President Roosevelt literally toed a chalk line for the boys, and stayed within a small square marked out for him by the cameramen." Notwithstanding the fact that Roosevelt could not have strayed from the podium unassisted even if he had wanted to, the point is that the symbiotic relationship was established. At this ceremony, as in other presidential speaking occasions, the newsreels allowed the citizenry to validate vicariously their president's investiture.[5]

The newsreels heightened the impact of the visual cues in FDR's delivery because he appeared before an audience on the screen as a person, not just as a detached voice from the radio grill. The acting out of the drama of the words on the reading copy, which FDR was very good at, made a great impact on the moviegoers. Arthur Molella noted: "FDR was as much a star of newsreels as he was on radio. 'In FDR we had the greatest single attraction,' said W.F. Githens of *Movietone News*. 'Announcement of his Fireside Chats . . . brought hundreds of patrons to the theater. Anti-New Dealers came to hiss. . . . ' " Lewis Jacobs realized the effects the newsreels had on the populace:

In fact, the very popularity of newsreels today makes them a far more potent factor in shaping American thought than they have ever been before. Moreover, because their images are so obvious, their message penetrates more easily than that of the story films; because they are generally accepted as the unalloyed truth, their effect is far reaching.

Where Hoover had been dour and uninspiring on film, Roosevelt was optimistic and animated: the image of hope became a reality for FDR's followers.[6]

Just as the movie moguls used the newsreels to help lure patrons to their picture palaces, so did Roosevelt use the newsreels for his purposes. Part of his success was in his message, but an important measure of his persuasiveness was due to his speech delivery. Perhaps understanding the efficacy of the newsreels, in which FDR so excelled, Robert Littell wrote:

What counts—and here is a valuable function of the newsreel—is the faces, the voices, the gestures, the personalities rather than the words spoken. For no matter how well prepared a politician's newsreel turn may be . . . the impression . . . will be good or bad according to whether or not the public likes what this glimpse of his face and voice reveals of the man himself.[7]

THE RADIO

Roosevelt on the radio immediately suggests the Fireside Chats. These certainly were among his most important radio addresses, but the president's other major speeches were broadcast over the air as well as being featured on the silver screen. Yet the chats were and have come to be Roosevelt's quintessential rhetoric. But what made them so? And for that matter, how many were there?

John Sharon defined the chats in terms of place, audience, content, and style. As for content, Sharon's observation that the speeches focused on a single issue, which Waldo Braden and Earnest Brandenburg seconded, could be applied to other addresses as well—the Victory Dinner Address, the "Four Freedoms" speech, the "Quarantine" speech, and so on. Actually, some chats dealt with one issue, but others dealt with more than one topic. The chats on May 26 and December 29, 1940, dealt with war preparation; however, the second chat, on May 7, 1933, dealt with a host of issues as did the fourth chat, on October 22, 1933, which focused on the New Deal alphabet soup agencies. Few of Roosevelt's significant speeches were confined to a single issue, as was the First Fireside Chat on the banking crisis, because, as will be demonstrated in the chapter on style, Roosevelt used an individual speech or chat for a variety of purposes. As for simple and understandable language, Roosevelt always crafted his words in that manner—the Fourth Inaugural Address comes immediately to mind. The audience could be a promising factor. Sharon differentiated between an informal audience—friends, family members, and close advisers—and a formal audience, invited to listen to a general radio broadcast. The latter situation, according to a letter from Robert Sherwood to Sharon, was not a chat. Yet the word *audience* in its rhetorical sense meant not the few people in the immediate room but the millions in their homes to whom Roosevelt spoke. Sharon's factor of place was accurate. Except for speaking on the Teheran-Cairo conference from Hyde Park on December 24, 1943, the president always addressed the country from the Diplomatic Reception Room in the White House.[8]

How many Fireside Chats were there? The Master Speech File listed twenty-one, the number FDR's people thought there were. Sharon calculated twenty-eight, the number Samuel Rosenman and the editors of *Public Papers and Addresses* said there were, and that is the number taken by Braden and Brandenburg. The problem of defining a chat is an example of what Thomas Conley called the "Linnaean Blues." Roosevelt was not concerned with aiding genre critics in precisely delineating the nature of the chats. Like the artificial fireplace before which FDR spoke, the chats do not fall easily into contrived categories. Trying to cast them into some generic form misses the point that FDR's purposes changed over time, that he addressed different issues and target audiences, and that he even responded differently to similar exigencies—for example, the pre-war chats from 1939 to 1941 progressed from a war of words against the Axis powers to shooting at them on the high seas upon provocation.[9]

For want of a better description, some of the Fireside Chats were pep talks. The ones of October 12, 1942, July 28, 1943, September 8, 1943, June 12, 1944, and November 19, 1944, were mediocre. With regard to these chats, Sharon believed the Third War Loan Drive, September 8, 1943, and the Fifth Drive, June 12, 1944, were firesides. But by the same reasoning of place, purpose, and medium, the Sixth War Loan Drive of November 19, 1944, should be termed the thirtieth and last Fireside Chat. (See Appendix 1 for a suggested canon of Fireside Chats.)

Some of the Fireside Chats were presidential responses to significant exigencies. In these messages, Roosevelt sought to calm the people and to utter a unified national response, even if it was only rhetorical bluster. The chat on European war on September 3, 1939, was poignant because the president was basically powerless to act. By May 26, 1940, Roosevelt was able to tell the American people that the Congress would appropriate huge sums of money for national defense. The "Arsenal of Democracy" chat, December 29, 1940, continued that appeal so that the United States could eventually support FDR's discourse with military deeds. Those chats on "Freedom of the Seas," September 11, 1941, and after Pearl Harbor, were the last ones that could be characterized as responses to Axis exigencies. In line with that kind of chat, the radio message delivered on May 27, 1941, should be called a fireside. This Unlimited National Emergency talk, delivered before an immediate audience in the White House of the governing board of the Pan American Union, followed, as others had, a presidential proclamation, and was spaced a reasonable length of time from the previous chat on December 29, 1940. Roosevelt heightened the effect of the National Emergency chat by telling his radio audience that the governing board was in his immediate audience.

Some of Roosevelt's best Fireside Chats were responses to his critics. Under fire, FDR rose to the challenge. He selected several potent rhetorical techniques and marshalled some of his most eloquent language in order to take his case directly to the people. For instance, in the Second Fireside Chat, May 7, 1933, he apologized for too much apparent presidential power over the Congress and cautioned people not to view the New Deal as control over business and industry but as a partnership. Republicans were not engaged by that euphemism. Responding in his Fifth Fireside Chat, June 28, 1934, to criticism that the New Deal had not materially altered the Depression, Roosevelt chose the best kind of defense—a good offense. He used a scapegoat technique to isolate his critics. He inveighed, in language reminiscent of the First Inaugural Address, against the few who were "characterized by a mad chase for unearned riches, and an unwillingness . . . to look beyond their own schemes and speculations," and who were known for their vocal complaints that their toes were being stepped on. Then to pit the people against his critics, he asked the now famous rhetorical question: "Are you better off now than you were last year?" FDR knew what the answer was. Almost all of the Sixth Fireside Chat, September 30, 1934, was a spirited defense of the NRA. The famous chat on the reorganization of the judiciary in 1937, to be treated in detail in chapter six, was an aggressive defense against the court-packing accusation. Other talks had elements of apology in them. For example, he refuted isolationists' arguments in the chats on national defense, May 26, 1940, and on "Freedom of the Seas," September 11, 1941. For the former, he used anaphora, beginning four paragraphs with "There is nothing in our present emergency,'' to assuage the audience's fears that the benefits gained under the New Deal would not be lost; and in the latter he vividly countercharged the isolationists: "But when you see a rattlesnake poised to strike, you do not wait until he has struck before you crush him.'' Until the "Freedom of the Seas" chat, Roosevelt's rhetoric was often contradictory and more bellicose than the reality of presidential action. During this time, as will be demonstrated in chapter seven, Roosevelt's responses to the isolationists were rhetorical catharses for him.[10]

Many of Roosevelt's chats were prime examples of a tenet of the rhetorical presidency. He used them to maintain and to enhance his presidential power by persuading the people to move the Congress. In his Third Fireside Chat, July 24, 1933, a broad appeal for the NRA, he reminded his audience that "It does not help much if the fortunate half is very prosperous.'' He used the bandwagon effect to entice employers to be on a patriotic Roll of Honor and offered a badge, "We Do Our Part,'' for those who cooperated, and in a chin-up affirmation, he challenged the people that they could pull themselves out of the Depression if they wanted to. On October 22, 1933, he assured his audience that the big and little chiselers would soon be out of business, and he prepared his audience for the legislation on gold he would soon propose to the Congress. He ended this chat with one of his famous lines: "Our troubles will not be over tomorrow, but we are on our way and we are headed in the right direction.'' Roosevelt spoke as the vox populi on April 28, 1935, when he plugged the social security act before the Congress and urged congressional legislation to extend the NRA. The chat on the reorganization of the federal judiciary, while functioning as an apologia, was also clearly an appeal to the people to press the Senate to pass FDR's bill.

After the Court fight, a victorious Congress was in no particular hurry to cooperate with the president, and thereafter his chats were edgy. The Fireside Chat calling the Congress to extra session, October 12, 1937, reminded the audience that the recession needed additional legislation to support the mired-down progress of the New Deal. In this chat, he credited the radio and the moving picture, or the newsreels, and not the newspapers, for having helped him to inform the people about the needs of their government. The chat on economic conditions, April 14, 1938, was a well-timed follow-up in the evening to a message the president had sent the Congress that day. To motivate the Congress, he used a favorite image, a nautical metaphor, as a clever concluding appeal to the people: "I propose to sail ahead. I feel sure that your hopes and your help are with me. For to reach port, we must sail—sail, not lie at anchor—sail, not drift.'' In the fireside on party primaries, June 24, 1938, in which he announced why the people should support his "purge," he openly sought their support: "In simple frankness and in simple honesty, I need all the help I can get.'' Another talk on economic policy, April 28, 1942, came on the heels of a message to the Congress. Lest conservatives miss his point, FDR used a series of questions that began with "Ask''; the objects of his interrogatories were the peoples enslaved by the Nazis. Roosevelt knew that if the American people could ask those people if the legislation he requested were worth it, their answer would be "yes." Then, in an eloquent series of statements framed by anaphora—"It must not be impeded by"—the president impugned the motives of those who would obstruct the war effort and endanger the gains of the New Deal. The president used his talk on inflation and war, September 7, 1942, to urge the Congress to pass a bill by October 1, and he reminded the people of its urgency. Toward the later part of the war, Roosevelt looked to the time after the peace was won, when presidents historically have had to surrender their powers to a restive Congress. In order to have a persuasive momentum after the war, he appraised the people about domestic issues he would address.[11]

One fireside deserves special attention. The two most effective speeches FDR ever delivered were his First Inaugural Address and his First Fireside Chat. Whereas the First Inaugural instilled hope and confidence that action soon would be taken, it may be said that in terms of audience response, the First Fireside achieved its immediate rhetorical goal of persuading Americans not to run re-opened banks. FDR's rhetorical strategy was brilliant but straightforward. To make certain that people would tune in to the chat, he issued on March 11 an announcement that he would address the nation the next evening. Having secured a national audience, he allayed fears by answering worrisome objections on the minds of his listeners. To the question of why would not all the banks open on Monday, he answered that he did not want another run on the banks. To defuse fears about what it meant if one's bank did not open on the first day—was it bankrupt? would it never open?—Roosevelt allowed that banks opening on sub-sequent days were just as sound. State banks, he assured, were opening on the same schedule as the national banks. Having calmed those concerns, he used levity to debunk any remaining reservations about hoarding and keeping one's money under the proverbial mattress. A remarkable aspect of this chat was Roosevelt's avowal that not all banks would reopen. The thread of honesty that he could not solve all the problems all the time was woven into many of his economic chats. He also took that tack in the pre-war chats, and he continued his honesty after the war began. Throughout these years, his persuasive credibility was enhanced by such frankness. He wisely eschewed promising the people more than he could deliver, and most people were willing to give assent to his per-suasion on what he could deliver.

Let us assume thirty Fireside Chats: FDR's timing of their delivery was sig-nificant in terms of the *kairos*, the right or propitious time. The following table gives their incidence on each day of the week:

Table 2
Firesides Delivered on Each Day of the Week

Sunday	Monday	Tuesday	Wednesday	Thursday	Friday	Saturday
12	6	6	2	2	2	0

Roosevelt chose Sunday, the most favored day, because he could address prime audiences. Sunday, Monday, and Tuesday, accounting for 80 percent of the chats, were excellent because Roosevelt would receive valuable news coverage on the following days. Conversely, it is instructive to observe that no speech was given on a Saturday, a light news day. FDR took care not to overuse the chats, and he timed them for maximum publicity in the press. Roosevelt revealed in a press conference on Saturday, August 27, 1938, that he was sensitive to rhetorical timing. He told the reporters that he refused to give a story that day because readers did not open the news section of their Sunday papers.[12]

The effects of Roosevelt's Fireside Chats, as well as of his other radio broadcasts, were due to a synergism of his rhetorical techniques, his careful timing and spacing, and his radio delivery. Over the radio, as on the newsreels, he ably communicated his ideas and presidential ethos. Rosenman pinpointed Roosevelt's great ability to identify with his audience: "I think his fireside chats gave you the impression, as you listened to them on the radio, that he was actually there, talking to you, and that you felt that he understood your problems, and that you were able to identify yourself with him, as he identified himself with you, as fighting a common cause." Sharon believed the chats exemplified "the full measure of his personality: his integrated purpose, his simplicity, his optimism, his sympathy, his courage, his ability to project himself to anyone's economic or social level." And Richard Strout said: "Roosevelt made radio his medium— his voice, calm, beautifully modulated, came right into the living room with you. You felt he was there talking to you, not to 50 million others, but to you personally."[13]

These critics' observations can be supplemented by frank reactions from Roosevelt's listeners. In response to FDR's First Fireside Chat, the chief justice of the Alabama Supreme Court wrote: "It was an inspiration and I believe will have a most salutary effect and that it will deter ninety per cent of the depositors from making withdrawals when the banks are opened." However, FDR's 1938 fireside on recovery drew criticism:

I am intensely opposed to the dangerous pump-priming plan as stated in your speech last evening.

You can't seem to realize that living beyond your means always results in trouble.

Once more you have proven the tongue is quicker than the brain.

There is very questionable elemental logic in any program which bespeaks enrichment through spending all the money one has.

Your unimpressive speech of last Thursday is further concern for lack of confidence.

FDR's May 1940 fireside drew mixed responses: "Did not care for speech. Is Hitler laughing?"; "As I was sitting and listening to your fireside chat last night, it seemed to me that an iron-clad cloak of fear lifted itself off my shoulders"; and "Your talk Sunday night did not make me feel that our defenses were adequate. I had the feeling that you had done all that you thought could be

Table 3
Newspaper and Voter Support for FDR in Presidential Elections

	1932	1936	1940	1944
Newspapers for FDR	41%	37%	26%	22%
Popular Vote for FDR	57%	60%	55%	53%

supported by public opinion to build up those defenses and perhaps you were right.'' In response to the efficacy of FDR's scapegoat technique to isolate the isolationists on December 29, 1940, at least one person appreciated it: ''With the exception of the small minority (to whom you expressed our contempt and condemnation so deftly and restrainedly) I believe the nation is behind you.'' But some of the persons thusly scapegoated still complained: ''You are breaking your pledge to keep us out of war . . . the English coal miner couldn't get a worse deal under Hitler than they now have''; ''Strongly protest your brazen attempt to drag the United States into this foreign war''; and ''Your message on Sunday night had a 'hollow ring.' ''[14]

THE PRESS CONFERENCE

So much has been written from so many perspectives about President Roosevelt's press conferences that one can only hope to fill a few lacunae. ''I have not tried to create a publicity bureau for the Administration,'' he wrote in 1938, ''or to 'plant' stories on its behalf.'' Notwithstanding Roosevelt's clever use of affirmation by denial—by claiming to deny a point he actually affirmed it—that is exactly what Roosevelt did in his conferences. B.H. Winfield has demonstrated how FDR tried to manage the conferences, and hence the reporting of the news, by manipulating format, rules of attribution that changed on an *ad hoc* basis, and conditions of attendance; moreover, Winfield detailed how FDR feigned surprise, pretended ignorance, or used elusive language to divert queries he did not want to answer. Additionally, Jill McMillan and Sandra Ragan discussed some of the factors that made Roosevelt the news reporters' friend in the White House.[15]

Yet, many critics have been so busy praising Roosevelt's admittedly adroit handling of the press, perhaps the best of any modern president, that most of them have not been troubled by a charge he made. FDR asserted that in the campaigns of 1932 and 1936 most of the publishers, especially the metropolitan ones, were against him and the New Deal. In a study of press reactions to Roosevelt's policies and speeches during his four administrations, Graham White demonstrated that the president's complaint apparently had merit (see Table 3).

Why was there such a disparity? There is an interesting parallel here. As mentioned earlier, Vice-President Spiro Agnew used his ''Television News Coverage'' speech, November 13, 1969, to charge that TV was not responsive to President Nixon's Vietnam War policy. Yet, Frank Stanton, president of CBS, countered in his "Reply to the Vice-President," November 25, 1969, that despite an alleged bias against the president's speech by anchormen, Nixon's speech was received favorably by the American people. George Wolfskill and John Hudson demonstrated in FDR's case that editorial bias in newspapers might not be as persuasive as is often imagined.[16]

But explaining the disparity, Roosevelt realized why much of the press was against him. He recognized that reporters might like him personally and might even sympathize with the social and political missions of the New Deal, but that their bosses, the editors and publishers, did not. He exempted the White House reporters who had to work for a living. But he held in special contempt columnists such as Westbrook Pegler, H. L. Mencken, and Walter Lippmann, not to mention newspaper tycoon William Randolph Hearst, whose Casa La Grande at San Simeon was proof enough there was profit in panning the New Deal.

Then why did Roosevelt continue to cooperate with the reporters by giving 999 news conferences in thirteen years? There are the obvious answers: he wanted to consolidate power by controlling the flow of information; he wanted to manage the news; he liked to pontificate with the press in off-the-record sessions. But one facet of FDR's handling of the press conferences has not been recognized. From a rhetorical standpoint, the press presented a convenient scapegoat to be used in times of political trouble. The president often blamed the newspapers for his bad press. He diverted the American peoples' attention from his policies to the press as the real culprit. FDR had it both ways: he used the press to purvey his political agenda, and when that agenda went awry for one reason or another, he charged the press with maligning the New Deal. The press handily supplied the president with the substance for his scapegoat attack.

Roosevelt began carping at the reporters soon after his landslide victory in 1936. He obviously believed they should march in lock-step behind the American people, who were with him. He was emboldened by the fact that he had won the presidency without the newspapers' assistance. Maury Maverick noted that the people repudiated the press: "To stupid bare-faced lies, gross intimidation and pay-envelope fraud, the people gave one long razzberry."[17]

As the second New Deal turned sour in 1937–38, the intensity of Roosevelt's attacks on the press grew truculent. Shortly after he announced his Court-packing scheme on February 5, 1937, he received a roasting from the press and he fought back. He told reporters on February 12 that the reception of his reorganization bill depended on the newspaper one read. He understandably failed to note that a sizeable segment of his own party was against him on the Court fight.

In his famous conference with the Society of Newspaper Editors, April 21, 1938, Roosevelt took the offensive. He indignantly attacked the editors for running an advertisement by the Southern Pine Association. Carried in papers throughout the South, the ad called farmers to arms over the wages and hour bill before the Congress. Roosevelt said the editors knew that it was a lie to warn farmers they would have to pay their field labor three dollars an hour, but the editors ran the ad anyway. Warming to his subject, Roosevelt traced the onus of unethical press practices to the owners. He knew eighty-five percent of the press was against him, but he still advised editors to eliminate their editorials because few people paid any attention to them. FDR coyly ended his conference, "I enjoyed all the shafts and I think I returned them with interest, so it is all right."[18]

As for the purge, which was not going well, FDR inveighed against the press to divert attention from the troubles he had caused. On August 16, 1938, he complained about the Tory press. He wisely chose the term *Tory* because it conjured an unpatriotic image, born during the Revolutionary War, of conservative economic royalists. A week later, on the twenty-third, he charged that the Tory press had overlooked an opportunity to educate the populace on political morality. Roosevelt chided the owners for not reporting how Republicans were crossing over to vote for Democratic candidates in the primary elections. He told a reporter for the *New York Herald Tribune* that this would be a "damned hard story" for the reporter's paper to print. During this conference, a reporter pressed the president on how strong the Tory press was. Roosevelt answered that 85 percent of the press was Tory, and, although the reporter offered a Gallup poll that suggested about three-hundred of the eight-hundred daily newspapers, or about 38 percent, supported the president, Roosevelt refused to believe that figure. Three days later, on the twenty-sixth, Roosevelt increased the tempo of his attack by indicting the *Boston Herald*, the *New York Herald Tribune*, and the *Baltimore Sun*, and he singled out "Frank Gannett, Bertie McCormick, and old man Hearst" for opprobrium.[19]

Roosevelt took a parting shot at the press over the purge. On August 27, 1938, he replied testily to a question about it. His response indicated sensitivity to criticism, and it also illustrated his awareness of how newspapers could malign his policy: "I would call it [the purge] one of those headline words, when you have to have a short word to illustrate an idea and, to go further, I would say it is an extremely immature word, either for headlines or leads." During his Fireside Chat on October 12, 1937, taking a sideswipe at the newspapers, he mentioned the contributions of the radio and the newsreels in educating the people. He omitted the newspapers purposefully because he thought they printed editorial viewpoints rather than real facts about the New Deal.[20]

On occasion, reporters could outwit Roosevelt. One such instance occurred during his conference on February 21, 1941. FDR complained that the press had published information leaked from the Senate Committee on Military Affairs before which General George Marshall had testified. Roosevelt came off badly in this exchange because a reporter trapped him into admitting that the press ought to publish documents that were obviously leaked by the Senate.[21]

However, faced with an urgent situation, Roosevelt usually rose to the occasion. His adaptability was never more in evidence than during his conference on Lend-Lease, December 17, 1940. Against a backdrop of attacks in the isolationist newspapers concerning whether Lend-Lease would violate neutrality and how it would be financed, Roosevelt mustered a masterful oral obfuscation. He reeled out the metaphor of the garden hose: after a neighbor used the hose, the lender only wanted it back intact; if the hose were damaged, the neighbor would merely replace it. To all sorts of queries—who would own the munitions, how would the British pay, would Lend-Lease move the United States toward war—FDR consistently hedged and refused to answer with a legalistic response. Instead, he parried with analogies that skirted the troublesome issues; nevertheless, these folksy images pressed the clear urgency that Great Britain had to be supplied for the sake of Western democracy.

CONCLUSION

Franklin D. Roosevelt was a rhetorician who realized the most effective way to communicate his speeches was through an unfettered medium. Radio was his prime tool, for it allowed him direct access to the American people on his terms and on a scale the public speaker, face to face, could never match. In a sense, his speaking was governing for many Americans. He told the audience what the government was doing to combat the Depression, which calmed fears and instilled hope. When the need arose, he enlisted the people behind him so that he could move the Congress as vox populi. Moreover, Roosevelt fashioned his delivery, especially his superb vocal modulations, to complement his words.

The newsreels, which David Halberstam noted were an important factor in American life at the time, allowed the president to communicate his total personality. Although the moviegoers saw and heard only clips, as compared to entire speeches and chats on the ratio, these short segments more than adequately portrayed the president's formidable delivery skills. Although there was some editorial selection by the newsreel editors, these clips managed to capture some of the most dramatic speeches and moments in FDR's speaking career. Thus, FDR was seen and heard by the movie-going public at his best. Whereas the radio allowed Roosevelt to achieve conversational intimacy, especially so in the Fireside Chats, the newsreels stressed the images of rhetoric and action.[22]

The newspapers were another story. Editors and publishers, the Tory press, were politicized behind the sacred trust of the First Amendment. On a less philosophical level, they disliked the codes of the NRA and Roosevelt's legislative program that curtailed their making money. Despite the fact that the conservative press printed his speeches and Fireside Chats, Roosevelt had to compete with snide headlines and unfriendly editorials. Increasingly after 1936, in his press conferences he cast the press in the role of scapegoat whenever his political policies were not going well. Some of Roosevelt's castigations were well founded but some were not. It served his rhetorical purposes to have Americans believe that eighty-five percent of the press was against him because it helped divert attention. His petulance against the press was purposeful; the figures were clear to anyone who wanted to read them. The newspapers did not have the persuasive power in the 1930s that their editors imagined or that Roosevelt wanted Americans to believe. Nevertheless, as James Pollard wrote, "Both were at fault and each used the other as a bogey to scare the public."[23]

On the basis of this chapter, there may be sufficient reason to add a corollary to the paradigm of the rhetorical presidency with regard to the media. Whenever the president uses the press for a scapegoat, critics may advantageously direct their attention toward the president's reasons for employing the technique. Though it is interesting to note that the president can portray the press as a scapegoat, it may be an altogether more useful finding to determine from what political matters the president is seeking to divert attention.

4

Four Campaigns to the
People

Campaign oratory was an integral part of FDR's rhetorical presidency. As a candidate, he took his New Deal directly to the people, and some of his greatest speeches were delivered in the heat of four campaigns. Only a handful of rhetorical phenomena, certainly Harry Truman's whistle-stop campaign of 1948, Dwight Eisenhower's ''I Shall Go To Korea'' speech in 1952, and John Kennedy's address on church-state relations to the Greater Houston Ministerial Association in 1960, can be mentioned in the same breath as Roosevelt's superb Madison Square Garden and ''Fala'' speeches.

THE 1932 CAMPAIGN

To begin her famous documentary ''The Triumph of the Will,'' produced in 1934, Leni Riefenstahl pictured Adolph Hitler coming as a savior to the German people by filming his airplane descending allegorically from the clouded heavens to Nuremberg. She might have taken the image from Roosevelt, who flew to Chicago in 1932 to accept in person his party's nomination to save the nation from the Depression.

Roosevelt's symbolic act, a public relations coup of the highest order, was a precursor of how he would use the technology of his time to enhance his political power, and of how he would not be bound by worn-out political traditions. But in reality, FDR's first campaign had all the vestiges of a time-tested rhetorical posture: define one's campaign by negation. If that seems confusing, it is meant to be, for it allows one to attack the opposition's policies with specific accusations while one talks in generalities about one's own political visions. Thus, Roosevelt continually identified unpopular policies with Herbert Hoover while maintaining latitude for himself. Part of this strategy was necessitated by the fact that Roosevelt and his "Brain Trust" crystallized his policies as he progressed toward March 4, 1933, and part was due to the expediency that is not accorded the incumbent: do not needlessly alienate voters by advocating specific programs that have the potentiality for divisiveness.

Governor Roosevelt delivered five important speeches in the campaign: two before the convention, the acceptance speech, and two after the convention. FDR delivered his famous "Forgotten Man" address over the radio from Albany on April 7, 1932, and his "Bold, Persistent Experimentation" speech at Oglethorpe University, Atlanta, Georgia, on May 22, 1932. He announced the New Deal, in what seemed to be an offhand manner at the time, on July 2, 1932. At San Francisco's Commonwealth Club, September 23, 1932, Roosevelt extended his hand to the business community, and at Pittsburgh, Pennsylvania, October 19, 1932, he gave an economic speech he came to wish he had never delivered.

THE "FORGOTTEN MAN" SPEECH

In this address, FDR attacked the Hoover administration for its commitment to what Roosevelt termed the trickle-down theory of enhancing the rich so that the poor would eventually benefit. Paying himself a compliment to build his competency as a contender, FDR used his experiences in World War I as a warrant for his credibility in battling the Depression. He pledged to solve the crisis "from the bottom to top and not from the top to bottom." Since there were considerably more down-and-out people than rich people in the country, those multitudes could easily identify with "the forgotten man at the bottom of the economic pyramid." Any forgotten man certainly would have appreciated the governor's sideswipe at the president. FDR reminded his radio audience that rather than helping the little man, Hoover had established a two-billion-dollar fund to help the corporations and railroads. Raymond Moley, the author of this speech, borrowed the phrase from William Graham Sumner's famous essay entitled "The Forgotten Man." Although Sumner had discussed the concept in terms of the average man who worked for a living, Moley used the term to encompass everyone who felt wronged by the Depression. The righteous anger Roosevelt stirred in this speech neatly covered some of the internal logical contradictions in his talk.

The governor condemned the president for expensive stopgap measures that would not solve the unemployment problem, scored him for the Hawley-Smoot tariff, and criticized him for not addressing the real problem of increasing purchasing power. Yet, what did Roosevelt advocate? He offered a vague panacea for increasing purchasing power without indicating how it would work; he mentioned a program to aid mortgage foreclosures without indicating it would cost a great deal of money; and he was for revising the tariffs as long as such revisions did not throw U.S. industries "out of balance," one of the reasons the tariff legislation had been passed originally.

Roosevelt concluded his speech with a precursor of the war metaphors he would marshall in his First Inaugural Address: "We are in the midst of an emergency at least equal to that of war. Let us mobilize to meet it."[1]

Although forgotten people in the country, particularly in the West and Midwest, and the newspapers they purchased, supported this speech, some complained that the speech was demagogic. In an outburst of his own, Al Smith vowed to fight against "any demagogic appeal" that set "class against class and rich against poor." Although the *New York Times* supported Roosevelt's candidacy, it noted he should not speak in "demagogic claptrap" and complained, "What the Governor himself would do for the man at the bottom he did not state." The conservatives understood all too well the implications of the forgotten man image. Sumner had wryly observed that monarchs complained their liberty to rule without check was infringed upon by constitutional legislation. Those wedded to the status quo realized that if someone started to remember the forgotten man, they would soon be forgotten. Although many at the bottom of the economic rung did not read the *New Republic*, it stated succinctly why the rich disliked Roosevelt and called him a demagogue, and why the poor saw through such plutogoguery: "The real demagogue is the politician who . . . in spite of the overwhelming evidence to the contrary, [says] that if government takes care of the rich, the rich will take care of all the rest of us."[2]

The next act of the Smith-Roosevelt drama was played out at a Jefferson Day Dinner at St. Paul, Minnesota, April 18, 1932. Hoping that sparks would fly as Roosevelt rose to Smith's challenge, Republicans and conservative Democrats were disappointed that Roosevelt did not deign to mention Smith even in a passing shot. Roosevelt did not want to divide the party unnecessarily; he had his sights on Hoover, the real competition. The governor continued some of the themes he would reiterate so eloquently in his First Inaugural Address. He repeated his belief that the national emergency was graver than a war, and he berated Hoover for trying lamely to assuage the nation's fears. As would have befitted his social class, in his concluding remarks FDR could have used the metaphor of a Cadillac V–16 engine that powered chauffeur-driven town broughams or alluded to a Dusenberg supercharged straight–8 motor that propelled dual-cowl phaetons to the then dizzying speed of 116 miles per hour, but Roosevelt went for the common touch by identifying with everyman's four-cylinder Ford: "If the old car in spite of frequent emergency repairs has been bumping along downhill on only two cylinders for three long years, it is time to get another car that will start uphill on all four."[3]

THE OGLETHORPE SPEECH

Candidate Roosevelt spoke at Oglethorpe University on May 22. Ernest K. Lindley composed this speech. Roosevelt must have been pleased with Lindley's draft because he made no changes on it. Lindley, a newspaperman, responded to a challenge FDR had issued to some newspapermen who had ribbed his speeches: if they could write a better speech, FDR parried, then write one. Lindley did.

The speech is a precursor for the speaking-is-governing tenet of the rhetorical presidency. It indicates that Roosevelt and Lindley understood that speech must prepare the way for action, but that in another sense, the deliverance of an important address was a symbolic action. Lindley had Roosevelt say "True leadership calls for the setting forth of the objectives and the rallying of public opinion in support of these objectives." Listeners and readers could easily infer that Hoover championed the wrong goals and was unsuccessful in gaining the nation's support for them. But what were Roosevelt's objectives? Aside from nostrums in the speech, the only policy he seemed to advocate clearly was a redistribution of income, which was a safe policy because the poor vastly out-numbered the rich, as the "Forgotten Man" speech demonstrated, but the re-distribution was vague because FDR did not specify how he would accomplish it. As policy addresses, the "Forgotten Man," the St. Paul, and the Oglethorpe speeches were, as the conservatives complained, platitudinous. But his critics missed a point that Roosevelt understood very well: his speeches were intended not for the critics who would not be won over anyway, but for the people. The efficacy of Roosevelt's rhetoric in these speeches was that by talking about problems, he appeared to offer solutions, even if he defined his solutions in terms of what they would not be—Hoover's. Rather than presenting tightly organized problem-solution speeches, Roosevelt used well-turned phrases to present an image of himself as a man of vision and action. Indeed, if one reads the literal rhetoric of the oft-quoted passage from the Oglethorpe speech, one is left with an indefinite pronoun: "The country needs and, unless I mistake its temper, the country demands bold, persistent experimentation. It is common sense to take a method and try it: If it fails, admit it frankly and try another. But above all, try something." Part of Roosevelt's vagueness was due to the fact that he had an advantage over Hoover: he was not identified with the Depression.[4]

THE NEW DEAL SPEECH

Roosevelt's acceptance speech at Chicago was, in many respects, a contin-uation of the rhetorical strategies he had developed in his earlier campaign speeches. He affirmed his image by negating Hoover's. This differentiation commenced almost immediately. He told the convention and the nation that he rejected the silly *modus operandi* of the status quo. His physical presence was demanded because the times were unprecedented and unusual. He said it was a "symbol" of his intention to be honest and to not shut his eyes to the truth as Hoover had, and it was "symbolic that in so doing I broke traditions."

However, the body of his speech suffered from the lack of coherence. To be sure, it contained the usual jibes at the Republicans, "If they claim paternity for one [prosperity] they cannot deny paternity for the other [the Depression]"; it called for action four times; and it called for repeal of the 18th Amendment. However, specific policies were notably lacking; he contradicted himself on the tariff issue; and he overused "just one word" as a transitional device. Yet all of that was overlooked when Roosevelt delivered Rosenman's famous peroration.

In his conclusion, he again defined his campaign by negation. He charged that the Republican leaders had failed in material things, in national vision, and in offering no hope. Whereas the people had hoped in vain under Hoover, Roosevelt offered forgotten man and women a phrase: "I pledge you, I pledge myself, to a new deal for the American people."

One does not gain a clear conception from Roosevelt's acceptance speech of what the New Deal would be, but that did not matter. What counted was that FDR held Hoover and the Republican leaders responsible for the Depression, offered hope where Hoover offered the status quo, and symbolically broke outdated traditions. The drafts of the acceptance speech are so incomplete that little can be reconstructed, although one item is worth mentioning. Rosenman's famous New Deal line was not originally placed as a peroration, but was handwritten as an insert on the fourth page of a twenty-page speech draft. Somehow, it was moved to its rightful place in the conclusion.[5]

COMMONWEALTH CLUB SPEECH

Whereas the acceptance speech excelled in symbolism, the speech to the Commonwealth Club, September 23, dealt with substance. The address was written by Adolph Berle and revised by the Brain Trust. The drafts of the speech are incomplete, and on the extant ones there are no emendations by FDR. The title of Berle's draft, "Progressive Government," dated September 9, 1932, is a good description of the address. In it, Berle used several rhetorical techniques to produce what Kenneth Davis called one of the few "extended coherent statements" made by candidate Roosevelt.[6]

Berle-Roosevelt used affirmation by denial in the introduction to make a partisan speech appear nonpolitical. In a classical *partitio*, or partitioning of the speech, Roosevelt told his audience he would not speak of politics but of government, not of parties but of universal principles. Roosevelt tried for most of the speech to be nonpolitical. However, the dichotomy he established early in the speech between Hamilton, who represented the Republican party, and Jefferson, who stood for the Democrats, belied his intention for those who understood the equation. He also scored the Republicans with the Reconstruction Finance Corporation, but this was far enough into his speech that the initial favorable impression he had created, by saying in the introduction he would be nonpolitical, had accomplished its goal. Roosevelt assumed this nonpolitical partisan posture in order to create a receptive context for his persuasions.

Wil Linkugel has convincingly demonstrated that Berle had FDR simulate the persona of the history professor in lecturing on the political implications of U.S. history to 1932. Thus, the ethos one would ascribe to Roosevelt-as-professor would be transferred to Roosevelt-as-candidate. That is why he denied he was giving a political speech. He wanted to build his credibility as a national figure. His speech accomplished that, but more.[7]

What critics have not observed in this speech on progressive government is how Berle-Roosevelt lucidly applied the method of residues to argue the philosophy, if not the detailed mechanics, of the New Deal. The method of residues is a rhetorical application of the disjunctive syllogism: either A, B, or C; not A, not B, therefore C. Berle-Roosevelt stated the thesis, a two-part disjunct, early in the address: either (A) men and women serve government and economics, or (B) government and economics serve people. Roosevelt developed disjunct (A) by negating Republicanism, Hamiltonianism, and rugged individualism. He let the audience conclude, by skillfully listing the credit, farm, tariff, and unemployment problems of the Depression, that people could no longer serve government and economic orders. "Put plainly," Roosevelt concluded, "we are steering a course toward economic oligarchy, if we are not there already." Thus, the only tenable disjunct was (B). In arguing that government should serve the people, Berle-Roosevelt adapted well to the listeners. This was a conscious effort to target appeals to a specialized constituent audience, a concept that Craig Smith refined in the rhetorical presidency. There was no "forgotten man" imagery or "bold, persistent experimentation" panaceas for his audience of business and civic leaders. Rather, Roosevelt talked about "an economic constitutional order" that was "the common task of statesman and business man." He was inclusive, not divisive. Yet, he gave his rhetoric some teeth. He applied the carrot-and-stick technique he would perfect in his First Inaugural Address. The carrot was the appeal that many businessmen already realized a new economic order was needed (the bandwagon effect) and that business leaders must suppress personal advantage for a greater common end. In a broad hint, Roosevelt scored the selfish princes of property for not assuming the social responsibility that went with their economic power. For the recalcitrant, the stick was a veiled threat: "Government may properly be asked to apply restraint"; "Government must be swift to enter and protect the public interest"; and "The Government should assume the function of economic regulation only as a last resort, to be tried only when private initiative, inspired by high responsibility, with such assistance and balance as Government can give, has finally failed." In the conclusion of the speech, Berle had Roosevelt speak as the vox populi. Subtly, Roosevelt let the audience infer that he had the power to produce his new economic constitutional order. For beyond the pleasant confines of the Commonwealth Club stood the "forgotten man": "Government includes the art of formulating a policy and using the political technique to attain so much of that policy as will receive general support; persuading, leading, sacrificing, teaching always, because the greatest duty of a statesman is to educate." In that one sentence, Berle captured the essence of the New Deal in relationship to the rhetorical presidency of Franklin D. Roosevelt. Indeed, Compton Mackenzie concluded that "if ever a speech prepared a country for a revolution, that Commonwealth Club speech did."[8]

THE PITTSBURGH SPEECH

On October 19, 1932, Roosevelt delivered a speech on the federal deficit that attests that rhetoric, like roosters, can come back to roost. The speech followed in the same vein as his earlier campaign talks. The attacks on Hoover were there, but more strident, and his policies were vague, even more so. In the earlier speeches, FDR had painted word pictures that stirred the emotions of his audiences, but when discussing the federal budget, he used numbers to appeal logically to his listeners. The problem was that Roosevelt was better with words that could mean different things to different people than with numbers that either compute or do not.

Roosevelt made two major attacks at Forbes Field. First, he indicted Hoover's policy of increasing the cost of government by a billion dollars from 1927 to 1931. Then FDR looked at the other side of the ledger book. He charged that Hoover estimated the deficit to be one hundred and fifty million when it was in fact three and three-quarter billion dollars for the two years ending June 1932. Sanctimoniously, Roosevelt allowed that the country, and he, could not stand that. Not content with attacking the president's policy, FDR went on to malign his character. He charged Hoover with a lack of "reasonable accuracy and reasonable prudence," said Hoover concealed "realities" and abused "confidence," and impugned Hoover's fear of trusting the American people with "the facts about their affairs." Lest he appear too disrespectful of President Hoover, whom he had implied was dishonest and deceitful, FDR sallied forth with an incredible affirmation by denial. Averring that he recited "this record with reluctance," Roosevelt coyly allowed: "I pay my tribute to the devotion of the President of the United States. It is not true to say that he has not been unremitting in his efforts, and I for one have never heard it said."

The real problem, however, in the Pittsburg speech was FDR's proposed solution. He pledged to reduce the cost of government operations by 25 percent. In pruning the "fungus growth" of boards and commissions and so forth, FDR claimed he would save thousands of dollars a year. He also claimed he would use the revenue, several hundred million dollars a year, that would accrue to the government from taxes on beer once the 18th Amendment was repealed. It was not clear how his savings—since he hoped not to raise taxes—would balance a budget so askew. (Perhaps the Democrats should not have taken such political umbrage when Ronald Reagan compared himself to Franklin Roosevelt in the 1984 campaign.)

This speech also stands as a good example of Roosevelt's tendency to say something for everyone in his speeches, a theme to be developed in chapter 8, "Writing the Rhetoric." Roosevelt's pledge to reduce the deficits was an example of a standard campaign tactic, "me too, me better." In this speech, Roosevelt appealed to conservatives in and out of the Democratic party by demonstrating how he was like Hoover, but how he was better than Hoover—FDR *would* balance the budget! Yet, what about the forgotten man whom Roosevelt seemed to have forgotten? In a humane but glaringly contradictory exception, FDR pledged to the poor that he would ask an authorization of funds, even if it meant keeping the budget out of balance, to stave off starvation.[9]

Before closing the 1936 campaign, a critic would be remiss in not excoriating Roosevelt's speech at Baltimore, Maryland, on October 25. The speech was equalled in spleen only by Senator Charles Sumner's "The Crime Against Kansas" speech, May 19–20, 1856, for which Sumner was bludgeoned on the floor of the Senate. Like Sumner's speech, FDR's philippic was excessive in venomous attack against Hoover, in vituperation against the Four Horsemen of Destruction, Delay, Deceit, and Despair (the speech was developed topically under each heading), and in vespine stings on rugged individualism. Amid all the acerbic assertions that could just as easily have been uttered by the Reverend Mr. Coughlin at his best (or worst?), one statement foreshadowed Roosevelt's battle with the Supreme Court in 1937. He charged the Hoover administration with deceit because the Republican party was in complete control of all branches of the federal government, and then he ad-libbed "the Executive, the Senate, the House of Representatives and, I might add for good measure, the Supreme Court as well."[10]

SUMMARY

The rhetorical purpose of Franklin Roosevelt's first presidential campaign was to win the election, which he did by 472 to 59 electoral votes and by 22, 800,000 votes to Hoover's 15,750,000. President Hoover bitterly campaigned on the complaints that FDR's New Deal was undeveloped and vague, which it was, and would therefore lead the United States down new and untested roads, which it did. But that did not matter to the American people. Hoover's policies were coherent but a continuation of the status quo; his image, cool and aloof, was identified with the Depression; and his speech delivery was insipid and uninspiring. Roosevelt, on the other hand, appealed effectively to different constituent audiences, never mind the contradictions from the "Forgotten Man" speech to the Commonwealth Club speech to the Pittsburgh address. He vigorously attacked a vulnerable administration at its Achilles' heel and, as Alfred Rollins so perceptively noted, "worked his way into the hearts of millions with a smile, a gesture, and promise of deep concern."[11]

THE 1936 CAMPAIGN

Roosevelt faced a different rhetorical situation for his second presidential campaign. The strategies he used for his first campaign were not entirely appropriate. As an incumbent, like Hoover in 1932, FDR had to defend the status quo. But Roosevelt made the most of the rhetorical situation. Whereas Hoover had been on the defensive throughout the 1932 campaign, Roosevelt seized the initiative and conducted an aggressive canvass. Thus, when Alfred Landon and his running mate, William Knox, attacked the president and the New Deal, Roosevelt defended and countercharged. This countercharge was a brilliant tactic because it turned the tables on the Republicans. Charges that the New Deal had not mastered the Depression became evidence that the New Deal had to accomplish more under Roosevelt's leadership. That is, Roosevelt realized, much better than the Republicans, that the American people had come to appreciate the difference between the government's serving the rich or the people. Thus, when Knox and Landon tried to argue "me too, me better," Roosevelt devastatingly outflanked that ridiculous posture. Franklin Roosevelt never let the American people forget the difference, not in degree but in kind, between him and the Republicans.

THE ACCEPTANCE SPEECH

Roosevelt delivered his second acceptance speech at Franklin Field, an open-air stadium in Philadelphia, on the evening of June 27, 1936. It was his best speech in the genre because of its tone and tenor.

The speech drafts are unnumbered and without initials to help identify their authorship. FDR had told Raymond Moley and Tommy Corcoran to prepare a draft, but had also told Samuel Rosenman and Stanley High to work on a draft. Roosevelt selected the Rosenman-High draft over the Moley-Corcoran one because he liked its fighting tone, but he nevertheless instructed Rosenman and High to incorporate the Moley-Corcoran draft into theirs. The speech was a pastiche of drafts, but what it lacked in coherence it more than compensated for in striking phrases. A draft titled "S and S" has the famous "economic royalist" phrase that has been ascribed to Stanley High. On another draft, the famous "rendezvous with destiny" phrase appears for the first time, and it has been attributed to Tommy Corcoran. Although the speech's most famous phrases were not Roosevelt's, he did make some emendations that illustrate his ideas on how to attack the Republicans.

On the basis of its anaphora and its sentiments toward the Tories, there is reason to believe that FDR dictated the following eloquently composed thought: "A small group had concentrated into their own hands an almost complete control over other people's property, other people's money, other people's labor—other people's lives." The sentence remained unaltered in the speech. And, there is no doubt at all that he penned the famous peroration that declared war on the economic royalists (FDR's additions are italicized and his deletions are bracketed): "We are [saving] *fighting to save* a great and precious [republican] form of government [for democracy] *for ourselves*. Re-enlist with me in that war. *I accept the commission you have tendered me. I join with you. I am enlisted for the duration of the war.''* Although the war was against the economic royalists, Roosevelt was sensitive to the nuances of language as is illustrated in the following example. Stanley High had used consistent imagery when he wrote about royalists and their thrones. Roosevelt was happy with the imagery of the economic royalists, but he went to the heart of the matter when he changed thrones to power, the real issue in the campaign: "What they really complain of is that we seek to [overthrow their thrones] *take away their power.* Our allegiance to American institutions requires the overthrow of [their thrones] *this kind of power.*[12]

Senator Harry Truman wrote Bess that Roosevelt's address was a masterpiece. A Republican from New York City thought so, too: "Mr. President I salute you. The spirit of your speech of acceptance shall never die. Permit me to state that with the sending of this dispatch one more Republican takes a walk." And from a compilation of messages assembled for FDR to read, there was a letter from a nine-year-old child from Kansas: "I heard your speech last night and it was a good one and I could understand it. My mother and father are for you because you are a good man."[13]

THE "I HATE WAR" SPEECH

In July 1936, the Spanish Civil War began with General Franco taking command of the revolting army units. In foreign policy Roosevelt's hands had been tied with the passage of the Neutrality Act of 1935 that was aimed at stopping intervention when Italy invaded Ethiopia in October 1935. So, at Chautauqua, New York, on August 14, 1936, Roosevelt gave a major speech. Although the campaign had not officially begun, the president clearly spoke as a candidate. Given that he wanted to win the election by not alienating any more voters than necessary, he decided to co-opt his critics by preempting the war issue: he would portray his image as more pacifistic than the isolationists. Given that his field of maneuverability was constrained by the Neutrality Act, it was a wise strategy to turn a disadvantage into an advantage. However, he would later pay for having so effectively identified himself for peace and against intervention.

Rosenman later apologized for the Chautauqua speech by asserting that in it FDR tried to educate the people to the dangers of dictatorships. A reading of the speech and the reactions to it suggests otherwise.[14]

Roosevelt created the bogy of war. His critics were not the interventionists but the isolationists, yet the Neutrality Act prohibited belligerency. Nevertheless, he created the straw issue that war profiteers wanted intervention and that only he could prevent war. In a false dichotomy—"If we face the choice of profits or peace, the Nation will answer—must answer—'We choose peace.' ''—FDR pledged to resist the clamor and work day-to-day for peace. Just who these warhawks were, FDR did not say, but he let his audience infer it must be the captains of industry who would produce the ships and munitions, in other words, the economic royalists. However, John Flynn wisely exposed FDR's rhetorical legerdemain:

One of the oldest stratagems in the world is the device of giving fair words to one faction and satisfactory deeds to another . . . The pacifists liked the speech; the warriors liked the ships and guns. Truly this is an unfailing technique. You do not have to give the liberals bread or even cake. "Let'em eat speeches" might be said of them.

Oswald Villard noted that Roosevelt's ploy, "mere rhetoric, however appealing," did not disguise the fact that the budget for naval armaments continued to increase under FDR's presidency; however, Villard's real coup was to state, with tongue in cheek, that he was pleased that Roosevelt had expressed himself so unequivocally for peace. The Americans who wrote the president supported his stand at Chautauqua: from Los Angeles, California, "More power to you as you scourge the Hearsterical Republicans and Jim Reds to their tombs"; from a professor at the University of Maine, "I feel better after what you said. We don't want the U.S. ever in another European War"; and from a minister in Sechlerville, Wisconsin, "I shall take pleasure in casting my vote for you again to become our Commander-in-Chief in the great war in behalf of social justice and Christian citizenship and Peace." However, an individual from Rochester, New York, perceived that Roosevelt's speech had no teeth to keep the peace with belligerents: "Diplomacy of a neutral nation which would deal effectively with belligerents must have the force and directness which warriors alone understand." Indeed, that individual might well have had in mind one of Roosevelt's obfuscations that said everything and nothing: "We are not isolationists except in so far as we seek to isolate ourselves completely from war."[15]

THE SYRACUSE SPEECH

President Roosevelt opened his second campaign at the Democratic state convention at Syracuse, New York, on September 29, 1936. Very early in his speech, he accused the Republicans of employing one of his favorite speech techniques: "There will be—there are—many false issues. In that respect, this will be no different from other campaigns. Partisans, not willing to face realities, will drag out red herrings—as they have always done—to divert attention from the trail of their own weaknesses." He then hooked one of those red herrings when he told the conventioneers that he was not a Communist, nor did he support any "ism" against American democracy. However, he turned the tables on the Republicans by implying that had it not been for him and the Democratic party, conditions congenial to Communism would have been spawned under Republican husbandry.

He also took a sideswipe at the patricians. FDR narrated a tale about an old gentleman who, wearing a silk hat, fell into a river and was certain to drown. A friend dived in and pulled him out, but the silk hat was gone. Three years later, Roosevelt complained, "the old gentleman is berating his friend because the silk hat is lost." A listener over the radio from Pasadena, California, reacted favorably to FDR's imagery: "You know we have lots of 'Silk Hats' here and maybe we can save some of those wearing them now that we have been informed that they really value that kind of head-gear. What a marvelous speech that was full of truth, sound logic and constructive thought." Roosevelt's parable illustrated, more so than any facts or figures, the irony in the Republican platform.[16]

In one of his greatest refutations of the Republican's "me too, me better" strategy, Roosevelt used sarcasm and an absolutely superb speech delivery to destroy that Republican stratagem:

Let me warn you and let me warn the Nation against the smooth evasion which says, "Of course we believe all these things; we believe in social security; we believe in work for the unemployed; we believe in saving homes. Cross our hearts and hope to die, we believe in all these things; but we do not like the way the present Administration is doing them. Just turn them over to us. We will do all of them—we will do more of them—we will do them better; and most of all, the doing of them will not cost anybody anything.

By constructing his phrases in anaphora and epistrophe, Roosevelt was able to deliver them in rhythmical cadences. Indeed, the above quotation is a good example of a rhetorical technique Hitler used: "Only constant repetition will finally succeed in imprinting an idea on the memory of a crowd."[17]

In one of his attempts to co-opt the followers of Father Charles Coughlin's Union for Social Justice, Roosevelt reminded them that the Republican leadership would never comprehend a need for "social justice." And finally, in the conclusion of his address, Roosevelt spoke one of his elusive aphorisms. It is a remarkable one because FDR used word inversion to imply that he embodied two opposing political philosophies simultaneously. People from all political perspectives could thus identify with him: "I am that kind of conservative because I am that kind of liberal."[18]

The responses to FDR's speech at Syracuse indicated that Americans appreciated his rhetorical techniques. To the red herring of Communism in the government, a person from Spring Lake, New Jersey, responded, "I am hoping it has submerged the malicious campaign propaganda of the enemies of free government"; to his attacks on the Republicans, an individual from Middletown, Ohio, wrote, "We are anxious to see how they take their medicine, it was a bitter pill for them, but all the truth," and from Salt Lake City, Utah, "your finesse in making the Republicans appear ridiculous was indeed clever."[19]

JOHN PAUL JONES AT MADISON SQUARE GARDEN

In a campaign that stressed Toryism and economic royalists, FDR culminated his canvass by using an image from the War of 1812 against the British. When asked to surrender by the captain of the British warship *Serapis*, John Paul Jones defiantly replied that he had just begun to fight. So had the Commander-in-Chief. His speech at Madison Square Garden in New York City on October 31 is a favorite speech and justifiably so.

The first draft, undated, was a joint effort by Samuel Rosenman, Tommy Corcoran, and Stanley High. Donald Richberg also contributed heavily to the speech's development. An interesting practice, evident on one of the drafts, is suggestive of how FDR worked with Rosenman. Rosenman would make FDR's dictated emendations on Rosenman's copy that would then go to the typist for the next draft. On the reading copy, there is evidence that Roosevelt must have read it aloud in order to time its delivery because the speech is marked off in intervals of ten minutes. There are many reasons why this speech was FDR's most famous and best campaign address.

In terms of something for everyone, the speech conveyed Roosevelt as militant at the beginning but Roosevelt as meek and mild at the end. The conclusion, with its references to "Peace on earth, good will toward men," Biblical allusions to altars of faith, and a quotation from a prophet, Mica 6:8, did not flow thematically from the speech, yet it was a wise move to temper the ferocity of the address with lip service to religious rhetoric.

In terms of style, the oration would have delighted Demosthenes. Anaphora and epistrophe abounded against Hooverism. FDR used "Written on the roll of honor" four times; he constructed three sentences of antithesis, beginning with nine mocking, crazy, mad years coupled to three equal epistrophes of three long years of scourge, breadlines, and despair; he gave six instances of "they tell . . . " juxtaposed to FDR's charges that these Republican statements were deceit; eight times he framed the New Deal's goals by "Of course . . . " and ended these certainties with the now famous phrase of "we have only just begun to fight," which was Roosevelt's idea and imagery.

In terms of his campaign themes, he framed them all in the speech. He called the roll of honor for those who had stood with him in 1932 and would stand with him in 1936 against the infidels. He inveighed against Hooverism with the famous monkey imagery—the "hear-nothing, see-nothing, do-nothing Government." He scored the war profiteers and government by mob rule (Communism). And then he threw down the gauntlet to the Tories:

Never before in all our history have these forces been so united against one candidate as they stand today. They are unanimous in their hate for me—and I welcome their hatred.

I should like to have it said of my first Administration that in it the forces of selfishness and lust for power met their match. I should like to have it said of my second Administration that in it these forces met their master.

Roosevelt had a personal hand in these oft-quoted lines because he emended the text: " . . . lust for power [found an enemy worthy of their hate.] *met their match.* I [would] *should* like to have it said of my second Administration that *in* it these forces [found] *met* their [oblivion] *master.*"

The master idea delighted the Democrats, but the Republicans responded to it with all the righteous indignation they could muster. From Warren, Ohio, came this typical complaint: "As an old time Republican, I have to admit that the President spoke truly in his Saturday night speech . . . when he said it was his desire to be known as the master of the American people." However, forgotten people responded warmly to FDR's emotionalism in his address. "This address," wrote a person from Reidsville, North Carolina, "was the greatest that ever fell from the lips of mortal man, so says scores that heard it over the radio," and from Cincinnati, Ohio, came a note "to congratulate you on the splendid, high type scholarship speech you made."[20]

SCAPEGOATS IN THE 1936 CAMPAIGN

In four of the most famous and oft-quoted speeches in the campaign, Franklin Roosevelt used the scapegoat technique to concentrate the people's ire on the captains of industry. As it served his purposes to have them believe the Tory press was against him, so it was useful to pit the people against the Tories themselves. According to FDR, the economic royalists impeded social and economic progress under the New Deal; these same people, the war profiteers in the Chautauqua speech, would drag the United States into foreign wars. Left to their own devices, the Republican leadership, so the country was informed at Syracuse, might have facilitated Communism by failing to fix the conditions that could breed it; and these same people, whom Roosevelt wished to master in his second term, would, if given the opportunity, turn the political clock back to 1933.

The strategem of the scapegoat served FDR's persuasive purposes effectively. As he determined in 1932, it was expeditious and higher drama to run against Hoover instead of for his own policies. In 1936, he ran for the New Deal, but he generated the real excitement by what he ran against. In reality, Roosevelt canvassed against Hooverism and Republicanism. Poor Landon was virtually ignored. Roosevelt played, like a Bach organ fugue, all of the themes of the economic royalist to raise the specter of the Depression, the trickle-down theory, rugged individualism, government for the rich, and so forth.

But one self-confessed economic royalist, E. T. Weir, chairman of National Steel Corporation, complained about being cast as a scapegoat: "He attempts to cut these men out from the main body of citizens and set them up as the visible enemies of the people . . . against which he, as the self-advertised champion of the people, tilts his lance." Weir's complaint was well taken: FDR's tactic worked: the people approved. In addition to Roosevelt's presidential rhetoric, part of his success was owed to his speech delivery. From the Forbes Field speech, which *Time* thought was "polished with every artifice of rhetoric, and delivered in his clear, golden voice," to the Madison Square Garden speech, which the *New York Times* thought portrayed Roosevelt in "his best oratorical form," with a voice expressing moral fervor, stern indignation, solemn and fighting tones, and an occasional tremble, Roosevelt delivered his speeches with a virtuosity unmatched by Landon's dry delivery. The synergism that obtained when Franklin Roosevelt campaigned to the people in 1936 was a landslide of 27,500,000 votes to Landon's 16,700,000, 46 states to 2, or, according to Jim Farley, "As Maine goes, so goes Vermont."[21]

THE 1940 CAMPAIGN

Although the campaign of 1940 lacked all the persuasive pyrotechnics of the one in 1936, it was nevertheless purveyed with a clever rhetorical posture. FDR's canvass was characterized by two distinct segments: the this-is-not-a-campaign campaign, from the acceptance speech in mid-July to mid-October, and the campaign from then until the election. During the first part, the basic rhetorical strategy was to speak as president, as often as not in the role of Commander-in-Chief, rather than as head of the party or as a partisan candidate. Roosevelt wisely capitalized on the prerogatives of the presidency and the functional ambiguities inherent in the office. The second part of the campaign was characterized by thematic rhetoric that Roosevelt recapitulated for the third time. However, there was one major difference. On the issue of preparedness for war, Roosevelt spoke with a clarity and assertiveness of purpose and position that were uncharacteristic of his former campaigns: he stepped on the isolationists' toes with a heavy foot.

THE ACCEPTANCE SPEECH, JULY 19, 1940

Non-candidate Roosevelt was nominated, much to Jim Farley's pique, for an unprecedented third term at Chicago. Whereas he had broken old traditions by flying there in 1932 to deliver in person his New Deal speech, Roosevelt now partially restored some of the old ways, to temper, at least symbolically, his breaking the unwritten taboo on a third term. He pretended that he had been drafted by the convention. He, as president, accepted the call from Washington, D.C., where he delivered his speech by radio to the convention. The imagery he established by that act became the reality of the non-campaign until a month before the election.

The speech was not a fighting address. Except for a swipe at "self-appointed commentators and interpreters," and some allusions to the social and economic gains under the New Deal, the speech was practically devoid of the generic rhetoric one would expect in such an address. Rather, half of the speech was devoted to a defense of why, despite his protestations to the contrary, he wanted a third term.

To be sure, FDR did not go as far as William T. Sherman did—"If nominated, I will not run, if elected, I will not serve"—but he ran a close second. In an effort to maintain the appearances of a draft, Roosevelt exercised some verbal gymnastics. Over the radio, he told the convention and the nation "that no call of Party alone would prevail upon me to accept reelection to the Presidency. The real decision to be made in these circumstances is not the acceptance of a nomination, but rather an ultimate willingness to serve if chosen by the electorate of the United States.'' Roosevelt came dangerously close to suggesting that being nominated was tantamount to being elected, and that the party could nominate someone who had no intention to serve if elected. Second, he contrived a compelling, yet transparent, apologia on why he should run. He allowed how he had often thought, while lying awake at night, that he had drafted Americans to serve their government. Patriotically, he averred ''that my conscience will not let me turn my back upon a call to service.'' ''Only the people themselves,'' Roosevelt announced, ''can draft a President.'' Thus, the charade Roosevelt played out in being drafted reinforced the imagery of his rhetoric.

The acceptance speech can also be read as a working paper on Roosevelt's campaign strategy. Consistent with the imagery of a reluctant candidate answering his country's call, Roosevelt announced that the press of presidential business would require his staying in Washington or close by—''where, if need be, I can be back at my desk in the space of a very few hours.'' Wendell Willkie could campaign on politics-as-usual, but Roosevelt would rise above partisan concerns to be a full-time president. In case this strategy would not suffice, FDR wisely gave himself an escape route. In being presidential, FDR cautioned: ''I shall not have the time or the inclination to engage in purely political debate. But I shall never be loath to call the attention of the nation to deliberate or unwitting falsifications of fact, which are sometimes made by political candidates.''

The major issue he presaged in his acceptance speech was preparation for war. FDR faced two arguments from his political opposition. One, charged primarily by the isolationists, was he would lead the nation into war. The other one, often joined by conservatives when they were not speaking as isolationists, was FDR had let the defenses of the nation dwindle, had neglected military preparedness. Helmsman Roosevelt steered a steady course between Scylla and Charybdis. He stated flatly he would not apologize for his sympathies with the allies' fighting aggression, for the materials the United States sent them, or for his arousing the nation to imminent danger. On the contrary, he said he would submit directly to the people his record on preparing the country morally and physically for any contingencies.[22]

To prove that point to the electorate, Roosevelt utilized the symbolism of his office. As a part of the non-campaign from mid-July to the election, he embarked on no less that twelve tours to defense plants and forts. Roosevelt's inspecting these places, as Commander-in-Chief, positively identified him with military preparedness better than his words could have and handily refuted the Republican's trumped-up campaign charges to the contrary.

The non-campaign continued into September. At the dedication of the Chickamauga Dam near Chattanooga, Tennessee, on September 2, Roosevelt reminded the audience that the philosophy of the New Deal was behind the regional planning, that certain forces would rob the people of the government's backing of such large enterprises, and, using the imagery of the Smoky Mountains, that defense industries were safer in the interior of the country than in its exposed seaboard. Roosevelt varied those themes slightly in his dedication of the Smoky Mountain National Park also on September 2.[23]

"I am in a sort of quandary tonight," Roosevelt told the Teamsters' Union convention in Washington, D.C., September 11, 1940. "I do not know whether this is a political speech or not." That was the giveaway, "whether you are talking American history or politics." Roosevelt's history was very current, concerned only with the past eight years. He reiterated how he had been busy inspecting the nation's defenses, and he reminded his constituent audience of all the benefits of the New Deal versus the pay envelope fraud the economic royalists had practiced in 1936. FDR captured the essence of the Republican's appeals to the working men when they "love the laboring man in November but forget him in January." On the issue that was uppermost in peoples' minds, Roosevelt reiterated his pledge at Chicago that the United States would not participate in foreign wars except in case of attack.[24]

Roosevelt continued his nonpartisan posture at the University of Pennsylvania, where he asked the audience to believe it was 1939, a nonelection year, rather than September 20, 1940. Roosevelt reiterated the Hamiltonian-Jeffersonian dichotomy and talked about the philosophy of the New Deal without mentioning it by name; thus, like his Teamsters' Union speech, this talk was more historical than political. Two stylistic devices adjusted this speech to its academic audience. One was an eloquent aphorism, "Eternal truths will be neither true nor eternal unless they have fresh meaning for every new social situation," and the other an application of chiasmus: "We cannot always build the future for our youth, but we can build our youth for the future."[25]

The last important non-campaign canvass speech Roosevelt delivered was his "hemisphere defense" speech at Dayton, Ohio, October 12, 1940. This was the first speech on which Rosenman, Harry Hopkins, and Robert Sherwood worked together. In the conclusion of the speech, FDR told his two-continent radio audience that the United States was arming for defense. Wayne Cole read in this speech an attempt to mollify the Italian-Americans who had been miffed at Roosevelt's swipe at Mussolini in the stab-in-the-back speech at Charlottesville, Virginia, in June 1940. To be sure, FDR did pay the Italian- and Spanish-Americans their respect. But what has not been recognized about this speech is how FDR gave the hyphenated Americans a not-so-subtle lesson on loyalty, in language that was uncharacteristically blunt:

It is natural that all American citizens from the many nations of the Old World should kindly remember the old lands where their ancestors lived. . . . But in every single one of the American Republics, the first and final allegiance, the first and final loyalty of these citizens . . . is to the Republic in which they live and move and have their being . . . . As we established our independences, they wanted to become citizens of America—not an Anglo-Saxon American, nor an Italian-American, nor a German-American, nor a Portuguese-American—but citizens of an independent nation of America.

Here, we do not have any dual citizenship. Here, the descendants of the very same races who had always been forced to fear or hate each other in lands across the ocean, have learned to live in peace and in friendship.

Aside from Roosevelt's appeal for citizens of the United States to be for America first, and not in the sense the America Firsters wanted, this passage also demonstrates a typically Rooseveltian rhetorical ploy to speak contradictory sentiments in a speech.[26]

Roosevelt may have continued his nonpolitical campaign, ignoring Willkie while attending to the business of government, but Willkie and the Republicans became desperate to forge an issue. They more or less conceded the New Deal to Roosevelt, and Willkie's "me too, me better" strategy attracted little attention. When Willkie favored the draft in August, FDR pressed the conscription legislation, so that was not an issue. Blithely ignoring the internal contradictions inherent in the charge, Willkie decided to attack Roosevelt at his Achilles' heel by portraying FDR as a warmonger—never mind that Willkie had earlier campaigned that Roosevelt had not prepared the nation's defenses adequately. Nor did Willkie have to worry about the press's calling him to task. I. F. Stone calculated the inches of space given to Willkie and FDR in the election: of the five major newspapers in the United States, the average support was 86.6 percent for Willkie and 13.4 percent for FDR; of these, the *New York Times*, which had supported FDR in 1932 and 1936, was the best with 33 percent for FDR, and the Chicago *Tribune* the worst with 4 percent. Moreover, polls indicated in mid-October that Willkie was making headway against Roosevelt's lead. Thus pressed to defend himself, Roosevelt launched a counterattack. The five speeches he delivered in the real campaign have generally been viewed by critics such as Cole and Robert Sherwood as equivocation. A reading of these speeches as rhetorical responses *in situ* suggests otherwise.[27]

NO. 1, PHILADELPHIA, OCTOBER, 23, 1940

Franklin Roosevelt seldom structured his speeches in a debate-like fashion, but the Philadelphia speech, which opened the campaign, like the other four of his subsequent campaign speeches reads something like a first negative's constructive speech. Defending the status quo, Roosevelt refuted, in a point-by-point fashion, reckless Republican charges. As he had in 1936, Roosevelt was at his best when he spoke in an offensive-defense style. As Landon had experienced Roosevelt's rhetoric, so would Willkie be subjected to his rebuttals.

Consistent with his non-campaign campaign, Roosevelt told his audience he had not entered a normal campaign because the national and international crises had kept him near Washington, D.C. Allowing that it was acceptable tactics to let the opposition call for the repeal of social security or the abrogation of the truth-in-securities act, FDR could not ignore deliberate falsifications of fact. He denied the Republican's ridiculous charge that he was responsible for Munich and that American democracy would end upon his election. He called the Republicans' campaign themes instances of dictators' propaganda, tricks of repetition until a lie becomes the truth, and he weighed in against part of the press that was closed to him. Then, admitting he was an old campaigner and loved a fight, he waved the bloody shirt that served him so well in 1936. Against the charge that the New Deal had not solved the Depression, he reminded the audience, with a clever anaphora of "Back in 1932 . . . ," that the Republicans had caused it. In a rebuttal reminiscent of his Syracuse speech four years earlier, Roosevelt sarcastically scored the Republican's "me too, me better" stance on New Deal programs: "If they could only get control of them, they plead, they would take so much better care of them, honest-to-goodness they would." He ticked off how much better employment was, how wages were better, how national income was up, and so forth. Then, in a devastating attack against the *New York Times* on the state of the economy, Roosevelt juxtaposed how the *Times*'s business experts praised the economic figures, with the sardonic jibe: "Wouldn't it be nice if the editorial writers of The New York *Times* [*sic*] could get acquainted with their own business experts?" Internal contradictions in evidence have always been a powerful persuasive tool, and Roosevelt played that flagrant violation to its hilt. Lastly, he recited his record in working for peace and pledged anew the noninterventionist platform on which he ran. Roosevelt did not equivocate on foreign policy: he admitted to arming the country in an effort to work for peace.[28]

NO. 2, MADISON SQUARE GARDEN, OCTOBER 28, 1940

Whereas Roosevelt paid considerable attention to domestic New Deal issues at Philadelphia, he now trained his rhetorical guns against the Republican's charges that he was rearming the United States slowly. Going for the broadside attack, Roosevelt aimed at Representative Hamilton Fish, former president Hoover, Senator Arthur Vandenberg, and Senator Robert Taft. In a typical debate strategy, he turned the tables on these Republicans by quoting their statements that the country's defenses were strong in 1938–39, but were somehow weak in 1940. His summarized his counterattack with the charge that they had played politics with national security in 1938–39 and were doing so during the election. Next, FDR examined the Republicans' votes on the battleships. In addition to Senator Vandenberg and Congressman Fish, FDR charged that Senator Charles McNary, the vice-presidential candidate, and Senator Gerald Nye had tried to scuttle the battleships with their votes. They, too, were playing politics with national security. His third main shot was against the Republicans' "me too, me better" position on aid to Great Britain. His recitation of their voting records refuted the Republicans' rhetoric. And then, with an ear to the possibilities of oral delivery, Roosevelt drew the audience's attention to his now-famous phrase: "now wait, a perfectly beautiful rhythm—Congressmen Martin, Barton and Fish." On the issue of equivocation, Roosevelt explicitly asked his audience to support his policies, which he clearly delineated, and to reject the reckless Republican charge that American boys were on their way to transports.[29]

Wendell Willkie had charged in Chicago on October 22, "If his promise to keep our boys out of foreign wars is no better than his promise to balance the budget they're already almost on the transports." This was part of Willkie's strategy to portray that only he could keep the United States out of war and that Roosevelt would lead the nation into war. As a matter of fact, Willkie charged at Baltimore, on October 30, that if the country reelected Roosevelt, "you may expect war in April, 1941."[30]

NO. 3, BOSTON, OCTOBER 30, 1940

"I have said this before," Roosevelt avowed, "but I shall say it again and again and again: Your boys are not going to be sent into any foreign wars." During a speech conference enroute on the train to Boston, Sherwood had cautioned the president that he should calm fears that Willkie had generated with the troop transport charge. Sherwood inserted the above phrase, but Rosenman noted it did not have the Democratic platform caveat of except in attack; FDR said to leave the caveat out, and the phrase was delivered without it. Sherwood ranked this speech below the Madison Square Garden one, but Warren Moscow believed the phrase was justified.[31]

The Boston speech was certainly the nadir of the campaign, but the problem was that Roosevelt faced both a local audience in Boston and a national audience. Boston presented some special problems that the national audience did not. Irish-Americans were Anglophobic, and Italian-Americans were rankled by FDR's anti-Mussolini rhetoric; moreover, Robert Divine noted that the isolationist sentiment among Catholic voters was worrisome. On the national level, Roosevelt could not tilt too much toward intervention or he would lose the issue to Willkie. Bombarded with pleas and telegrams from worried Democrats, Roosevelt heeded the warnings and left off the proviso about armed attack. But, as Sherwood and Rosenman both remembered, the president was prickly about not uttering the caveat, because he wanted the votes.[32]

On the other hand, FDR did not pander for those votes. Although he paid an obvious compliment to Ambassador Joseph Kennedy, the president openly told the audience he was requesting an additional twelve-thousand airplanes for the British. If he had wished to equivocate, he could have deleted that announcement in order to curry favor with the Irish-American block. Roosevelt also used the bandwagon effect. He addressed Seattle with its Boeing airplane plant, Douglas aircraft in Southern California, Curtiss plants in Buffalo and St. Louis, Hartford's Pratt and Whitney plant, and Curtiss-Wright at Patterson, to inform his Bostonian and national audiences that he was moving forward with arming the country.

Thus, the speech transcended the constraints of the immediate Bostonian audience to his national constituency. Moreover, commentators on this speech have overlooked the fact that the president devoted approximately 30 percent of his speech to the agricultural issues that had been alleviated under the New Deal. Attesting to the power of the newsreels, FDR opined that American farmers would not be deceived "by pictures of Old Guard candidates, patting cows and pitching hay in front of moving picture cameras." Before closing his address, FDR used *argumentum ad personam* (for good reasons, he generally eschewed such character assassinations) against Congressman Joe Martin of the Bay State. As an example of "all that is finest in American public life," Roosevelt listed the agricultural bills Martin had voted against, prophesied sarcastically that Martin would probably be rewarded with the title Secretary of Agriculture, and then let the audience join him in refrain against the trio: "Martin, Barton and Fish."[33]

NO. 4, BROOKLYN, NOVEMBER 1, 1940

The Brooklyn speech was not as famous as the Boston speech because the president did not make any promises about war, with or without the attack proviso. Nevertheless, it contained invective against the Republicans on a scale that bears examination.

On the offensive, FDR charged that in the last days of the canvass, extreme radicals and extreme reactionaries had formed an "unholy alliance" against the American people and Christianity. His warrant was the fact that Republicans had placed an advertisement against the Roosevelt administration in the *Daily Worker*, the newspaper of the Communist party. Although the Republicans clearly did not advocate Communism, Roosevelt cleverly used guilt by association to illustrate the length to which the Republican party would go to get votes.

In his previous speeches, the president had responded in the main to the Republican party's attacks against the New Deal and against his steady course of arming for defense but avoiding war. In this address, Roosevelt attacked the motives of the Republican leadership. Without naming names (like Landon, Willkie was never recognized by Roosevelt), the president presented in searing language a personalized indictment against the corporate characters of the plutocrats. In terms the average person could clearly understand, Roosevelt said the "New Deal was no mere rescue party to restore to a chosen few their old power over the people's savings, the people's labor, the people's lives." Exposing their innermost desires for selfish privilege and power, Roosevelt maligned the plutocrats' patriotism: "They feared the legitimate forward surge of their own common people, more than they feared the menacing might of foreign dictators." To substantiate that accusation, he then asked a compelling series of rhetorical questions, crafted with the anaphora of "Do you want to abandon . . . ," to elicit a positive vote for the New Deal, its party, its president. Roosevelt was quick to capitalize on gaffes by his opponents, and none served his purposes better than a charge that Roosevelt's only supporters were paupers who earned less than $1,200 a year. FDR turned the tables by letting the audience infer that his charge about the plutocrats was substantiated by one of their number, and by suggesting that millions of Americans supported him "by the dictates of their hearts and minds, and not by the size of their bank accounts."[34]

Before moving to his last major campaign speech, we should tie up a dangling end. On the same day FDR delivered his Boston speech, Willkie charged that Roosevelt would have the country in war by April 1941. Since the president did not rebut the charge at Brooklyn, did he acquiesce to the attack? Rather than refute the charge directly, FDR quoted Secretary of State Cordell Hull that the president was not leading the United States into war. That reply was given from the rear platform of the president's campaign train in Rochester, New York, and at Buffalo on the same day, November 2, on the way to Cleveland, Roosevelt himself spiked Willkie's charge by once again averring, without the Democratic platform's attack proviso, "Your President says this country is not going to war."[35]

NO. 5, CLEVELAND, NOVEMBER 2, 1940

Candidate Roosevelt closed his campaign at Cleveland, but in a "non-campaign" manner, he gave a final radio talk from Hyde Park on November 4. The Cleveland address was a pastiche of campaign themes presented in an elevated rhetorical style. The only discernible structure in the speech was FDR's itemizing of the four tenets of his foreign policy: to keep the United States out of war, to keep war out of the hemisphere, to aid countries resisting aggression, and not to appease dictators.

Usually, FDR took credit for his New Deal. In this speech, he praised Americans for creating the New Deal. With eleven anaphoristic phrases that began with "You," he complimented his audience for enacting all the accomplishments of the past eight years. Harkening back to his First Inaugural, he reminded them they had even driven "money changing from the temple." His ploy was a clever rhetorical strategy. By asking the people to support their program rather than his, he subtly implied that if they voted against him, they would, in effect, vote against themselves.

In an extended peroration, FDR looked to the future. By eloquently framing seven paragraphs with "Of course," he alluded to the historical continuity of his Madison Square Garden address in 1936. Interspersed in these paragraphs were the epistrophes "For there lies the road to democracy that is strong." Lastly, he used seven times the phrase "I see," reminiscent of his Second Inaugural, to give continuity to his presidential visions. These stylistic devices gave the speech a statesman-like elegance that transcended his earlier, earthy campaign talks.[36]

SUMMARY

In steering his campaign between Charybdis and Scylla, Roosevelt ran, in terms of the constraints he faced, a most astute campaign. The image of "drafting" the president and the ploy of "non-campaign" speeches served him well until he was forced in late October to debate Willkie's reckless charges. Of course, it is understandable why Willkie had to find an issue that would draw presidential blood: the third-term issue figured, but not prominently enough to elect Willkie; his "me too, me better" strategy on the New Deal, which was at odds with the old guard's desires, did not fool Democrats or please Republicans; and his charge that Roosevelt had neglected the country's defenses was patently absurd. But when Willkie finally went for war, following the advice of the Republican leadership, he motivated FDR to respond.

"In place of issues," the *Nation* editorialized, "the Republican Party was forced to resort to devices, and they were not pretty." It is worth remembering that Willkie initiated the war issue by making many spurious claims, of which the most damaging to Roosevelt, and damning to himself, were allegations about Munich, the troop transports, and war by April 1941.[37]

On the whole, Roosevelt conducted a credible campaign. He unapologetically avowed aid to Great Britain, even in his speech in Boston. He acted symbolically, by inspecting defense plants, and spoke candidly about arming the nation for defense. He time and again starkly contrasted himself to the appeasers who would accommodate or capitulate to Hitler and Mussolini. Excluding only those speeches in Boston and Buffalo, he ran on the except-for-attack proviso of the Democratic platform. FDR realized the American people, or at least enough of them to elect him, wanted and supported his policies of armaments and of no appeasement for dictators, yet these same people were unwilling to face the implications of their and Roosevelt's stand. In a sense, Willkie capitalized on the inconsistencies inherent in the American people's wishful thinking one year into World War II. He presciently perceived that the president's policies for short-of-war defense would eventually lead to hostilities. Thus, he forced FDR's position to its logical conclusion in order to raise the fear of a foreign war. Roosevelt realized it would be political suicide to ask the American people to follow him logically where they were unprepared emotionally to go. For better or worse, the American audience had its own ambiguity about the implications of short-of-war aid to Great Britain, and Roosevelt adapted to that paradox as best he could. He did not equivocate, because the logic of his stand was apparent to anyone who wanted to complete it (as Willkie tried to do). Indeed, the *New Republic* focused on Willkie's failure to trick the voters: "The people may not be able to cope with all the technicalities of argument or the subtleties of propaganda, but in the end a democratically trained people usually understand the main issues even better than its critics and befuddlers." To his credit, Roosevelt did maintain his Boston-Buffalo pledge until December 8, 1941, although he admittedly stretched it to its limit.[38]

The president gave the American people other good reasons to vote for his New Deal. The ferocity of his counterattack was indicated by the invective and *ad personam* attacks he targeted against specific Republicans, especially Martin, Barton, and Fish. As he proved in 1936, Roosevelt could turn any Republican table.

From an oratorical perspective, Roosevelt outclassed Willkie. Divine noted the Hoosier "was least effective on the radio, where his high voice sounded shrill in contrast to FDR's reassuring baritone." For the Chattanooga speech, *Time* found FDR's voice "sonorous and flexible," his delivery "easy." "Only television," *Time* opined, "could have shown the nation the relish, the skill of his performance before 22,000 screaming Democrats in the Garden"; *Time* also testified to the oral quality of Roosevelt's speeches that was "more telling when given the benefit of his accomplished delivery than when read or quoted." And even the *New York Times*, which bolted Roosevelt in 1940, captured the president's expertise at Philadelphia: "The President was never in better form. With all the force of tonal inflection, irony and bitter humor, he revived his campaign technique of 1932 and 1936 and carried to a high pitch of enthusiasm the crowd which had gathered in the hope of hearing the type of talk he delivered."[39]

THE 1944 CAMPAIGN

On the surface, the parallels between the campaigns in 1940 and 1944 were numerous. The president accepted a metaphorical draft from the Democratic convention; there was a period of non-campaign activity during which Roosevelt acted and spoke as Commander-in-Chief; he was finally goaded into a direct confrontation with Governor Thomas Dewey of New York; the campaign became bitter and vituperative; and FDR won.

Upon closer examination, FDR faced some serious constraints in 1944. Although the fourth-term issue did not figure any more prominently in the debate than it had in 1940, it raised a related issue that was genuinely worrisome to the voters. In comparison to the certainty of Dewey's vitality in canvassing cross-country, the question about the president's health and vigor for a campaign and a fourth term needed addressing. Due to Dewey's shrewd and aggressive campaign, Roosevelt had to enter the campaign much earlier than in 1940; typical Republican falsifications had to be rebutted and the age issue assuaged. Whereas Willkie had scored Roosevelt's past record on armaments and interventionism, Dewey mounted an attack against the president's assumed foreign policy. The sole purpose of Dewey's approach was to raise fear in the voter's minds. This was a smart calculation because it put Roosevelt on the defensive in supporting a foreign policy that had yet to occur; thus, once FDR had committed himself, Dewey could further attack from whatever angle that was most harmful. But at the right moment, Roosevelt seized the ground, turned the strategy back on the Republicans, left Dewey sputtering "me too, me better," and proved, once again, his superb sense of rhetorical timing and strategy.

THE ACCEPTANCE SPEECH

The result of the 1944 Democratic convention was foregone as far as FDR was concerned, although Henry Wallace had to give way to Harry Truman, but FDR played another charade. Whereas the military metaphor he had appropriately used in 1940 was the draft, the analogous one in 1944 was the war-time duty of following orders. In an exchange of letters with Robert Hannegan, chairman of the Democratic National Committee, Roosevelt wrote he would follow the order of "his superior officer—the people of the United States."[40]

President Roosevelt addressed the convention audience in Chicago on July 20, 1944, by radio from his private train in San Diego, California. Soon, he left for Hawaii for military conferences. As in 1940, he bowed to his obligation to serve the country and allowed he would not campaign in a partisan sense except— and note the change of wording from "falsifications" in 1940—"to correct any misrepresentations."

The speech was statesman-like with only a hint of partisan attack. When FDR took notice of the opposition, he did so in an elegant style that was above the foray. Finally vindicated, FDR told his Chicago and national audiences, "The isolationists and the ostriches who plagued our thinking before Pearl Harbor are becoming slowly extinct." He pledged himself to three goals: (1) to win the war, (2) to form an international organization with armed forces to prevent another war, and (3) to provide the returning veterans and all Americans with employment and decent standards of living. With the aid of seven anaphoristic phrases, beginning with "They will decide," he then listed the records of the New Deal and his conduct of the war for the people's perusal. Remarkably, in a rare admission from Franklin Roosevelt, he admitted that he had made mistakes and that things were not always perfect (he would develop this theme in the Fourth Inaugural), yet he believed his administrations were progressive and their records clear. He ended the speech by quoting the peroration from Abraham Lincoln's Second Inaugural Address to indicate, as Lincoln had in 1865, that Roosevelt looked forward to the coming peace.

Lincoln's statement was added at FDR's direction on draft two. The speech went through five drafts prepared by Samuel Rosenman and Elmer Davis. On the fifth draft, Roosevelt made an interesting addition to the text. Not only did his emendation make the context of his record more concrete, it also preempted possible Republican charges that might arise about preparedness and the conduct of the war: "They will decide it on the record—*the record on the seas, on the land and in the skies.*"

The reception of Roosevelt's speech revealed that people reacted to it in kind. A person from Hollywood, California, thought the speech "was inspiring, kind, and renewed our hope for security," whereas an individual from Madison, Wisconsin, wrote, "Particularly I appreciate your fairness in referring to political opponents . . . let the Republicans do the mud-slinging." In another vein, in an early hint of the age issue—even before the Bremerton speech—the *Christian Century* sounded the alarm about "a tired man, a desperately tired man, whose health has been giving increasing concern during the past year or more."[41]

THE BREMERTON SPEECH

Upon his return from consultations with General MacArthur and Admiral Nimitz, the president spoke from the deck of a destroyer at Bremerton, Washington, on August 12. This speech, a rambling discourse with no particular significance or quotable line, would not be remembered except that Samuel Rosenman panned its delivery, and subsequent critics joined the chorus. Rosenman, and others following his lead, implied that Roosevelt's delivery of the speech, in conjunction with a photograph that pictured the president at his worst for his radio acceptance speech at San Diego, set the health issue in motion. Rosenman used the Bremerton speech as a foil for the famous Fala speech. Yet, as the *Christian Century* indicated, the president's health was a minor concern long before the Bremerton speech. It is true that the photograph was unflattering: in a photographic essay, *Time* juxtaposed the bad one, which Dewey's papers had published, with a vibrant one, featured in the president's papers. But, the address evidently had a negligible impact on the American audience. The problem is that one cannot find any damaging allusion to the speech, except that *Time* called it a "rambling, folksy account" but did not mention FDR's delivery. Moreover, FDR's health was not a major issue in the campaign. Before the Fala speech but after the Bremerton address, a poll on September 7 indicated that only 1.6 percent of the respondents would switch to Dewey because of FDR's health; in October, less than .5 percent were concerned about his health. The oft-stated relationship between the Fala speech and the Bremerton address is an example of *post hoc ergo propter hoc*. Rather, the Fala campaign speech was motivated by far more serious considerations.[42]

THE TEAMSTER UNION OR FALA SPEECH

President Roosevelt faced two constraints in the 1944 campaign that account for the nature of his rhetoric in the Fala speech better than the old-man, poor-health, poor-delivery-from-Bremerton explanations offered by Rosenman and subsequent critics. First, FDR faced a formidable foe in Dewey, particularly in the governor's ability to communicate over radio. Dr. James Bender compared Dewey's and FDR's radio voices and found them "evenly matched in speaking prowess." Although Dewey spoke faster than FDR, at 128 wpm vs. 102 wpm, Bender observed that Dewey had mastered the pauses and modulation that characterized Roosevelt's mastery over radio; moreover, the quality of Dewey's voice might have had a slight edge over Roosevelt's because Dewey had a stronger baritone voice to FDR's tenor range. These findings were also corroborated by the views of some NBC commentators. Richard Harkness noted that for the first time, FDR faced a candidate who was in in the "same league with him" in the use of radio; H. V. Kaltenborn noted that both men had "radio voices to translate ideas"; and Morgan Beatty believed Roosevelt might be at a disadvantage because there was "little desire for the old-fashioned rip-roaring appeal in wartime." The second factor leading to the Fala speech was that Roosevelt faced the possibility of a low turnout, and that could only help the Republicans.[43]

The rhetorical brilliance of the Fala speech was due to what Roosevelt did best. What he did best was to analyze the needs of the electorate in an election, and then to innervate those needs. Notwithstanding what Morgan Beatty believed, Roosevelt must have sensed that war-weary Americans needed some old-fashioned campaign oratory to revive interest in the campaign; moreover, Roosevelt needed to answer the charges Dewey was spreading in his canvass. The president pooled his resources: he chose a highly partisan constituent audience—the Teamsters' Union—for a favorable audience response; he adopted an aggressive defense, which had served him well in 1936 and 1940; and he used scathing sarcasm and invective, which he had perfected in the two previous campaigns, to rebut Republican misrepresentations. And then he did something that only a Franklin Delano Roosevelt could do: he used humor, as one might do in an after-dinner speech, aided by an absolutely superb delivery, to present one of the best campaign speeches of all time and probably his third-best speech.

To be sure, the Fala speech alluded to FDR's age—he facetiously allowed that he was actually four years older than he had been the last time he spoke to the Teamsters, and he admitted he was too old to speak out of both sides of his mouth (as the Republicans did); he scored the Republicans for their duplicitous platform, their attempt to persuade the nation that the Democrats were responsible for the Depression, and in a continuation of the Syracuse and Philadelphia attacks on the Republican's "me too, me better" appeals, their attempt to co-opt his military policy. Inveighing against the Republicans, FDR said:

Don't leave the task of making the peace to those old men who first urged it and who have already laid the foundations for it, and who have had to fight all of us inch by inch during the last five years to do it. Why, just turn it all over to us. We'll do it so skillfully— that we won't lose a single isolationist vote or a single isolationist campaign contribution.

Later in the speech, Roosevelt delivered the coup de grace to the Republicans when he revealed their libelous statements about Fala. *Time* ironically noted the Fala speech as "one of the main campaign speeches [that] was mainly remembered as being about the candidate's dog." But the most important factor in the speech's impact was Roosevelt's delivery.[44]

Time was simply rapturous about Roosevelt's radio mastery: "He was like a veteran virtuoso playing a piece he had loved for years, who fingers his way through it with a delicate fire, a perfection of timing and tone, and an assurance that no young player, no matter how gifted, can equal." It also noted that when Roosevelt spoke "botched," he gained an even greater effect by spelling it out: "b-o-t-c-h-e-d." The *New Republic* noted how FDR consummately delivered his humorous lines: "There have been few politicians in America who have been sure enough of themselves to use laughter and keep their dignity, and Mr. Roosevelt is one of them; and here he used humor against a humorless opponent, which made the contrast all the more striking." The audience for the rhetorical presidency responded to FDR's delivery of the speech: from St. Louis, Missouri, "Each four years your speeches get better, every body says that was the best one they ever heard yet"; from New York, "Your sense of humor you injected into this speech was a delight for the heart''; from Philadelphia, ''Your speech tonight was a humdinger''; from St. Petersburg, Florida, ''That was a perfect knock out speech Saturday''; from Cleveland, Ohio, ''There never was a campaign speech equal the one you made''; and from the Bronx, ''Your speech should be re-broadcast as often as possible—for if it is done—the Republicans will only receive the votes of the National Manufacturers Assoc. and the American Bankers Assoc., and those who insist on being blind, deaf, and dumb.'' However, one unreconstructed Republican from Los Angeles, California, telegraphed the president: ''Invective, billingsgate, high-school-kid wisecracking constitute a poor substitute for statesmanship. What we deprecate in your first campaign becomes abhorrent from the lips of a President running for reelection, and constitutes a new low in campaign tactics.'' As intended, the Fala speech reinvigorated the campaign. The Des Moines *Register* observed Roosevelt ''wanted to give the country precisely the impression of jovial and confident energy that he did give.'' He clearly demonstrated his mastery over the radio, according to the Atlanta *Constitution*: ''[Roosevelt] successfully defended his title as the world's most effective radio speaker. Even the most prejudiced of his critics are conceding that following his magnificent speech of Saturday night.'' And the height that Roosevelt attained in his speech can be gauged by the depth of Westbrook Pegler's column in the *Times Herald*:

The corny aside about Roosevelt's dog . . . was in the true, Fountleroy humor of a man who was in the charge of nursemaids until an age when others of his generation were playing jiggers-the-cop, and whose mama held him so precious that he never went to public schools with the uncouth sons of the common man because the lower classes have B. O.

The Fala speech stands as eloquent testimony, as it did *in situ* in 1944, that rhetorical technique, yes, even delivery, moves public opinion.[45]

POLITICIZING THE WHITE HOUSE: RADIO CAMPAIGN SPEECH # 1

President Roosevelt had used the image of addressing the nation from the White House as a symbol of executive authority in the Fireside Chats and in other radio addresses, but he had not politicized the White House for partisan campaigning. On October 5, he took to the airwaves, cleverly alluding to the authority of the presidency by beginning his talk with ''I am speaking to you tonight from the White House.'' By appearing to speak as the president of all the people, Roosevelt used the speech to accomplish two campaign goals. He artfully tried to mask his intentions, but they were still transparent.

Roosevelt spent the initial one-third of his talk on the topic of registering to vote and voting. In an Olympian attitude, FDR opined that registering and voting should ''be open to our citizens irrespective of race, color, or creed—without tax or artificial restriction of any kind. The sooner we get to that basis of political equality, the better it will be for the country as a whole.'' Yet, neither he nor his party nor the Republicans had sponsored any legislation to effect that lofty presidential lip service to the principle of equality. He also allowed there should be a large turnout at the polls in order to make a clear presidential mandate from a majority of the voters. This appeal would help his chances for reelection, especially with the pivotal independent vote.

The latter two-thirds of his talk was devoted to a refutation of Dewey's campaign attacks. Dewey had made some headway with a fear appeal that Roosevelt would maintain the troops in uniform after the war in order to keep unemployment down. A campaign slogan said it slyly: ''Bring the boys home quicker with Dewey and Bricker.'' FDR adroitly laid that bogy to rest. He detailed legislation that mandated speedy demobilization, and he added that ''you do not need legal training to understand it.'' Then he counterattacked the patriotism of anyone, that is, Dewey and his bunch, who would mislead and weaken the morale of the fighting soldiers abroad and the civilians at home.

In an effort to gain votes by any means, Dewey dipped to Red-baiting. When Earl Browder, released from prison by FDR, urged his Communist followers to support the president, Dewey was delighted with a windfall of apparent proof for his reckless charge. FDR handily denied the absurd charge and turned the whole argument on the Republicans who had franked the bogus literature on the Communist charge through the mails at taxpayer's expense. Nor did FDR shrink from avowing his support for the people of the Soviet Union. He wisely refrained from mentioning Stalin or the Communist party, and he used the term *Russia* twice: *Russia* somehow connotes less Communist-associated negative images than the term *Soviet Union*.''

As a precursor of an issue that would become pivotal in the canvass, Roosevelt also adamantly affirmed, with no equivocation, his commitment to a world organization dedicated to keeping the peace—''if necessary by force.''[46]

FOREIGN POLICY ASSOCIATION SPEECH, NEW YORK, OCTOBER 21

The importance of what Roosevelt said in his radio speech before the Foreign Policy Association dinner meeting was related to what Dewey did not say in his major speech at the *New York Herald Tribune* Forum on October 18.

Senator Joseph Ball, a leading Republican internationalist from Minnesota, challenged Dewey and Roosevelt to answer three questions about a world peacekeeping body. The critical question was whether the president could commit U.S. military forces, under the aegis of the United Nations, without further congressional approval. The answer to the question was critical to different constituent audiences. A negative reply would doom the United Nations to a debating society but would please the Old Guard isolationists; an affirmative answer would give military authority to the United Nations but would antagonize the isolationists. In an effort to placate both polarities in his own party—both the isolationists and internationalists—Dewey dodged the issue in the Forum speech. Even Walter Lippmann attacked Dewey's stance in his address.

When Roosevelt's turn came, he did not dodge Ball's question. FDR's unequivocal answer was designed to lure the independents and the Willkie internationalists into his camp. FDR effectively used the rhetorical technique of contrast, and he made it stark. Playing on the age issue, he claimed he was too old to bear false witness against his opponents, even in a campaign. Then he reminded the American people, that in the event of a Republican victory in the Senate (a subtle appeal to get out the vote), Senator Hiram Johnson, a leading isolationist from California, would be chairman of the Foreign Relations Committee. Moreover, he read the rogue's gallery: Senator William Borah, who according to FDR practically invited Hitler to invade Poland; Senator Gerald Nye from North Dakota; and Representatives Hamilton Fish and Joseph Martin (much to FDR's great glee, Fish was defeated in the election).

But the crux of the speech was presented in one of those garden hose-type analogies from Lend-Lease days that Roosevelt was so good at. He reiterated his keep-the-peace-by-force argument he had made during his White House radio talk on October 5, and then said even more. Although he did not detail exactly how U.S troops would function in United Nations forces, he went further on the subject than Dewey did. Roosevelt used the analogy that when a policeman sees a felon entering a house, he does not first go to the Town Hall to call a town meeting to determine if he could issue an arrest warrant. The answer was good enough for Ball, who announced for the president. Roosevelt was lucky because Dewey could have beat him to the punch, thus leaving FDR to argue "me too, me better," which, as it worked out, was precisely the position in which Dewey found himself—too little, too late. Roosevelt's speech also drew praise from other quarters. The *Nation* appreciated FDR's candor: "Mr. Roosevelt again provides the inescapable answer." And the *New Republic* thought his address was "one of the great speeches in his career." In terms of votes, which counted in the election, the Willkie internationalists and independents, relieved by Roosevelt's forthrightness on that major issue, swung to the president.

The speech in the evening to the Forum was preceded by a symbolic *tour de force*. He was scheduled to motor through the burroughs of New York City during the day, but unfortunately the weather did not cooperate. FDR ordered the convertible top on his touring Packard lowered but kept the bullet-proof windows up, and he drove for forty miles in the rain and cold. As his visits to munitions factories had demonstrated his commitment to arm the country in the 1940 campaign, this symbolic action answered the health question more effectively than words could have: "Well—this was the answer to the whispering campaign about his health. . . . It was a silly but very gallant spectacle."[47]

DOING UNTO DEWEY

As the campaign neared the finish line, Roosevelt canvassed vigorously. His attempt to identify Dewey with the isolationists worked to the governor's disadvantage, but FDR had to do more than that to capture people's attention and votes. To be sure, he aggressively defended himself against Dewey's campaign by ellipsis, turned the tables whenever he could; waved the now tattered and torn bloody shirt from the days of 1932; and pledged a United Nations organization and a just peace. His latter campaign speeches were in a sense some of his best ones because he addressed the nation's future. Realistically, Roosevelt was forced by Dewey to focus on domestic issues because FDR was weakest there, but the president's persuasive perspicuity did not fail him. He wisely buttressed his remarks on domestic issues by constantly mentioning his success in foreign issues, where he was clearly superior to Dewey.

At Philadelphia on October 27, Roosevelt used the occasion of Navy Day to deliver a broadside against Dewey. Taking Dewey's charge that there were not five civilians in the government who had the confidence of the American people, Roosevelt turned the tables easily enough. FDR proudly reminded the people that every battleship, all but two of the heavy cruisers, and all of the aircraft carriers that had participated in the battle of Leyte Gulf, October 23–26, were authorized during his administration. After reciting the Republican voting record for appropriations for the Army Air Corps in 1939, Roosevelt allowed how Hitler and Hirohito must have laughed. Against Dewey's ludicrous charges that Roosevelt had not given the armed forces enough supplies and munitions, FDR listed a history of the war and then clinched his argument with one of those word pictures that he could so eloquently paint: "The facts speak for themselves. They speak with the thunder of tens of thousands of guns on battle fields all over the world. They speak with the roar of more than a million tons of bombs dropped by our air forces." For the recency effect, Roosevelt saved his best salvo for last. In an attempt to argue "me too, me better," the Republicans floated an interesting appeal: a Republican president and a Republican-controlled Congress could better cooperate in waging peace. Roosevelt concisely reduced that clever strategy to "vote my way or I won't play," thus impugning the Republicans' patriotism to win the war and the peace that followed. In a conclusion that made the comparison stark, FDR used the anaphora of "May . . . " six times to revile the Republicans who would use the war and peace for selfish political gain.[48]

On October 28, Roosevelt delivered one of his better speeches of the campaign before 110,000 people at Soldiers' Field in Chicago while another 150,000 listened on loudspeakers outside. He began his attack on Dewey by using the same ploy that had worked so well at Syracuse in 1936, at Philadelphia in 1940, and in the Fala speech earlier in 1944: a sardonic rendition of Republican "me too, me better." The "blunderers and bunglers" passed the New Deal, but the Republicans would not change it; "tired old men" built the war machine, but the Republicans would not change it; Roosevelt laid the groundwork for peace, but Dewey would not change it. Then came Roosevelt at his sarcastic best:

"But," they whisper, "we'll do it in such a way that we won't lose the support even of Gerald Nye or Gerald Smith—and this is very important—we won't lose the support of any isolationist campaign contributor. Why, we will be able to satisfy even the *Chicago Tribune*.''

The attack on the *Chicago Tribune*—FDR named the McCormick, Patterson, Gannett, and Hearst presses as bastions of isolationism at the Foreign Policy Association speech on October 21—was a continuation of the press-is-against-me argument that he had used so effectively in the mid- and late 1930s. He then turned his attention to the future of the United States after the war. Comparing what things were like in 1932 to the gains by 1940, to the necessities of a full life after the war, the president reviewed the accomplishments for labor, the farmer, small and large business, and government projects such as TVA. Thus, he cleverly waved the bloody shirt under the guise of looking to the future. In his conclusion, Roosevelt masterfully employed the metaphor of the winning team to appeal for votes. A vote for Roosevelt would mean peace, security, and decent jobs after the war. He openly implied that a vote for him would repay the fighting men and their families for their sacrifices, and he closed with his famous appeal, ''We are not going to turn the clock back!'' One could easily infer Dewey was not for Roosevelt's Economic Bill of Rights (announced in the State of the Union Address, January 11, 1944), one would be ungrateful to vote for Dewey, and despite Dewey's protestations to the contrary, the Republicans would return the country to conditions circa 1932.[49]

President Roosevelt delivered his second and final radio broadcast from the White House in November 2. Acknowledging that he had intended to follow his speech at Chicago with ones at pivotal places, Cleveland for Ohio and Detroit for Michigan, FDR apologized that his Commander-in-Chief duties kept him in Washington, so that was why he spoke from the White House. In a coy appeal for the women's vote, Roosevelt praised their contributions to the war effort in military and civilian capacities. This was the first time FDR singled out the female voter for special rhetorical attention. His first partisan punch was a reiterating of a theme he had hammered at Chicago: how the Congress, according to the other party, could only cooperate with a Republican president. Sensitive to charges that he was proceeding without the Congress, he countered that the House and Senate had both voted to cooperate in an United Nations–type organization for peace. He then used affirmation by denial to denigrate ''certain types of newspapers'' whose whispers and rumors he would not answer in kind. This ploy dovetailed with his more-presidential-less-candidate posture he tried to establish in this speech. Again referring to a campaign theme of teamwork, he looked forward in the latter part of his address to a new and varied life in the United States that included, interestingly enough, television. In his conclusion, he stated that only he could avert ''another war in another generation,'' build a better United States than before, and keep ''the faith with our boys.'' He broadly implied that a vote for him was patriotic, a vote for Dewey was not.[50]

In the final swing of the canvass, FDR whistle-stopped through Connecticut on his way to Boston for a major speech on November 4. The speech was rhetorically fine tuned to meet the diverse needs of his Boston and national audiences. Al Smith, who had broken with FDR for Landon in 1936 and Willkie in 1940, was nevertheless a figure who served FDR's persuasive purposes in his speech's introduction. If the audience inferred his implications, the evocation of the "Happy Warrior" sobriquet could serve as an analogy for Roosevelt as war leader; the bigots who had gunned for Al Smith when he ran for president in 1928 could also stand for those Republicans who attacked FDR in 1944. Nor would the Catholic constituency, both in Boston and the country, have missed the allusion to religious bigotry; and to identify with the mass audience, much as Smith had done in his better days, FDR listed names with obvious ethnic derivations to include all constituents. Finally, he pledged to overcome racial and religious intolerance and snobbery.

The most famous line in the Boston address was a vindication of his speech made there four years earlier. Then, he had left off the except-for-armed-attack proviso when he assured the people that their sons would not be sent to a foreign war. But in 1944, reflecting back to 1941 "when our own soil was made the object of a sneak attack," which was a precise fulfillment of the proviso, Franklin Roosevelt declared he would do the same thing "again and again and again."

As for the New Deal, Roosevelt turned the tables on Dewey and the Republican campaign orators. He asked a series of rhetorical questions centering on the theme that if the Republicans had fought against him for twelve years, then how could the people now trust their "me too, me better" rhetoric? Continuing the same line of attack, Roosevelt ridiculed the Republicans' calls for a change. He identified five Republican allegations and ended each with the epistrophe of "that it is time for a change," delivered sardonically. With that, he appealed for fifty million voters to cast a ballot (forty-eight million actually voted).

Roosevelt also accused Dewey of talking from both sides of his mouth. FDR used the device of horns of a dilemma to snare the governor. Pardoning himself for quoting Dewey correctly—a jab at Dewey's campaign by ellipsis—Roosevelt quoted Dewey's saying at Boston that Communists were seizing control of the New Deal; yet at Worcester, Massachusetts, Dewey had pledged to remove the threat of monarchy in the United States. Roosevelt rightly exclaimed: "Now, really—which is it—Communism or monarchy?"

Midway into his speech, Roosevelt made a rare admission. "This Administration," he said, "has made mistakes. That I freely assert. *Assert*. And I hope my friends of the press will not change that to *admit* [italics in original]." Although many might have appreciated his swipe at the press, only dyed-in-the-wool Democrats would have been duped by that verbal prestidigitation. But he turned that admission, or assertion, to his advantage. He claimed he had a pretty good batting average in trying to help the masses, and he never made the mistake of "substituting talk for action when farms were being foreclosed, homes were being sold at auction, and people were standing in breadlines.'' As he was preparing his Fourth Inaugural Address Roosevelt must have recalled that thought, because he wanted it in his speech.[51]

Roosevelt received 25,600,000 votes to Dewey's 22,000,000.

SUMMARY

Roosevelt was elected by the smallest margin of his four campaigns. This was not so much attributable to the quality or quantity of his speeches as it was to other factors—such as that any politician makes enemies the longer he is in office and that the war, which benefited FDR, was ending, and to Dewey's astute, well-organized campaign.

Still, FDR demonstrated that his rhetorical acumen to deal with the issues and images had not diminished with age. He hit the ground running with the Fala speech to invigorate interest in the campaign and to demonstrate his own mental and physical vitality. He reiterated his three themes—peace, the United Nations, and jobs after the war—at every opportunity. He showed that at his age he could still take it, in his drive through New York in the cold rain, and he turned the old age argument back on the Republicans with an avenging twist. He ran against the Old Guard for the forth time. He was lucky to be able to seize the high ground on the United Nations armed forces issue when Dewey ducked his golden opportunity. He successfully identified Dewey with the isolationists, thus wooing the independents and Willkie internationalists. He played the role of the dutiful president to its utmost capacity, and perhaps as an indication of the closeness of the race, he politicized the once neutral image of the White House in two partisan radio talks. Dewey's delivery was a match for FDR's and the governor had the creators of public opinion at his disposal, which motivated FDR to attack the friend of his enemy—the newspapers. Yet, Roosevelt and his rhetoric prevailed.

CONCLUSION

A number of Roosevelt's great presidential addresses were forged in the crucible of four campaigns to the people. Some speeches were examples of the lofty ideals of teaching and statesmanship he had communicated in the Commonwealth Club speech in 1932, but most of them were pedestrian political persuasions designed for one purpose: to be elected and re-elected. On that singular criterion, Roosevelt succeeded admirably well, and the occasional flashes of eloquence were that much more to his rhetorical credit. Roosevelt always did what it took to win.

In 1932, FDR ran against Hoover. It was the nature of his language that sustained the attack. His catch phrases—the "forgotten man," "bold experimentation," and the New Deal—symbolized for the masses all that was amiss in the Depression. If the campaign was short on specific policies to ameliorate the crisis, Roosevelt, as an articulator for the peoples' feelings, nevertheless spoke in powerfully emotive language that tapped and directed the nation's need for hope and a solution to the crisis. The imagery of flying to the convention to break outworn traditions, coupled with the dynamism of his delivery in public speeches and mastery over the radio, promoted Roosevelt's optimism and confidence that he could shape the nation's destiny.

In 1936, Roosevelt ran against Hooverism, whose stand-in was Landon. FDR waged the canvass at the zenith of the New Deal with a campaign rhetoric at its apotheosis. He developed and deployed the basic strategy in 1936 that worked again in 1940 and 1944: an offensive-defense. With such a posture, one always seemed to learn more about Roosevelt's Republican opponents than about him. Whether attacking the New Deal or arguing "me too, me better," which was a contradictory stance, the Republicans invited the kind of rhetorical responses Roosevelt excelled in making. His turning the tables on them was sometimes downright funny but always telling. He used the scapegoat device to divide the people from their enemies—the economic royalists, the 85 percent Tory press, and the Old Guard—while concomitantly reminding his constituents how they had benefited morally and materially from the New Deal. As with Hoover, Landon was no match for Roosevelt's radio technique and his newsreel presence.

In a desperate attempt to force Roosevelt from running against Hooverism again in 1940, Willkie probed for weaknesses. He tried to make the third term an issue, but Roosevelt countered with the imagery of a draft for the president. He tried tinkering with the New Deal on a "me too, me better" basis, but Roosevelt easily ridiculed that attempt. When the domestic strategy did not perform as expected, Willkie charged that the country was not armed sufficiently for war. So, the Commander-in-Chief visited munitions factories and gave non-political campaign speeches along the way. At last, the Hoosier found an issue to scare the people; the boys are almost already on the troop transports. It was a low trick, which motivated Roosevelt to reply in kind at Boston and Buffalo. *Tu quoque*, you too, is one of the oldest defenses in political rhetoric, but it is worthwhile always to remember who initiated the falsifications.

Misrepresentations played a pivotal role in 1944. By now a seasoned campaigner in that kind of refutation, Roosevelt ridiculed Dewey's campaign by ellipsis. Similarly, he dispatched the governor's transparent attempt to better carry on the New Deal, the successful prosecution of the war, and the peace to come, all of which were the president's accomplishments. To Roosevelt's debit, he did not champion the United Nation's armed forces issue, but his better-late-than-never affirmation, albeit in oblique language, was a credit to Dewey's artfully dodging the question.

Franklin Roosevelt excelled in negative or defensive campaigning. He was in his best form when running against Republicanism, when responding to his Old Guard adversaries. At a time when Americans actually went to mass meetings, thronged around campaign trains at whistle-stops, and tuned to nationally broadcast speeches, FDR's kind of rhetoric generated dramatic excitement, demarcated good and evil, pleased his partisans, bedeviled his opponents, and fulfilled ward workers' efforts to produce a crowd to cheer their champion. In another sense, Roosevelt's campaign strategy was a safe gambit. By reacting to other candidate's rhetoric, he diverted attention from his camp to his opponent's. Except for generalized more-of-the-same appeals for the New Deal in 1936 and 1940 and the war in 1944, whatever Roosevelt did not campaign for, he did not have to defend. This was especially true in 1936 when he did not raise the Supreme Court issue, in 1940 when he tried to remain above partisan campaigning, and in 1944 when it could have cost him dearly had Dewey beat him to the punch on the United Nations armed forces issue. Lastly, FDR's campaigns, particularly his last two, revealed, as his press conferences did, an underside facet of his rhetorical personality that was not reflected in his other presidential addresses. The ridicule, sarcasm, and personal invective that increasingly characterized his campaign speeches disclosed how and why Roosevelt could deal with his enemies in the fray of campaign combat. Like his cousin Theodore Roosevelt, who as president shook hands with the *hoi polloi* on New Year's Day at the White House and then bathed afterwards, Franklin Roosevelt resumed some of the themes of his campaigns, although not their style of language, as he regained his presidential image in his inaugurals.

5

Inaugurating the Presidency

Into the foreseeable future, Franklin Roosevelt will hold the distinction of being the only U.S. president to have delivered four inaugural addresses. But he did not excel in quantity alone. FDR's First Inaugural is one of the greatest inaugurals ever delivered. As a rhetorical response to a crisis situation, his address in 1933 equaled, if not surpassed, Abraham Lincoln's First Inaugural in 1861. Although the two speeches were grounded in different rhetorical situations, and were differentiated by Roosevelt's purpose to unify the country behind his leadership as contrasted to Lincoln's attempt to keep the Union from disuniting, both inaugurals were state papers of the highest order for their times and posterity. However, for sublimity of thought and elegance of expression, not even FDR's First reached the Olympian height of Abraham Lincoln's Second Inaugural Address. Yet, in terms of catchphrases that captured Americans' attention and imagination, can any president's inaugural speech best the famous line from FDR's First Inaugural—the reader already knows it—or the tag line from his Second Inaugural, "I see one-third of a nation ill-housed, ill-clad, ill-nourished"? Roosevelt delivered one of the two best presidential inaugurals in the nation's history; his Second Inaugural surely stands among the better of the lot; and his third and fourth were good inaugurals, although the fourth portrayed his personal and political philosophy in an intimate and revealing manner.

In treating FDR's four inaugurals, one could be guided deftly by Karlyn Campbell and Kathleen Jamieson's seminal essay entitled "Inaugurating the Presidency." Their study of the genre determined that an inaugural performs the following functions: "1) unifies the audience by reconstructing its members as 'the people' who can witness and ratify this ceremony; 2) rehearses communal values drawn from the past; 3) sets forth the political principles that will govern the new administration; 4) demonstrates that the President appreciates the requirements and limitations of his executive functions; and 5) achieves these ends through means appropriate to epideictic address. . . . ''[1]

The problem with a generic theory on inaugurals is that Franklin Roosevelt and his speech writers did not sit down with a theory in mind to compose his inaugurals. Indeed, as will be demonstrated, different elements are missing in his different inaugural speeches. As in the case of the Fireside Chats, it is difficult to construct a generic Rooseveltian inaugural because he faced different issues, a different United States, and a different world from 1933 to 1945. Moreover, a generic theory needs to account for the continuity of campaign themes that may be woven into the inaugural fabric. For in some sense, the inaugural can also be viewed as the last campaign address. In Roosevelt's case, at least, it is instructive to isolate the themes he carried forward, or dropped, in his inaugural addresses.

Given the fact that a generic theory of inaugural addresses must cast a net wide enough to engulf all the average inaugurals floating on the surface of history, it may not seine deep enough to capture the weightier catches of FDR's inaugurals. Despite these caveats, despite each speech being sui generis, Campbell and Jamieson's theory offers a methodology to criticize the merits and failings of FDR's four addresses. Each speech failed or succeeded in its rhetorical situation, and the generic theory can help explicate each speech *in situ*.

THE FIRST INAUGURAL ADDRESS, MARCH 4, 1933

Historian David Potter's observation that, by historical hindsight, the critic might not perceive events as contemporaries comprehended them is germane to a study of FDR's First Inaugural Address. Although he had large majorities in the Congress, FDR could not know the ''Hundred Days'' legislation would pass without congressional demurral. To assume he knew of his forthcoming legislative successes when he fashioned the speech is mistaken, and such an assumption causes the critic to miss some valuable insights concerning FDR and his speech.[2]

The First Inaugural was Roosevelt's premiere persuasion. Harry Hopkins concisely caught the essence of FDR's address: ''With that one speech, and in those few minutes, the appalling anxiety and fears were lifted, and the people knew that they were going into a safe harbor under the leadership of a man who never knew the meaning of fear.''[3]

THE PRODUCTION OF THE SPEECH

The following drafts are extant: the first draft in FDR's handwriting; a second draft, a typed copy of the first with a variety of emendations; a typed third draft that includes additional changes; and a final typed reading copy from which the president delivered his speech on that blustery March day.[4]

The existence of Roosevelt's handwritten draft, in conjunction with a note that FDR had attached to this draft (the note stated he wrote the first draft at Hyde Park on February 27, 1933), has led some to conclude that FDR authored his own speech. Although FDR wrote this first draft, he was not responsible for its authorship. Rather, Raymond Moley composed the first draft. Moley related how he had prepared it, how FDR had copied his draft in longhand at Hyde Park, and how Moley had tossed his own draft into the fire with the words, "This is your speech now," after FDR had finished copying Moley's draft. Moley's version of the speech writing is verified independently by an investigation of FDR's handwritten draft. Several of FDR's pages suggest that he did copy from another source. Instead of the speech text's filling each successive page, there are lacunae on pages three, five, and seven. These lacunae suggest that FDR took more pages to write than did Moley, or to put it another way, the ten pages of copy could be reduced to approximately eight pages if FDR had written his text seriatim on each page.[5]

As for the famous fear statement, "the only thing we have to fear is fear itself," a variety of sources have implied that it, too, was FDR's. However, the phrase was undoubtedly Louis Howe's handiwork. Howe was FDR's personal secretary, something of the man-behind-the-president. Howe dictated a whole beginning paragraph for the third draft, on which the phrase appears for the first time. If the phrase were not original with Howe, then his original source has eluded later researchers.[6]

Only one major revision appeared on the handwritten draft (FDR's copy from Moley's draft). In the second paragraph, Moley wrote of leadership in past national crises and how the people's support of that leadership "on every occasion has won through to." FDR crossed out the quoted phrase and substituted "is essential to victory." Not only was FDR's phrase more concise, but it also linked leadership with victory in a military-like manner.[7]

The third draft (the second typed one) is replete with Roosevelt's handwriting and contains some significant alterations. In the fear paragraph, Howe wrote "nameless, unreasoning, unjustified terror which paralyzes the needed efforts to bring about prosperity once more." With a definite emphasis on military words, FDR produced "which paralyzes *needed* efforts *to convert retreat into advance.*" Later on, the text read: "The standards of the money-changers stand indicted"; however, Roosevelt denigrated the bankers by writing: "*Practices* of the *unscrupulous* money-changers stand indicted." *Practices* sullied the loftiness of "standards," and *unscrupulous* spoke for itself. Treating the bankers in the same vein a bit later, FDR charged "They know of no other ways than the ancient rules" to "They know *only* the rules *of a generation of self-seekers.*" He further strengthened the text to cast additional ridicule on the bankers. "The moral stimulation of work must no longer be submerged in the sham of evanescent profit scouring" became "The moral stimulation of work *no longer* must be

forgotten in *the mad chase* of evanescent profits.'' All these emendations demonstrate that Roosevelt took particular pains (pleasure?) in denigrating and deprecating the bankers, more than Moley's draft had done.[8]

In the latter part of his address, Roosevelt turned to his personal leadership
as president. In a number of places on this draft, he strengthened or clarified
Moley's language in order to enhance the positive nature and vigor of his intended
leadership style. The following examples illustrate the point. ''Because without
such discipline no progress can be made, or any leadership really led'' became
''Because without such discipline no progress *is* made, *no* leadership *becomes
effective*.'' The future tense of Moley's thought was brought into the present
tense by FDR's change, stressing the immediacy of his leadership, and *effective*
looked for immediate and tangible results. ''I am prepared under my constitutional duty to indicate the measures'' became ''I am prepared under my constitutional duty to *recommend* the measures.'' *Recommend* has a stronger sense of
positive advocacy than ''indicate,'' which suggested merely pointing out. Roosevelt wanted to stress his leadership role by taking the lead in recommending
to the Congress his measures, rather than merely indicating to the Congress what
legislation he thought was appropriate. But, interestingly, FDR deleted ''sword
of'' in the following passage: ''With this pledge taken, I assume unhesitatingly
the sword of the leadership of this great army of our people.'' Perhaps the term
sword sounded too militaristic, and perhaps he wanted to stress his personal
leadership rather than a symbolic role. All these emendations demonstrate that
FDR wanted to state clearly the active and personal leadership with which he
would assume the presidency, and that he wished to strengthen Moley's draft
in those respects.[9]

While waiting in the Senate Committee Room for the inaugural ceremonies
to begin, Roosevelt added in longhand an opening sentence on his reading copy:
''This is a day of consecration.'' When he delivered the address, he verbally
inserted ''national'' before ''consecration.''[10]

In summary, one might wish that FDR had authored his own first inaugural,
but he did not. The famous ''fear'' statement, which is so intimately associated
with him and his inaugural, also was not his. Nevertheless, he did make emendations on three of the four drafts, and most of those changes demonstrated his
desire to use militaristic words to evoke military-like associations for his listeners.
He paid special attention to the bankers by utilizing language that purposefully
defamed them and their practices. Lastly, he managed his language to strengthen
his leadership role. He would act immediately to lead the nation in its crisis.
The philosophical significance of this textual investigation is that although the
forthcoming exegesis of FDR's rhetorical purposes is concerned with some of
Moley's and Howe's ideas, Roosevelt was satisfied enough with the text to make
it his inaugural speech, and many of the changes were expressly his word choices.

In an accompanying notation for his inaugural address, FDR wrote that in his
speech he attempted primarily to allay the nation's fear: ''I sought principally
in the foregoing Inaugural Address to banish, so far as possible, the fear of the

present and of the future which held the American people and the American spirit in its grasp." Indeed, his famous fear phrase made an indelible impression on the American mind. Yet, however popularized and catchy the fear statement was, it was not the crux of his speech, nor was it the solitary theme on which commentators based their evaluations of his speech's efficacy with his reading and listening audiences. A close examination of FDR's First Inaugural reveals that he used three rhetorical techniques to aid him in announcing his implementation of the New Deal within the inaugural context.[11]

THE SCAPEGOAT TECHNIQUE

In early 1933, Americans' preeminent concern was the banking crisis. Almost five thousand banks had failed since 1929, and twenty-two states had closed their banks prior to March 4. The spiraling effects of margin and then more margin, stock losses, foreclosures, and ultimately bank failures probably had at their epicenter the bankers and brokers. Rexford Tugwell indicted them specifically: "Wall Street was again the wicked place it had been during the progressive era. The financial establishment was being blamed for what had happened." Finis Farr concurred, "It was true that most of the guilt belonged to the money changers, who probably had something to do with the Stock Exchange."[12]

FDR's coup in his inaugural was to make the moneychangers the scapegoat for the Depression. The scapegoat had its derivation in Jewish antiquity, when the people symbolically placed their sins on a goat's head and then allowed the goat to escape into the wilderness, thus relieving them of their guilt. It has been demonstrated how FDR purposefully used language to denigrate the moneychangers. In his speech, he unflinchingly proclaimed what was believed by the average American: the moneychangers were culpable for the Depression. He used the scapegoat technique to channel the American people's anxieties from themselves to the bankers. The speech text leaves little doubt that Roosevelt utilized the scapegoat device: "The rulers of the exchange of mankind's goods have failed through their own stubbornness and their own incompetence, and have abdicated. Practices of the unscrupulous money-changers stand indicted in the court of public opinion, rejected by the hearts and minds of men." And again: "Yes, the money-changers have fled from their high seats in the temple of our civilization. We may now restore that temple to the ancient truths." William Leuchtenburg noted that the president's delivery matched the mood of his language: "Grim, unsmiling, chin uplifted, his voice firm, almost angry, he lashed out at the bankers." Having castigated Wall Street, the president then indicated he would direct his New Deal toward checking it and its practices. In order to stop a return to the "evils of the old order," he announced there would be banking reform: "There must be a strict supervision of all banking and credits and investments. [Applause.] There must be an end to speculation with other people's money. [Applause.] And there must be a provision for an adequate but sound currency. [Applause.]" To these ends, the Congress passed the Emergency

Banking Act on March 9; the Civilian Conservation Corps, March 31, put people to work; and the fear of foreclosure was alleviated by the Emergency Farm Mortgage Act, May 12, and the Home Owner's Loan Act, June 13.[13]

Various contemporary signs indicated that Roosevelt struck a responsive rhetorical chord with the scapegoat device. When he said he would restore the "temple to the ancient truths," his inaugural audience applauded for the first time. Editors from Universal Films and Pathe News included FDR's attack on the bankers in their newsreels. Tugwell noted that FDR "tramped hard on those who were responsible." The media also supported the president's application of the scapegoat technique. The *Christian Century* noted, "the 'false money-changers' deserve all the condemnation that can be heaped upon them"; *Nation* observed that FDR dealt bankers a "verbal scourging"; and *News-Week* stated, "It was an assault on the bankers, against whom the voices of the distressed are raised in an ever-swelling chorus as the depression endures." As promised at Oglethorpe University, FDR remembered the forgotten man, as indicated by his effect on the business community. *The Times* (London) noted that FDR was "likely to rouse the opposition of a good many vested interests." Thus, the president used the device to blunt possible opposition from those laissez-faire sympathizers who might attack his New Deal banking and investment measures. Basil Rauch indicated that FDR was successful in disarming his banking critics: "The bankers were in a chastened mood. . . . They had lost the cohesion of a vested group."[14]

The scapegoat technique served as one of the epicenters around which several of the elements of inaugural oratory devolved. It is important to note what values Roosevelt stressed and how he defined them. To be sure, he attended to traditional mores, in a vague manner, by mentioning "social values," "the joy of achievement," and "honesty . . . honor . . . the sacredness of obligations." But the emotional impact of his speech was accomplished in the manner in which he defined other values. Rather than emphasizing what values he would inculcate, he stressed the ones he would exterminate by listing the vile practices of the money-changers. As a continuation of his practice in the canvass to attack Hoover, while being vague on his own policies, Roosevelt affirmed the nation's true destiny, not by indicating what it would be, but by asserting what it would not be: he defined and then rejected the negative values held by Wall Street. He elevated the tried-and-true moral values of the average American over the tried-but-found-wanting material values of the self-seekers. The scapegoat device figuratively reconstituted the people by cleansing them while concomitantly excluding from their midst the moneychangers. Roosevelt could not lead, nor could the people follow, until he, as saviour, symbolically purified them so that they could reenter the temple. After the people had been cleansed by driving away the scapegoat, they, in company with FDR, could "restore that temple to the ancient truths." By assenting to the efficacy of the scapegoat device, the people vicariously shared in the victory over their vanquished nemesis, and they implicitly supported the president in the subsequent actions he proposed against the enemy in the New Deal.

FDR's First Inaugural was action-oriented. His emendations demonstrated that he would work in the present for specific policies. The scapegoat device was an application of the leadership criterion he had set forth in the "Forgotten Man" speech about rallying public opinion in support of objectives. Roosevelt did not ask the American people to contemplate how they might overcome fear, he led the way. In his acceptance speech, he partially blamed the American people for the Depression:

Blame not Governments alone for this. Blame ourselves in equal share. Let us be frank in acknowledgment of the truth that many amongst us have made obeisance to Mammon, that the profits of speculation, the easy road without toil, have lured us from the old barricades. To return to higher standards we must abandon the false prophets and seek new leaders of our own choosing.

Although it was certainly true that average Americans had played the stock market, Roosevelt wisely overlooked that fact in his First Inaugural. By blaming only a small minority of people on March 4, the president was able to divert attention to Wall Street and away from the American people. Roosevelt realized that one never points the accusing finger at one's constituents, but at one's enemies.[15]

Available evidence from the inaugural audience, from contemporary newsreels and media, and from later commentators suggests that FDR was successful in obtaining his persuasive purpose.

THE MILITARY METAPHORS

Militaristic language was posted throughout FDR's campaign speeches, especially so at Oglethorpe, and he advanced that theme on March 4. Although Americans had elected Roosevelt, questions still remained about the nature of his personal leadership and the New Deal. Since it was not particularly clear from the canvass, Americans avidly awaited his inaugural speech to determine how he proposed to lead the country out of the Depression.

Knowing that his program would need mass support and that the New Deal would bring broad and at times radical departures from conducting government as it had been until 1933, Roosevelt endeavored to garner that support by deploying military metaphors. Approximately 50,000,000 Americans listened to FDR's presidential rhetoric on the radio, and the immediate inaugural audience numbered about 150,000. William Leuchtenburg studied the era's values and concluded that Roosevelt responded to the Depression crisis by purposefully using military imagery: "Roosevelt's inaugural address . . . reflected the sense of wartime crisis," and "President Roosevelt sought to restore national confidence by evoking the mood of wartime.'' The military metaphors centered on values that arise from needs during wartime, but the nation was not at war. FDR skillfully played on the emotional evocations of militaristic language in order to declare a figurative war on a serious economic condition. Now at war, as it were, he indirectly asked citizens to follow him as Commander-in-Chief. Given that a war implies some loss of freedom for the greater goal of victory over the enemy, the military imagery served as a precursor of broad executive power, and in giving assent to such a definition, the people acquiesced to the kind of executive action Roosevelt proposed.[16]

The careful listener or reader would have noted that FDR deployed an advance guard of military metaphors in the early parts of his address: ''retreat into advance,'' ''victory,'' ''direct recruiting,'' and ''emergency of war.'' But when the president directly urged support for and acceptance of his personal leadership in the latter three-fourths of his speech, his language was replete with militaristic imagery:

If we are to go forward, we must move as a trained and loyal army, willing to sacrifice for the good of a common discipline, because without such discipline no progress can be made, no leadership becomes effective. We are, I know, ready and willing to submit our lives and our property to such discipline because it makes possible a leadership which aims at the larger good. This I propose to offer, pledging that the larger purposes will bind upon us, bind upon us all a sacred obligation, with a unity of duty hitherto evoked only in times of armed strife. With this pledge taken, I assume unhesitatingly the leadership of this great army of our people dedicated to a disciplined attack upon our common problems.

The repetition of ''discipline'' four times and of ''leadership'' three times, and the use of other value-laden words such as ''duty,'' ''sacred obligation,'' and ''armed strife,'' reinforced the desires that yearned for action against the Depression.

The effect-oriented responses from private persons and the press were favorably impressed with FDR's appeals. From all quarters came support for Roosevelt's bid for quasi-military leadership power, and that support was often couched in the president's infectious military imagery. Republican Alfred Landon of Kansas affirmed: ''If there is any way in which a Republican governor of a midwestern state can aid the President in the fight, I now enlist for the duration of the war.'' Landon evidently believed his enlistment expired in 1936, when he decided to run for president. Myron C. Taylor, chairman of United States Steel Corporation, declared, ''I hasten to re-enlist to fight the depression to its end,'' and James Hagerty wrote, ''In the phraseology which ran all through his [FDR's] speech he indicated that he regarded the United States as in an economic war.'' The *New York Times* capsulized other newspapers' comments, parts of which are included here: the *Plain Dealer* in Cleveland responded to FDR's military metaphor and characterized the speech as ''fighting words, fit for a time that calls for militant action''; in Des Moines, the *Register* believed ''it is the rallying of the country to a renewal of a courageous and sustained war on the depression." In its inimitable manner, *The Times* (London) also noticed the military-like words: "What is important to note is the spirit which inspired it throughout. A high and resolute militancy breathes in every line."[17]

But this military image, which had been prominent in the "Forgotten Man" speech, could also hurt FDR if Americans misperceived his intent. In inaugurals, Campbell and Jamieson found that presidents should communicate their aware-ness of the requirements and limitations of their executive power in a democracy. Given that Roosevelt may have tipped that delicate balance away from limitations toward apparently unlimited power with the military metaphors, he needed to reassure the American people that they had little to fear of a nascent dictatorship in his New Deal. He hastened to allay Americans: "Action in this image, action to this end, is feasible under the form of government which we have inherited from our ancestors. Our constitution is so simple, so practical, that it is possible always to meet extraordinary needs by changes in emphasis and arrangement without the loss of essential form." The critic might have challenged FDR's assertion that changes in emphasis and arrangement can ensue without a loss of essential form, but Farr believed the assertion sounded fine to most of FDR's listeners, and anyway, there was little time to raise that question because Roo-sevelt's confident voice continued on.[18]

However, Adoph Hitler's Fuehrer-principle was fresh in some American's minds, and they were not so easily beguiled. Partially indicative of this thinking was Hearst's *New York Mirror* issue of March 6, which headlined its story: "ROOSEVELT ASKS DICTATOR'S ROLE." Indeed, Chancellor Hitler dem-onstrated that he appreciated the efficacy of Roosevelt's inaugural address by the language he chose in his congratulatory cable:

The Reich Chancellor is in accord with the President that the virtues of sense of duty, readiness for sacrifice, and discipline must be the supreme rule of the whole nation. This moral demand, which the President is addressing to every single citizen, is only the quintessence of German philosophy of the State, expressed in its motto "The Public Weal Before Private Gain."

Benito Mussolini's *Il Giornale d'Italia* saw in FDR's inaugural a reaffirmation of its views:

President Roosevelt's words are clear and need no comment to make even the deaf hear that not only Europe but the whole world feels the need of executive authority capable of acting with full powers of cutting short the purposeless chatter of legislative assemblies. This method of government may well be defined as Fascist.

However, Franklin Roosevelt was not a Hitler or a Mussolini. On the first day Hitler assumed the office of Reich Chancellor, he said he would never relinquish it: "No power in the world will ever get me out of here alive." Juxtaposed to

Hitler's statement is an interesting emendation FDR made on the third draft of his inaugural address. He added *present* to the following sentence: "They have made me the *present* instrument of their wishes." His change suggests that FDR had a more reasonable and limited conception of his leadership role. The term *present* implies the four-year term, and it does not preclude some other president four years later.[19]

Although some people were less comfortable with Roosevelt's military imagery than were most of his contemporaries, he successfully evoked in the American people a patriotic duty to support his quasi-military leadership in his symbolic war on the Depression. Lest this military metaphor smack too much of an incipient American Caesar, Roosevelt took pains to assure his audience that the Constitution would survive.

THE CARROT-AND-STICK TECHNIQUE

President Roosevelt enlisted the country in his symbolic army with his military imagery, he used the scapegoat device to subdue Wall Street, he had a favorable press until the honeymoon was over, and now he had only to deal with the Congress.

During the interregnum, November 1932 to March 1933, the president-elect received advice from many quarters, including even President Herbert Hoover, on how he could help to stop the deepening Depression. Of particular concern here is the advice FDR received on how to cope with the Congress. In a letter, Senator Key Pittman of Nevada warned FDR in early February 1933 that the Congress could be difficult to control because Democrats had grown restive under the Hoover administration. Of these typical warnings, James Patterson wrote, "Such predictions of an unruly congress in a time of social and economic crisis were commonplace in the months prior to Roosevelt's inauguration."[20]

Accordingly, Roosevelt resorted to the carrot-and-stick device to move the Congress to follow his executive leadership. He presaged this device in his famous Commonwealth Club address at San Francisco. His carrot was a clever cajoling of the Congress to act either on its own or in tandem with him:

And it is to be hoped that the normal balance of executive and legislative authority may be wholly equal, wholly adequate, to meet the unprecedented task before us. But it may be that an unprecedented demand and need for undelayed action may call for temporary departure from that normal balance of public procedure. I am prepared under my constitutional duty to recommend the measures that a stricken nation in the midst of a stricken world may require. These measures, or such measures as the Congress may build out of its experience and wisdom, I shall seek within my constitutional authority to bring to speedy adoption.

If the carrot were not motivation enough, then the stick would be:

But in the event that the Congress shall fail to take one of these two courses, in the event that the national emergency is still critical, I shall not evade the clear course of duty that will then confront me. I shall ask the Congress for the one remaining instrument to meet the crisis: broad executive power to wage a war against the emergency, as great as the power that would be given to me if we were in fact invaded by a foreign foe.

The tumultuous applause that immediately followed, and it was the greatest applause of any passage in the speech, could not have been mistaken by listening members of the Congress. Eleanor Roosevelt thought the applause was "a little terrifying. You felt that they would do *anything*—if only someone would tell them *what* to do." (Italics in original.) The *News* in Dallas supported FDR's carrot-and-stick device by suggesting that "if Congress fails him, the country will strongly back him in his demands for virtual war powers"; moreover, the conservative Boston *Transcript* even agreed with FDR: "The President's program demands dictatorial authority. This is unprecedented in its implication, but such is the desperate temper of the people that it is welcome."[21]

In hindsight, the Congress was anything but intransigent, but FDR did not know that when he fashioned his address. Although the carrot-and-stick technique admittedly did not directly cause the Congress to cooperate, it did nevertheless serve a vital function. The device's efficacy ensued from a tenet of the rhetorical presidency: speaking is governing. President Roosevelt conveyed his willingness to use the stick if it were necessary. Alfred Rollins believed that if Roosevelt had not demonstrated his ability to act and to lead, he might have faltered on inauguration day: "What Roosevelt did do, with monumental success, was to preserve the faith which vague commitment or partial action might have shattered." In other words, a contemplative inaugural in 1933 would have been inappropriate.[22]

SUMMARY

In his First Inaugural Address, Franklin Roosevelt unified and reconstituted the people for the task before them. He scapegoated the bankers and brokers for the Depression. He marshalled military metaphors to evoke in the American people a sense of duty and discipline, communal values that are salient and needed in a time of national crisis, and to persuade citizens to support his quasi-military leadership in his symbolic war on the Depression. For the Congress, he deployed the carrot-and-stick device to demonstrate his desire to act either in tandem with Congress or alone if it failed him. These techniques were successful rhetorical devices because he articulated the attitudes of the immediate and national inaugural audiences, of most of the contemporary news media, and perhaps most important, of the members of the Congress. Cleveland Rodgers realized the effect of FDR's presidential rhetoric on the American people, that it "first won for him the support of the great masses of people and put behind his efforts the full force of an overwhelming public opinion."[23]

The inaugural eloquence that Roosevelt spoke on that cold day in March 1933 in order to move public opinion was a function of rhetorical technique. As the vox populi, he assuaged the deep needs of the people and represented before them in efficacious language the restored values that would lead them forward and out of the Depression. He displayed his mastery over the crisis by selecting active words that fulfilled concomitantly the exigencies of the rhetorical situation as well as the requirements of the inaugural occasion. By adroitly defining his desire to work with the Congress, he made certain the audience appreciated his allegiance to the doctrine of separation of powers. On the other hand, by conjuring the military-political crisis in which he would act if the Congress did not, he allowed the American people to ascertain the necessity of executive ascendancy over the legislative branch if it came to that. The American audience appreciated his action-oriented New Deal and his determination not only to talk eloquently about action but also to act expeditiously.

Closing remarks are perhaps best left to Roosevelt. His three rhetorical techniques coalesced in his inaugural conclusion: "The people of the United States have not failed. In their need they have registered a mandate that they want direct, vigorous action. They have asked for discipline and direction under leadership. They have made me the present instrument of their wishes. In the spirit of the gift, I take it."[24]

THE SECOND INAUGURAL ADDRESS
JANUARY 20, 1937

FDR's second inaugural is more noteworthy for what he did not say than for what he did communicate it it. With regard to what he did say, two general reasons may explain why the address, except for the famous "one-third" statement, was not an ideal one. First, the initial draft was prepared by Donald Richberg, and it was not a particularly eloquent effort on which to base an elegant speech. However, the president made some interesting emendations on the various speech drafts, which dramatically improved them, and these will be analyzed presently. Although government is often proclaimed to be the problem in the 1980s, Roosevelt's changes on the drafts clearly indicate what values he stressed in order to argue that government was the solution to the nation's problems in the 1930s. The second reason is that the nation FDR faced in January of 1937 was not a nation in crisis, and consequently there was no need to give a striking rhetorical response to a desperate situation. In that sense, and perhaps unfairly, FDR's other inaugurals are bound to suffer when compared to his First. For some unknown reason, FDR did not even bother to allude to the historical significance of the new inauguration date of January 20, which resulted from shortening by some six weeks the old date of March 4 by the 20th Amendment to the Constitution (which was finally ratified in February 1933—too late to have altered the date for the First Inaugural Address).

WHAT ROOSEVELT DID SAY

The president reconstituted the people by beginning his speech with a reference to the communal values that would be carried over from his first term to his second one: "When four years ago we met to inaugurate a President, the Republic, single-minded in anxiety, stood in spirit here. We dedicated ourselves to the fulfillment of a vision. . . . We did those first things first." He additionally noted, "This year marks the one hundred and fiftieth anniversary of the Constitutional convention which made us a nation"; therefore, "Today we invoke those same powers of government to achieve the same objectives."

Some of FDR's emendations demonstrate that he would shape his second term along the same general lines as his first term. He had made, and would again make, government work for the people rather than for special interests: "On the day [it] *we* dedicated [itself] *ourselves* to the fulfillment of a vision—to [bring about a day] *speed the time* when [the people] *there would be for all the people that* [in the] security and peace [in the] *essential to the* pursuit of happiness"; "*Our covenant with ourselves did not stop there.* [But] *I*nstinctively we [also accepted] *recognized* a deeper need—the need to find [in] *through* government [as] the instrument of our united power and purpose"; [These had more and more] *Attempts at their individual solution had left us more and more* baffled and bewildered"; "We have [learned] *decided as a people* that [private economic power, uncontrolled by public obligations, can not be relied upon to] *we must work together to* meet common needs and [to] preserve the general welfare." In the example just quoted, FDR excised language that hinted of economic royalists: perhaps he wanted to shed the role of campaigner and to reassume the stature of president.

More important, Roosevelt stressed the communal values that had informed his leadership of the country since 1933. The following are examples of this value-laden rhetoric: "to promote the general welfare and secure the blessings of liberty to the American people"; "Our tasks in the last four years did not force democracy to take a holiday"; "With this change in our moral climate and our rediscovered ability to improve our economic order, we have set our feet upon the road to enduring progress"; and "In this process evil things formerly accepted will not be so easily condoned. Hard-headedness will not so easily excuse hard-heartedness." These values demanded that the country and he should not be deterred by certain old values that had characterized the election race just finished: "Many voices are heard as we face a great decision. Comfort says, 'Tarry a while.' Opportunism says, 'This is a good spot.' Timidity says, 'How difficult is the road ahead?' " But Roosevelt rejected these old values with a rhetorical question: "Let us ask again: Have we reached the goal of our vision of that fourth day of March, 1933? Have we found our happy valley?" President Roosevelt believed not, so he eloquently cast his answer in the famous anaphora for which the speech is justly remembered:

I see millions of families trying to live on incomes so meager that the pall of family disaster hangs over them day by day.

I see millions whose daily lives in city and on farm continue under conditions labeled indecent by so-called polite society half a century ago.

I see millions denied education, recreation, and the opportunity to better their lot and the lot of their children.

I see millions lacking the means to buy the products of farm and factory and by their poverty denying work and productiveness to many other millions.

I see one-third of a nation ill-housed, ill-clad, ill-nourished.

The invention of the one-third statement is an example of Roosevelt's rhetorical acumen. He made the necessary changes on a mediocre draft to produce a stylistic masterpiece: "I see [those] millions who live their daily lives in city and on farm [amid] *under* conditions [outlawed by a so-called] *labelled indecent by a so-called* polite society half a century ago. I see [conditions where these] millions [are] denied [the] education, [and] *recreation and even* the opportunity to better their lot and the lot of their children. I see [those] millions lacking the [economic power to consume] means to buy the products of farm and factory and [thereby denying] *by their poverty denying* work and productiveness to many other millions." At this point on the draft, Rosenman wrote "I see a . . . ," but unfortunately the rest of his thought is indistinguishable because FDR erased it. FDR wrote over the erasure, "one-third of . . ." (the rest is also unclear). Finally, Roosevelt crossed out the entire "I see one-third of" and wrote: "I see one-third of a nation ill-housed, ill-clad, ill-nourished." The third draft indicates that FDR divided the long "I see millions" paragraph into one-sentence paragraphs in order to give the necessary visual cues to deliver the lines, which he did with his usual aplomb. Also, the close observer might note that the quoted paragraph above does not exactly match the speech text as delivered: the few minor changes were made on the third draft.[25]

The one-third statement, which is to the Second Inaugural Address as the famous fear statement is to the First Inaugural, merits attention. Some controversy exists over whether the eloquence was exaggerated. Although recent critics include the one-third statement in their accounts without disapprobation, contemporary writers were more judicious in their reception to the thought. Rauch recalled: "The statement came as a shock to most Americans. It implied that the recovery which had been achieved was superficial." Donald Richberg, who was one of the collaborators on the speech, complained that the figure was fanciful: "I ventured to suggest that if one were going to pull a figure out of the sky it would at least be safer to say one-fourth rather than one-third. But F.D.R. had a certain feeling for numbers which had been commented on by other observers. He liked the one-third and he wasn't particularly bothered by using a fraction which, even if it could not be supported, could not be disproved." The public reaction mail to the Second Inaugural Address indicated that some people saw conditions as FDR portrayed them while others perceived improvement. A Carmel, California, person praised FDR for painting America as it was:

"Your honesty and courage in painting a true picture of conditions in the U.S.A. as they exist after you served four years as President ('I see one third of a nation ill-housed, ill-clad, ill-nourished'), when it would have been so easy to have omitted mentioning these terrible facts, is probably without parallel.'' Similar sentiments were repeated from Rockford, Illinois: ''It shows that you are in very close touch with conditions as they really exist. Unfortunately, all cannot see it in that light.'' But other writers communicated their gratitude to FDR for their general improvement under his New Deal. A Works Progress Administration worker from Providence, Rhode Island, compared life under President Hoover to life under President Roosevelt: ''Since you have been President I'm starting to get back on my feet because it takes me time because I have to pay back all the bills I had to make in the time of the Hoover administration which we were all going back instead of forward. But now we could look forward.'' A denizen of Denver, Colorado, wrote: ''My thoughts go back four years ago, March 4, 1933. Then I sat looking out upon the drout stricken prairies of Eastern Colorado *sad ill* and *discouraged* in fact I longed to die. . . . My health has improved, my finances and economic condition are really better, due to your *constructive policies* [italics in original].'' A farm couple from Buffalo, Minnesota, knew things were better for them: ''It was a happy idea to compare the inaugural day to the inaugural day four years ago. We who live out on the farms know that conditions are better and we are glad to give the President the credit he deserves.'' It is difficult to prove or disprove FDR's one-third statement with statistics. The unemployment rate had dropped from a high of 24.9 percent in 1933 to 16.9 percent in 1936, but that was no match for the 3.2 percent of 1929, before the crash; moreover, it is worth remembering that in 1935–36, 43.5 percent of the families and unattached individuals made under $1000, whereas a poll taken in January 1937 suggested that 48 percent of the respondents felt that a family of four needed $1050 to $2049 a year to live in health and comfort. Although figures may never resolve what the exact fraction was, such quibbling seems to miss the point FDR made in the triad of his speech: the past had demanded New Deal measures, those measures were working in the present, but more measures were needed in the future to solve the nation's pressing problems so that Americans could reach their happy valley.[26]

Before we examine how Roosevelt intended to lead the people to their happy valley, an observation is worth making about an insert that was placed in the fourth draft. The emendation is an example of the give-and-take between FDR and his speech staff. Rosenman had written, ''The test of our progress is not whether we add to the abundance of those who have much; it is whether we provide enough for those who have little.'' Roosevelt struck ''whether'' and replaced it with ''what'' in the first part of the compound sentence. But Rosenman had his way by restoring his original language and adding a ''more'': ''The test of our progress is not [what] *whether* we add *more* to the abundance. . . . '' Rosenman's rendition was better than Roosevelt's because it kept the parallelism of the conjunction ''whether.'' Also, those students of President Kennedy's rhetoric might wish to compare Rosenman's thought with one of the famous lines from JFK's Inaugural Address: "If a free society can not help the many who are poor, it can not save the few who are rich."[27]

Unlike the First Inaugural, which was, in certain key elements, a thematic rhetoric of the 1932 campaign, the Second Inaugural made a relatively clean break with the canvass in 1936. Given that Landon and Republicanism were so thoroughly repudiated at the presidential level in 1936, the speech is noteworthy for the lack of gloating rhetoric. One sees shades of economic royalists lurking in a few sentences, but the blatant attempts to cast them as a scapegoat are lacking; nor is there any John Paul Jones rhetoric against the Old Guard Tories. Since the 1936 campaign was an offensive-defense of the New Deal, which FDR promised to continue in a second term, he took a more contemplative posture in the inaugural speech. In the last fifth of his address, he looked to the future and assured his audience: "We will not listen to Comfort, Opportunism, and Timidity. We will carry on." But how and where he proposed to carry on was a mystery.

WHAT ROOSEVELT DID NOT SAY

The close reader would note that Roosevelt did not enunciate in his inaugural Campbell and Jamieson's elements on political principles and on appreciation of executive powers and limitations. He did not mention the significant problem of the Supreme Court's harmful rulings against the New Deal, the political ways by which he would seek to alleviate those rulings, or how he proposed to treat the Court via his executive power. By not defining his policy against that body, the people could not understand his vision of how he proposed to obtain a more compliant Court. Yet, language along those lines was expected in the inaugural setting. *Time* noted that Roosevelt delivered "an address which presented no programs, no plans," and the *New York Times* also noticed the omission: "Those who looked for a detailed outline of the President's proposals for the next four years, especially for an elaboration of his new program for the new Congress, were in part disappointed." How Roosevelt proposed to carry on was rumored to be on the justices' minds, as they expected something from the president on the Court issue: "There was no secret among the court officers that some direct allusion to the court was anticipated from Mr. Roosevelt, but if the justices had this expectation they were surprised, for the message was devoid of anything of this kind," and "Some may complain that his inaugural address was disappointingly vague. It laid down no new policies. It called for no added legislation." Nathan Miller questioned why Roosevelt did not mention the Court: "But how would he deal with the Supreme Court, which seemed bent on dismembering the New Deal? . . . No specifics were forthcoming in his second inaugural speech."[28]

It may be objected that January 20, 1937, was not the appropriate time nor was the inaugural the right occasion to lay the argumentative foundation for an attack against the Supreme Court. Roosevelt cannot be realistically condemned for not raising the issue in the campaign, the purpose of which was to get elected and not to hand Landon an issue that would undoubtedly help the Tory cause. The genre theory would suggest the inaugural was the appropriate time. The validity of the theory is supported by the fact that contemporary and later critics complained about the omission. Even if one wished to waive aside those critics, there is additional proof. If one could demonstrate that the lack of language on the Court issue helped to contribute to the downfall of the Court scheme, then the theory would be vindicated. It will take an entire chapter on the Court fight to prove that point, but the basic argument follows.

The lack of language as expected on the Court problem cannot be dismissed. The American people were not prepared for FDR's surprise attack on the judiciary two weeks later because they had not been enlightened to its necessity or told the values upon which such an attack would be mounted. As will be demonstrated in chapter 6, FDR's problems with the people and the Congress could have been rectified, or at least alleviated, by communicating the values that would impel action against the judiciary as required by custom and tradition in an inaugural speech.

President Roosevelt's Second Inaugural Address was good but not stellar. Its saving graces were the famous one-third statement and the anaphora of "I see millions." These elegant stylistic devices displayed his eloquence and enlightened the people to the conditions in the nation as he perceived them in 1937. But for all its stylistic panache, the speech did not reveal the political principles nor the executive functions and limitations on how he would deal with the Supreme Court, whose judicial wrecking of the New Deal arguably contributed to Roosevelt's frustrations in not being able to solve the remaining one-third problem. Eloquence in language without mastery over policy was not enough.

THE THIRD INAUGURAL ADDRESS
JANUARY 20, 1941

"The inaugural address was hailed by some New Deal enthusiasts as comparable to Lincoln's Gettysburg Address, or to Mr. Lincoln's second inaugural message." If that had been said in 1933 about FDR's First Inaugural, it would have been a just comparison; if said in 1937 of the Second, it would have been flattery; as actually written about the Third, it was hyperbole. The Third Inaugural Address is probably the most unfulfilling of FDR's inaugural speeches, for a variety of reasons.[29]

The rhetorical artifacts under scrutiny are FDR's handwritten draft, some significant emendations on five subsequent drafts (although there were six drafts—the first one was actually a typed version of FDR's handwritten one), and the final reading copy. Upon a close examination of these documents, the address lacked in the generic characteristics, was too philosophical in tone and treatment, and was a muted rhetorical response to the war in Europe. The emphasis is not so much on determining deficiencies, but rather on the fact that these omissions indicate how and why Roosevelt responded to certain exigencies in 1941. The speech has an interesting tension. FDR wanted to fulfill the logical and practical implications of his thoughts as he wrote them out in longhand, and as he later emended the drafts, but he felt constrained from doing so by his gauging of the isolationist forces in and out of the Congress. Thus, the speech is a kind of battleground between belligerency, what FDR wanted, versus non-belligerency, what he gave the isolationists. He advanced toward but stopped short of enunciating the values that would serve as a precursor to American intervention in a world at war. His inaugural speech was thus constrained by the paradoxes of the canvass and by his pledge at Boston not to send American boys to war, even assuming the except-for-armed-attack language of the Democratic platform. He devoted too much verbiage on a philosophical treatment of domestic communal values at the expense of rehearsing the political principles that would guide a third term at home and abroad, and he was vague on the values Americans should hold toward our allies and the aggressors.

ROOSEVELT'S HANDWRITTEN DRAFT

In the first paragraph he penned on yellow legal paper, FDR obviously alluded to the timely and imminent dangers in Europe and hinted that he would address the current situation: "Always it is worth while in the midst of swift happenings to pause for a moment to take stock of our thoughts. If we do not we risk a pitfall or a wrong turning." This paragraph could easily have functioned as an introductory lead to a discussion of the political principles on which he would rely in order to avoid problems in his third term. It was a good beginning.

But abruptly, he moved from the present tense in the first paragraph to past tense in his next two paragraphs. This shift in tense was inappropriate because the nature of his language in the beginning implied that he would speak to the future and not about the past. Also, this change of scene from the current war crisis to past domestic history was not thematically related nor logically implied:

Eight years ago a danger hung over our land; we were in the midst of it; we knew its shock and its actual immediate bearing upon our daily lives as individuals and as a nation. We sensed its causes, and we were in agreement that quick action, unwonted action, bold action, was not merely desirable but urgently requisite.

These eight years have been long years, crowded with new things. They have been fruitful years for the people of our land; for they have brought to us a more marked security and, I dare to say, a better understanding of life's ideal than we had had in times before.

The impelling image of action, modified by three strong adjectives, could have eloquently functioned as a guiding principle to deal with the crisis in Europe, yet the idea was not developed nor applied to any executive actions.

Roosevelt did reasonably continue the train of thought from his second and third paragraphs to the fourth one, but there still was no revelation of how he would avoid pitfalls or wrong turns:

Most vital to our present and our future stands out the picture of a democracy which has conquered a crisis at home; put away many evil doings; built new structures on enduring lines; and at the same time has preserved the fact of its democracy. For action has been taken within the framework of the Constitution of the United States. The coordinate branches of our government give every evidence of continuing to function. The Bill of Rights remains inviolate; the freedom of elections is wholly maintained; and the dire prophets of the downfall of America have seen their evil predictions come to naught.

The allusion to Nazi Germany and Fascist Italy is clearly implied by a democracy still functioning here despite predictions to the contrary.

Then, without warning or hint, Roosevelt again veered off in another direction by introducing the metaphor of the soul and then fleshing it out:

A nation has a soul.

Like a person a nation has a body too—a body that must be fed and clothed and housed and given the means of locomotion that fit our day.

Like a person a nation has a mind—a mind too that must fit our day in its relation to those minds of other nations which are so near to us *now* in the whole circle of the world [italics in original].

But it is the soul of a nation which matters the most to its future, which calls forth the most sacred guarding in its present.

Our soul is the product of centuries. It was born in the multitude of souls living in many lands, souls of some high degree, but mostly souls of very plain people who sought a thing called freedom—who sought it under several forms of governings in other lands, but came hither early and late to attain more freely.

The last paragraph was a distillation of his speech at Dayton, Ohio. Moreover, what was left of America's allies in Europe was clearly on FDR's mind when he wrote they were near us now. Indeed, in this dire situation, how he proposed to actuate for America a "most sacred guarding" of its present or future was a mystery.[30]

The inaugural situation demanded a response to the war in Europe and its related domestic exigency. After the fall of France to Hitler on June 14, 1940, England stood alone against the Axis. In order to save her by helping in her war effort, FDR delivered his famous "Four Freedoms" speech on January 6, 1941, and followed it with the Lend-Lease Act that would circumvent the neutrality legislation by sending American war munitions to England. Although that speech is discussed in chapter 7, suffice it to say that Roosevelt ignited a bitter fight with the isolationists. Yet, he did not hint in his draft at the serious need in England for this critical legislation, nor reiterate the values on which such help should be based, nor issue a clarion call for unity behind his proposal. Indeed, the draft seemed to approach the exigency of the situation but avoided any concrete language that hinted at action. The metaphors Roosevelt used to convey the need for the nation-as-human to be sustained in mind, body, and soul were good ones; however, he failed in this handwritten draft to indicate how he proposed to nourish the soul, either at home or abroad, in his third administration.

THE PROGRESSION OF THE SPEECH DRAFTS

Using Roosevelt's handwritten text, Samuel Rosenman revised and enlarged the speech. Not until the fourth draft (actually the third) do certain revisions merit attention. Although it is impossible to determine who composed it, a new introduction appeared on the fourth draft. This new material was a good addition because it stressed the idea that the inaugural would speak to the European exigency. It heightened that crucial issue by juxtaposing past communal and domestic values, which had informed previous precursors to actions, with the present concern for foreign matters:

On each national day of Inauguration since 1789, the people have renewed their sense of dedication to the United States.

In Washington's day the task of the people was to create and weld together a nation.

In Lincoln's day the task of the people was to preserve that nation from disintegration from within.

In this day the task of the people is to save that nation and its institutions from assault from without.

The new introduction was an appropriate beginning. First, it adequately reconstituted the people in ratifying an historic occasion by acknowledging the needs inherent in the country's survival from times past. Second, it served as a reasonable premise for the business of a "pitfall or wrong turning" because it developed an historical precedence for the kind of action it hinted. Yet, the rest of the speech continued to veer away from fulfilling the introductory material.[31]

On the fifth draft, FDR made an emendation that supports the thesis he wanted to address the war in Europe. He changed his own language in the following sentence: "If we do not, we risk [a pitfall or a wrong turning] *the real peril of inaction.*" This change lends credence to the thesis because he used the opposite of action or a precursor to action, namely "inaction," which he believed was the "real peril," to reinforce the sense of "risk." As Washington and Lincoln had acted appropriately in their historical settings, the nature of FDR's language indicated, by analogy, that he would act accordingly in response to the situation in 1941. A few sentences later, still in the introduction, he strengthened the text in order to take a rhetorical shot at Hitler and Mussolini: "There are men [abroad - and here -] who doubt this. There are men who believe that democracy, as a form of government and a frame of life, is limited or measured by a kind of mystical and artificial fate: that, for some unexplained reason, tyranny and slavery have become the [new order of the world] *surging wave of the future*— and *that* freedom [old and outmoded] *is an ebbing tide*. But [the vast majority of] *we* Americans know that this is not true."[32]

This passage is important for a variety of reasons. An examination of the drafts contradicts Rosenman's version of how the above material was invented. Rosenman had Roosevelt dictating the entire thought as it was finally emended on draft five. One cannot prove or disprove that FDR dictated the thought because it appears anew on the fourth draft. The original idea is as follows (with Rosenman's emendations italicized): "[Others may] *There are men abroad - and here - who* doubt this. [Others may] *There are men who* believe that democracy as a form of government and a [way] *frame* of life is limited or measured by a kind of mystical and artificial fate: that, for some unexplained reason, tyranny and slavery have become *the* new *order of the world* and freedom old *and outmoded*. [We in this country] *But the vast majority of Americans* know that this is not true." If, as Rosenman suggests, FDR wanted to allude to Anne Lindbergh's *The Wave of the Future* by choosing "surging wave of the future," he did not do it in the fourth draft but in the fifth, and the passage was not dictated *in toto* as Rosenman said it was.[33]

The fifth draft has another interesting Rooseveltian revision. The President was sensitive to the meanings of words, and he made a change on the draft to defuse an oft-made charge that he was a quasi-dictator. As the line stood, it inadvertently supported allegations that he had wielded unlimited and unwonted power in the New Deal. Given that he was being inaugurated for an unprecedented third term, he certainly did not want to aid and abet his political enemies' accusations; accordingly, he struck the troublesome phrase and substituted a delightful action adverb that completed the thought admirably well: "We acted quickly, boldly, [and beyond the limits of tradition.] *decisively*."[34]

The nature of the concluding language in the sixth draft demonstrates some of the deficiencies in the speech. The introduction and body of the speech had portrayed the problem of the nation-as-human, and Roosevelt finally indicated in the conclusion how he would address a solution. The conclusion reads as follows:

If we lose that sacred fire—if we let it be smothered with doubt and fear—then we shall reject the destiny which Washington strove so valiantly and so triumphantly to establish. The preservation of the spirit and faith of the nation does, and will, furnish the highest justification of every sacrifice that we may make in the cause of national defense.

In the face of great perils never before encountered, our strong purpose is to protect and to perpetuate the integrity of democracy.

For this we muster the spirit of America, and the faith of America.

We do not retreat. We are not content to stand still. As Americans, we go forward, in the service of our country, by the will of God.

Yet, even the conclusion is problematical. The first conditional sentence does not affirm a future goal or value, but merely raises the possibility of a rejection of American values without indicating the negative outcome of the "if-then" situation. The next sentence on sacrifices for national defense finally fulfills the expectations of the introduction, but it is the only sentence in the speech that does so, and it is too little too late. This kind of fulfilling language, in conjunction with the exigency of Lend-Lease, deserved more attention and more substantive language. The next thought on protecting and perpetuating democracy sounded good, but how did he propose to do it? The following sentence told how, but in mixing the metaphors, FDR confused the language and blunted the impact of his key verb, for one "musters" armies, weapons, and munitions, not pacifistic and religious terms such as "spirit" and "faith." And though he continued the militaristic verbs in the very last sentence, the image of action is undirected because one does not know how or where "we go forward."[35]

When he delivered the speech, Roosevelt made a verbal slip. On the reading copy, the president wrote about the word *inaction*: "(I misread this word as 'isolation,' then added 'and inaction.' All of which improved it!) FDR." *Isolation* does not look much like *inaction*. But if one were frustrated in wanting to address values and political principles that could serve as precursors to action, such as Lend-Lease, but felt constrained from doing so, then the misreading may be more than just a mistake. A close listening to the speech as actually delivered suggests that FDR did not misread *inaction*. As he delivered the line, he seemed to pause to gather his thoughts, to think before speaking. FDR said "we risk the real [slight pause and halt] peril of isolation [slight pause, but no halt] the real peril of inaction." Given the relative tameness of the text, his uttering the word "isolation" may have been a kind of vocal catharsis he allowed himself at a time when he was otherwise powerless to act.[36]

THE EFFECT OF THE SPEECH

One may infer from negative evidence that the Third Inaugural was not particularly eloquent or noteworthy. The contemporary media reception to the message was cordial but lackluster. There was little to say about the speech. *Newsweek* noted: "What could Mr. Roosevelt say to those millions? Only that he believed democracy will not fail." The *New York Times* nodded in agreement that it "was little more than a simple, solemn declaration that the President would carry out a program already evident in detail." Rosenman remarked, "It did not make such a popular impression." Nor is the speech afforded much scrutiny or praise at the hands of later writers and critics.[37]

The inaugural theory can explain the reception and deficiencies of the Third Inaugural. By defining the past domestic issues in the same New Deal language heard twice before, FDR did rehearse old (outworn?) values, but the audience gained no new understanding from this speech. Indeed, a thirteen-year-old from Dayton, Ohio, poignantly praised the president for his past policies, and for not inaugurating a new administration: "Thanks for the help you gave my daddy and a lot of other men who were out of work when you started 8 years ago."

As to the foreign exigency, Roosevelt was so vague on values that would serve as precursors to action there, especially with regard to Great Britain, that one senses disappointment in not fulfilling the expectations of the speech's introductory material. An enthusiastic supporter from Willoughby, Ohio, inadvertently pinpointed a deficiency in the speech: "The only people opposed to your policy apparently are those who either dislike you, dislike Britain, or dislike democracy because it puts a crimp on their selfish aims." The speech did not address why Americans should help sustain the British war effort or how American security was linked to Britain's survival. Nor were the selfish aims of the isolationists discussed in relationship to the greater good of the country's survival as a democratic nation. FDR did unify the audience, but it was a static kind of unity that went nowhere and did nothing. He hinted, vaguely, at political principles that would guide him in a world at war in the introduction and conclusion of the speech, yet these few sentences were so nebulous and nondirected that it is understandable why it was difficult for the contemporary audience to share Roosevelt's vision of the future or to be enlightened by his language. The *New York Times* recognized the significance of the lack of straightforward language in the speech: "Although conceived and delivered under the stress of the international crisis, the address did not chart by specification the future course of the Administration." It is not surprising, but is quite understandable, that Rosenman reported that Roosevelt was disappointed with its weak impact. In short, the weakness of the Third Inaugural stems from the fact that Roosevelt wrote a draft that was saddled with the burden of start-stop or advance-retreat. Such ambiguity was conceived in the campaign and given birth on inaugural day in 1941. Rosenman noted that the first or second draft of a speech often determined its final quality. That was his discreet but accurate way of saying that FDR's Third Inaugural was not an especially good address because the beginning draft was the Boss's.[38]

THE FOURTH INAUGURAL ADDRESS
JANUARY 20, 1945

The exigencies of World War II impinged upon FDR's Fourth Inaugural Address in a variety of ways. In a press conference held in November 1944, Roosevelt indicated his decision to keep his fourth inaugural ceremony brief. A reporter asked him, "Are you going to parade any on inauguration day?" FDR replied, "No. Who is there here to parade?" Consequently, the nation was alerted that "President Roosevelt's fourth inaugural will be one of the simplest and soberest in the nation's recent history." The long-standing tradition of holding the inaugural ceremony at the Capitol was suspended because Roosevelt believed holding the ceremony at the White House was more in keeping with the war effort. His immediate audience was the smallest on record: fewer than five thousand persons were on the White House grounds for the ceremony and perhaps another three thousand people were outside the gates. After George

Washington's Second Inaugural Address, Roosevelt's Fourth was the briefest. Arthur Krock wrote, "The few hundred words to which he wisely confined his inaugural address yesterday were in keeping with the nature of the occasion." Until the 22nd Amendment to the Constitution is repealed, a fourth inaugural occasion will not be repeated.[39]

THE COMPOSITION OF THE DRAFTS

The original materials are ten speech drafts, some significant carbon copies of those drafts, and the final reading copy. The ten primary drafts can be divided into five sets: (1) two drafts of random thoughts dictated by FDR, (2) one draft prepared by Archibald MacLeish, (3) two drafts written by Samuel Rosenman, (4) two drafts prepared by Robert Sherwood, and (5) three drafts from which the final reading copy ensued.

Rosenman shed some light on the composition of Roosevelt's speech, but part of his analysis is misleading. Rosenman recalled that drafts had been submitted by MacLeish, Sherwood, and himself, and that FDR took the drafts, including his own dictation, and combined them into his own speech. Rosenman's recollection is supported by the fact that each writer's submitted draft had its pages fastened together with a blue ribbon. Roosevelt took these drafts, plus his own blue-ribboned dictation, under presidential advisement. Rosenman is misleading in implying that Roosevelt himself combined all of the drafts into his own reading copy. First, there is no textual evidence to indicate that FDR worked over the drafts with his emendations as he had done in his other speeches because, except for one minor emendation to be discussed later, Roosevelt's handwriting does not appear on any of the drafts. Second, Roosevelt's final reading copy was developed in three stages solely from Sherwood's submitted draft. In the first stage, Roosevelt dictated his own thoughts as Rosenman recalled. The fact is verified by the drafts. Roosevelt's initials (FDR), although not in his handwriting, appear on FDR's drafts so these thoughts are *his*. In the second stage, he directed each of his speech writers to use his dictated thoughts to write a draft. Accordingly, MacLeish, Rosenman, and Sherwood worked on their respective drafts with an eye toward submitting them to the president. FDR directed that a division of labor be maintained and that each writer be responsible for his own submission. The drafts imply this. Rosenman's initials (SIR) are on his drafts, Sherwood's initials (RES) are on his, and MacLeish's abbreviation (A MacL) is on his. The third stage began when FDR selected Sherwood's submitted draft, and they fashioned the final address. Grace Tully, FDR's secretary, noted that Sherwood "did considerable work" on the speech.[40]

FDR'S DRAFTS

Two typewritten drafts represent Roosevelt's thoughts. The basis for the address is on a one-page, legal-sized draft entitled "Some Thoughts For Inaugural

Speech,'' January 6, 1945. Two ideas are worth noting. The first was a quotation that Roosevelt remembered from his schoolmaster at Groton: ''I remember that my old schoolmaster said in the early days, 'Things in life will not always run smoothly—life is a series of ups and downs. Sometimes we will be rising toward the heights—then all will reverse itself and start downward. The great fact to remember is that the trend of civilization, like the trend of the individual, is on the average upward; that a line drawn through the middle of the peaks and valleys through the centuries always has an upgrade trend!' '' The second was the following thought: ''At a time like this most of us need the confidence which flows from conviction.'' FDR's mind was obviously on the war when he dictated these ideas. He wished to reassure the American people that the trend of the war was positive and the United States would eventually triumph. Even in the campaign, Roosevelt had assiduously eschewed speculating on the end of World War II. Looking beyond the war, he envisioned that the peace would place civilization on an upward trend once again. He also intimated that the country's confidence that the war would be won would be rewarded because of its conviction in its civilized war aims.

The second draft, consisting of three legal-sized, typewritten pages, is titled ''Other Thoughts For Inaugural Speech,'' January 13, 1945. FDR's initials, although again not in his handwriting, appear on this draft, and Edgar Robinson believed it reflected Roosevelt's thinking. This draft was fastened together with the blue ribbon. Carried over from the January 6 draft were the schoolmaster quotation and the confidence from conviction sentiment. Two additions are salient. The following thought was reminiscent of his famous fear statement from 1933: ''Twelve years ago I said in a day of stress that this country had to fear fear itself.'' He also made an observation about the Constitution: ''The Constitution of 1787 was neither perfect nor complete. It was the best that could be obtained at that time.'' These four thoughts—the schoolmaster quotation, the confidence from conviction idea, the fear statement, and the Constitutional thought—were FDR's and he wanted them included in his address.[41]

MACLEISH'S DRAFT

This set consists of a five-page typed original and a carbon copy. Both are dated in the same handwriting 1/15/44 (*sic*) and carry MacLeish's abbreviation. The only difference between the original and the carbon copy is that MacLeish evidently forgot to make an addition on the carbon copy that he had made on the original. MacLeish's original draft has a blue ribbon attached to it that signifies it went to FDR for his consideration. For three pages, MacLeish discoursed in some detail on the military aspects of the war. His last two pages looked forward to the freedom of the future, which was communicated in militaristic terms. Except for one instance, there is no discernible trace of MacLeish's thoughts in FDR's final address. Some of MacLeish's language appears to have been used in the final address, but it is strikingly similar to Sherwood's. In a

line-by-line comparison, one can perceive these similarities (Sherwood's handwritten draft is italicized):

"You will understand and, I believe, agree with my wish that the
"You will understand   my wish that the
forms of this Inauguration should be simple and its words brief.
forms of this Inauguration should be simple and its words brief.
There is no need to say in words what [all] mankind has seen and
There is no need to say in words what all the world has seen
experienced in action. The meaning of our Republic has been
              in action. The meaning of our Republic has been
declared upon every continent of the earth and on the seas and
declared upon every continent of the earth and on its seas and
on the islands.
in the islands.

Because Sherwood's drafts are not dated, it is impossible to tell whether his
handwritten draft predates MacLeish's. An equally plausible case could be made
for one man's "copying" from the other. What can be determined is that Sherwood's language from his handwritten draft was chosen by FDR. FDR probably
rejected MacLeish's draft because it stressed too much militarism at a time when
FDR wanted to stress peace and because it did not include any of the president's
dictated thoughts.[42]

ROSENMAN'S DRAFTS

This set consists of two drafts, but neither is dated. The first, consisting of
five pages, is handwritten and has on its upper right-hand corner a notation of
the number of words: 742. This numerical notation indicates that Rosenman was
fulfilling FDR's desire that the inaugural address be brief, for he insisted that
the address "not be more than five minutes in length." From the original handwritten draft, a typed original and two carbon copies were produced and these
carry Rosenman's initials (SIR). The typed original was fastened with a blue
ribbon, indicating that it was sent to the president.

The typed original illustrates how Rosenman relied on FDR's core thoughts.
Rosenman used Roosevelt's confidence from conviction thought, but he gave its
skeletal frame some flesh and muscle: "The assurance of that world peace will
not come overnight—it will not come easily. It will take hard work, it will take
patience, it will take tolerance and mutual understanding. Above all, it will take
conviction—unshakeable conviction that it can be done and that it will be done."
If Rosenman's specific and concrete words improved FDR's basic thought, his
terseness sacrificed the imagery of Roosevelt's schoolmaster quotation: "We
must remember the truths we learned from childhood on—the course of life is
not always smooth and level. Mankind can attain great heights—and can sink
to low depths. But through the centuries, the trend of civilization—like the trend

of the individual—has been forward and upward.'' Rosenman did improve FDR's Constitutional thought by enlarging it with specificity: "Our Constitution itself was not a perfect instrument in 1787—nor a complete one. But in 1787 it was the best that human beings had up to that date been able to achieve. The framers of the Constitution knew that they had not achieved perfection—nor did they insist upon perfection before they signed it.'' Finally, he revised Roosevelt's fear statement. He simplified the awkward verb-noun construction (''had to fear fear itself'') and made the thought reminiscent of the actual First Inaugural statement: "As in every day of crisis, the principal thing to fear is fear itself— fear that we cannot accomplish the high objectives we seek.'' Except for the schoolmaster quotation, Rosenman's use and revision of Roosevelt's core thoughts generally improved the president's original dictation.

Two other points about Rosenman's draft are worth making. First, nowhere in his draft did Rosenman have the MacLeish-Sherwood idea about the words and form of the inaugural being brief and simple. One can assume either that Rosenman did not see their drafts or that he did see them but chose not to use their thoughts. Second, there is evidence to indicate that both Rosenman and Sherwood got the following thought from FDR himself or that one of them "copied" the thought from the other. Although it is impossible to determine the thought's origin, the similarity of Rosenman's and Sherwood's sentence strongly suggests a common source (Sherwood's sentence is italicized):

"The Almighty God has blessed our land in a thousand ways."
"God Almighty   has blessed this land in a thousand ways."

On one of the carbon copies of the typed original, Rosenman made numerous revisions. The perplexing fact is that none of Rosenman's revisions on this carbon copy were on the typed original that was submitted to FDR, nor, for that matter, is there extant a new draft that should have ensued from Rosenman's revisions on this carbon copy. The fact that Rosenman revised the carbon copy indicates that he intended to polish the text but, for some inexplicable reason, did not.

Very little of Rosenman's submitted draft is identifiable or recognizable in the final speech. FDR evidently did not like Rosenman's version of the fear statement. The Constitutional thought was so changed that it did not resemble Rosenman's writing. FDR apparently wanted the schoolmaster quotation to remain similar to his original. Likewise, the confidence from conviction thought was partially restored in the speech to its original form. FDR probably rejected Rosenman's draft because it strayed too far from his dictated thoughts. He evidently liked Sherwood's submission better.[43]

SHERWOOD'S DRAFTS

This set consists of a three-page hand written draft that is undated and a three-page typed original of the handwritten draft. The typed original has a blue ribbon fastened to it. There are also two carbon copies of the original. One is designated "FIRST DRAFT" and will be discussed later.

In his handwritten draft, Sherwood utilized all of FDR's core thoughts. He took the basic Constitutional thought and reshaped and redirected it: "Our Constitution of 1787 was not a perfect instrument—it is not perfect yet. But it provided a firm base upon which all manner of men, of all races and colors and creeds, could build the great and powerful and eternal structure of democracy." He also used the schoolmaster quotation. In fact, Sherwood pasted the quotation, which was excised from a carbon copy, to his handwritten draft, and then revised it (his deletions are bracketed, his additions italicized):

I remember that my old schoolmaster said in [the early] days *that seemed to us then to be secure and untroubled*: "Things in life will not always run smoothly—life is a series of ups and downs. Sometimes we will be rising toward the heights—then all will seem to reverse itself and start downward. The great fact to remember is that the trend of civilization *itself* [like the trend of the individual] is *forever* [on the average] upward; that a line drawn through the middle of the peaks and valleys through the centuries always *has* [had] an *upward* [upgrade] trend."

Sherwood's schoolmaster quotation more closely approximated FDR's dictated original than did Rosenman's. As for the fear statement, Sherwood retained only the word *fear*, and hence FDR's statement lost its impact from its First Inaugural sense: "Those goals cannot be achieved if we proceed with suspicion and mistrust and with fear." Immediately following this sentence, Sherwood used FDR's confidence from conviction thought. He evidently inserted it as an afterthought because he squeezed two lines of writing into one ruled line and denoted his interlinear addition with a caret: "They can be achieved only if we proceed with understanding and confidence—and with courage." Sherwood treated understanding and confidence and courage as separate, with an emphasis upon courage; hence, FDR's original dictation lost some of its meaning. Except for the schoolmaster quotation, Sherwood's choice of words changed the emphasis and meaning of FDR's core thoughts. Sherwood seemed to pay lip service to the thoughts by including them in his draft, but his renditions retained little fidelity to FDR's thoughts. So why did FDR select Sherwood's draft? Rosenman's draft strayed too far from FDR's dictation, and it is moot whether Sherwood's draft approximated the dictation better than Rosenman's. The answer to the question of what tipped the balance in Sherwood's favor is in the nature of the language in his draft.

FDR probably liked Sherwood's draft better for the following reasons: (1) since he wanted a brief speech, he evidently appreciated Sherwood's introduction about the brief and simple form and words, which Rosenman did not include in his work, (2) since he liked anaphora, and since Sherwood's draft was replete with anaphora and Rosenman's was not, FDR evidently preferred Sherwood's style; (3) although Rosenman discussed the war in less militaristic terms than

MacLeish did, FDR probably chose Sherwood's draft because it was practically devoid of war language; and (4) at 674 words, Sherwood's draft was shorter than Rosenman's draft, at 702 words.[44]

THE FINAL ADDRESS

This set consists of three drafts from which the reading copy developed. Sherwood has written that FDR paid close attention to the speech's composition: "He worked it over with more care and more interest than he had shown in the preparation of any speech in two years." It is difficult to distinguish FDR's dictated emendations from those of Sherwood because all of the changes appear in Sherwood's handwriting. Yet, the fact remains that Roosevelt accepted all the emendations, and one can treat them as if they were FDR's.[45]

The foundation of the final speech began on a carbon copy of Sherwood's submitted draft. Sherwood crossed out his initials and printed instead "FIRST DRAFT." It was as if the speech ceased to be Sherwood's and instead became the president's. Several changes were made on this draft, and two merit discussion. FDR's confidence from conviction thought was substantially restored to its original intent: "They can be achieved only if we proceed with *the* understanding and confidence [—] and [with] courage *which flows from conviction.*" It is probable that the president dictated this change to restore his stress on conviction. Two inserts were produced for this draft, and one of them was in the final address. Sherwood's handwritten insert was further revised in his hand: "We may and probably shall make mistakes—but they must [not] *never* be *the kind* of mistakes [that] *which* result from faintness of heart or [the] *from cynical* abandonment of moral principle." Again, FDR may have dictated this insert to establish that mistakes were inevitable, but that he believed action was preferable to inaction. He spoke similar sentiments in his radio acceptance address from San Diego and in his final campaign speech at Boston. Indeed, he stressed in his last three presidential campaigns that he had acted and the other party had not.

A new draft titled "First Draft" developed from the above one; actually, this was the second draft of the final address, and it was worked over extensively. The following selected examples demonstrate FDR's desire to achieve brevity: "You will understand and, I believe, agree with my wish that the form of this Inauguration [should] be simple and its words brief"; "We Americans of today, [—and our brothers of many lands who fight at our side—] *together with our allies,* are passing through a period of supreme test"; "We can and [we must and] we will achieve such a peace [despite all the doubts that may dilute our confidence or all the formidable obstacles that may be placed in our path]"; "The Almighty God has blessed our land in [a thousand] *many* ways." Excess verbiage was also excised from the schoolmaster quotation without sacrificing its imagery: "Things in life will not always run smoothly [—life is a series of ups and downs]. . . . a line drawn through the middle of the peaks and *the* valleys [through the centuries] *of the centuries* always has an upward trend.'' In the following selection, care was taken to delete pessimistic words and make the thought more optimistic: ''We shall strive for perfection. We [may] *shall* not achieve it *immediately*—[not in this generation nor the next one—] but we still shall strive. We may [and probably shall] make mistakes—but they must never be [the kind of] mistakes which result from faintness of heart or from cynical abandonment of moral principle.'' Notice that ''immediately'' effectively and concisely replaced its eight-word counterpart. Although some words were added to make the thoughts more specific or optimistic, the effect of the emendations was an overall reduction of words to achieve brevity. Consistent with FDR's aim, this draft was reduced from 779 to 604 words.

From these emendations on the typed ''First Draft'' (actually the second draft), a new typed ''Second Draft'' (actually the third) was produced. The emendations on this draft were less extensive than those on the second draft. The main changes were the insertion of the formal handwritten salutation, the deletion for brevity of two paragraphs, and some minor word changes for better felicity of expression. These changes reduced the word count from 604 words to 560.

From this draft, a typed, triple-spaced ''Final Reading Copy'' was prepared. President Roosevelt's handwriting appeared twice on the reading copy. In an exceedingly shaky hand, FDR wrote his name and noted that the text was the ''orig. reading copy.'' The other instance was the insertion of his schoolmaster's name: ''I remember that my old schoolmaster *Dr. Peabody* said. . . . ''[46]

AN EVALUATION OF THE FOURTH INAUGURAL ADDRESS

Roosevelt's vigor in delivery of the speech seemed still to be with him and he often gestured with his head. But he looked very old and very tired. His reading of the speech still had his superb phrasing, but the rate was slower and more cumbersome than one might expect, and this was especially so toward the latter part of the address. He made numerous changes from his reading copy, and hence several texts of the speech are in error.[47]

The reaction to the speech was mixed. Roosevelt's close admirers reacted favorably. Frances Perkins wrote that ''it was short but good. It was in the Roosevelt style.'' Grace Tully believed that ''in finished form it was simple, succinct and impressive in its philosophical sincerity.'' Others saw in the address FDR's attempt to preview the peace that would follow World War II. Indeed, this was a continuation of his ''a just peace'' rhetoric he had stressed in the campaign. Denis Brogan believed ''the brief inaugural speech was devoted to the great problem of peace. It was also an appeal for the banishing of suspicion.'' *Newsweek* noted his address was ''a promise and a prayer.'' Others reacted less favorably. *Time* observed, ''It would probably never be considered a great speech, but it indicated the President's mood and temper''; FDR's assistant and omnibudsman William Hassett believed it was ''hardly a notable address''; and

Finis Farr flatly stated, "The Fourth Inaugural Address was labored and platitudinous." The speech was labored, but not in Farr's pejorative sense.[48]

SUMMARY

Robert Sherwood composed the draft from which the inaugural address evolved; the speech was not, as Rosenman stated, a combination of all the drafts by FDR into his own composition. As in the case of his First Inaugural, FDR did not compose his Fourth Inaugural.

He did, however, make a choice from among the submitted drafts. He rejected MacLeish's submitted draft because MacLeish stressed militarism too much at a time when Roosevelt wished to focus on the future peace rather than on the past glories of war. The president not only properly eschewed discussing the progress of the war, the newspapers did that daily, but he also appropriately stressed the new value of magnanimity in victory and peace that would replace the old value of vengeance at Versailles, which had helped contribute to a second world war. In some respects, FDR used his Fourth Inaugural as Lincoln did his Second Inaugural Address—to turn the audience's attention from the immediate situation of war to a philosophical discourse on the meaning of the war for the future. Although Rosenman wrote a good draft, FDR rejected it because Rosenman strayed too far from FDR's dictated thoughts and because Rosenman included some militarism in his draft. The fact remains that Roosevelt selected Sherwood's draft, probably because its thoughts and its style more closely resembled his original dictation, and because it was shorter and contained few allusions to the war. Roosevelt wisely read the inaugural occasion as an opportunity to shape the nation's and the world's future in terms of the values of a "just and honorable peace, a durable peace," so that Americans could share his vision of the future. He would fulfill a campaign promise.

Although much of the final reading copy developed from Sherwood's submitted drafts, the final address nevertheless had FDR's imprint on it. Although his original fear statement had lost its impact from its First Inaugural sense, FDR retained the word itself. In 1933, Roosevelt's fear statement allayed the fears of a stricken people in the midst of a Depression, but in 1945, he appropriately used it to remind Americans that the coming peace should not be approached, as it had been after World War I, "with suspicion and mistrust—and with fear." In this address, as in the First Inaugural but not in the Third, the exorcism of fear served as a precursor to action in the coming administration. It implied that the kind of activist political principles that had served the country advantageously during the Depression would be applied analogously to the coming peace. Although Sherwood had altered it on his draft, the dictated confidence from conviction thought was returned to a close approximation of FDR's original dictation. Given the enormous task of rebuilding a peaceful postwar world, Roosevelt communicated to the American people his belief that they should be sustained and motivated in that effort "with the understanding and confidence and courage which flow from conviction.'' These value-laden words served as a kind of bridge from the past and present to the future by welding these values, which had sustained a successful prosecution of the war, to the same kind of success in the peace; thus, the people could understand the efficacy of his coming administration. Although the Constitutional thought was redirected and reshaped, it was unmistakably from FDR's original dictation. He communicated in his Constitutional thought his political belief that the Constitution was not perfect in 1787 or in 1945, but that it was a solid structure upon which he had attempted to build his essential democracy. Implicit in that thought was the vague hint that he intended to improve democracy in his fourth administration: ''it is not perfect yet'' seemed to imply an attempt at fulfillment in the coming years. Although there were a few minor changes in the schoolmaster quotation, they did not appreciably alter the imagery of FDR's original thought. He aptly used the schoolmaster quotation to summarize the progress of his administration and the prosecution of World War II. Franklin Delano Roosevelt stated his belief that under his leadership he had achieved his goals by leading the line upward.

Roosevelt's image of the ''upward trend'' gave a philosophical unity to the speech that has not been hitherto appreciated, nor conceived as contributing to the eloquence of the inaugural occasion. The idea of progress is a salient American value. Progress implies movement, action, attainment. The upward trend image in the inaugural served as the precursor for the political principles FDR would pursue. The anaphora of ''We have learned'' eloquently vindicated FDR's stand against isolationism, which stand he was unable to address with mastery in the Third Inaugural. These ''We have learned'' parallel sentences had as their objects the lessons or values that would actuate policies, such as leading the United Nations.

Traditionally, it is *de rigueur* for presidents to refer to the deity in their inaugurals, and FDR did so in all four of his. Yet, the obligatory reference to God is best realized thematically in the Fourth. In his First, he asked for protection of the American people, and an especial favor for himself, ''May he guide me in the days to come''; in the Second, he again sought ''Divine guidance'' primarily for himself; and in the Third, he invoked the diety almost as an afterthought and probably inappropriately for the militaristic verbs he used. But in the Fourth, the allusions to the deity reinforced the idea of the upward trend as it pertained to improving the domestic lives of the citizenry and to guiding a nonisolationist America in the foreign scene, by giving a recurring unity to the main values stressed in the speech. These lessons served as precursors for action as summarized by his allusion to God in the last sentence of the inaugural: ''So, we pray to Him now for the vision to see our way clearly—to see the way that leads to a better life for ourselves and for all our fellow men—and to the achievement of His will to peace on earth.''

Roosevelt fused the elements of the genre theory to the inaugural occasion of 1945 in an eloquent manner. He unified the people especially well in his introductory language about keeping the inaugural ''simple and its words brief,'' and by noting that "we . . . are passing through a period of supreme test" and "we shall perform a service of historic importance." Moreover, the additional mentioning of the pronoun *we* throughout the speech served constantly to reconstitute the people in a new and positive direction. After the First, this speech is the most unified thematically. Where the First served to actuate, the Fourth functioned to forecast action. Like the First, it discussed the old communal values that would serve as principles in achieving a better America; for a world at war, it discussed also the new values, learned "at a fearful cost," that would attain a lasting peace. But most important, Roosevelt rose above the immediacy of the war, by choosing Sherwood's draft over the others' more militaristic ones, in order to celebrate the future peace. President Harry Truman's radio announcement of VE Day is a fitting epitaph for FDR's fine Fourth Inaugural Address: "This is a solemn but glorious hour. I only wish that Franklin D. Roosevelt had lived to witness this day. . . . The flags of freedom fly over all Europe."[49]

CONCLUSION

Richard Joslyn has opined that inaugural addresses, in relationship to other presidential persuasions, are relatively unimportant. Although his assessment of run-of-the-mill inaugurals may be apt, surely there are exceptions. In recent times, John Kennedy's Inaugural Address and Ronald Reagan's First Inaugural Address come immediately to mind. Nor is his assertion applicable to FDR's addresses. His First Inaugural Address is a state persuasion of the first water. Even his Second, Third, and Fourth are substantial cuts above most other twentieth-century inaugurals. In the pantheon of FDR's other persuasions, certainly the First is at the pinnacle. Given the amount of time Roosevelt devoted to developing their drafts, he obviously thought his inaugural speeches were important. He even stood in pain to deliver his Fourth Inaugural. (That was a gauge of his deference to the inauguration of a United States president. In the early years, he habitually wore his braces, so standing for his other three investitures presented no more problems than he was normally accustomed to. However, with the advent of the war, he did not wear his braces, and his address at Bremerton in early August 1944 was the only wartime occasion that Roosevelt stood for an address, even for critical campaign addresses when his age and health were issues.)[50]

With regard to the First Inaugural, the main deviance from the genre theory was the stress on action, not contemplation. As demonstrated, the scapegoat device prepared the way for direct action, for which FDR made a clarion call against the enemy; the military metaphors evoked a war on the Depression that FDR began to lead that day; and the carrot-and-stick made straight paths for legislative action. These devices could not serve a useful function or make rhetorical sense if they were not fashioned and employed to actuate the American people and especially the Congress to support his New Deal. It may be that in pedestrian inaugurals, presidents ask their listeners to contemplate the ceremony.

But in four other important inaugurals, including FDR's First, presidents spoke about action. In his First Inaugural Address in 1861, Abraham Lincoln urged the secessionists to consider closely the courses of their past, present, and future actions, with the very clear admonition that they, and not he, would be responsible for the outcome of his Constitutional reaction to their actions. Concomitantly, his speech prepared the northern audience for the implied action, based on the value of keeping the Union intact, necessary to sustain his veiled threat. John Kennedy's Inaugural Address in 1961 precursed new courses of political action, and he openly urged Americans to support his New Frontier: "In your hands, my fellow citizens, more than mine, will rest the final success or failure of our course"; "Will you join in that historic effort?"; "And so, my fellow Americans: ask not what your country can do for you—ask what you can do for your country." Robert Ivie also demonstrated that Reagan's First stressed action, as seen in the following excerpt: "We must act today in order to preserve tomorrow. And let there be no misunderstanding—we are going to act, beginning today." It may be that particularly noteworthy or eloquent inaugurals transcend the genre, or it may be, as Joslyn accurately stated, that all such speeches have "action as a pervasive, enduring, and consequential goal."[51]

Certain elements in the Second Inaugural were deficient. Political principles were weak and executive powers and limitations absent. It could be argued the political principles were implied in Roosevelt's re-election for a more-of-the-same New Deal. But one can search in vain for language that alluded to the executive function. Indeed, given FDR's hubris, engendered by the landslide, one might not expect him to notice the Congress or the Court. But, as was outlined above and will be argued further in the next chapter, it was precisely this hubris that helped account for FDR's rhetorical problems with the Court, the Congress, and the American people.

In a sense, the Third Inaugural was too contemplative or philosophical. As demonstrated, political principles were vague, executive functions unclear, and communal action forestalled. The problem was, of course, that FDR could not act on the great issue of the day—the war in Europe—and his address reflected his inability to contemplate or actuate any value other than isolationism. In all fairness to Roosevelt, though, he could not fulfill the expectations of inaugural eloquence in 1940 because he was ruled by national law and international restraints over which he had virtually no control. That does not erase the claim, however, that his inaugural is not illustrative of the genre theory.

Interestingly, FDR's Fourth Inaugural Address conformed the closest to the theory. Although it was contemplative in tone, its language precursed the political actions FDR had implied in his campaign and doubtless would have pursued if he had lived. Yet, even the Fourth is without language on executive powers and limitations.

And so, this chapter ends as it began. Neither FDR nor his speech writers had any generic theory in mind as they composed four inaugural addresses— one or two of which were exemplars of the art and all of which bore the hallmark of artistic craftsmanship over pedantic workmanship.

6

Roosevelt vs. the Supreme Court

President Roosevelt, as well as the Americans who voted for the New Deal and the Congress that enacted it, faced a serious threat from the Supreme Court's anti–New Deal rulings. From 1790 to 1930, the Court overruled only sixty congressional acts, yet in FDR's first term it voided twelve New Deal laws. The coup de grâce came on Black Monday—a bitter and dark metaphorical allusion to Black Thursday, October 24, 1929, when the stock market crashed—when, on May 27, 1935, the Court struck down the National Recovery Act and the Frazier-Lemke farm mortgage foreclosure act. In response to these rulings, FDR made a swipe at the Court in his press conference on May 31: "We have been relegated to the horse-and-buggy definition of interstate commerce." With the Wagner Act, which legalized collective bargaining, and the Social Security Act on the Court's docket, Roosevelt had reason to fear the Court would continue to make its adverse rulings. The issue was whether the New Deal could do anything under the Constitution, as interpreted by the Court, to solve a national economic Depression. Herman Pritchett posited that "a Court whose politics and values lead it to the proposition that an economic depression is constitutional and that efforts to combat it are unconstitutional puts itself in the grave peril of being neither right nor representative." Roosevelt did not move against the Court in his first term, but his landslide victory over Landon convinced him that he could move on the Court in his second term.[1]

One proceeds on the premise that Roosevelt lost both the battle and the war with the Court. Although Roosevelt claimed success and Leonard Baker concurred, Dixon Wecter, Herman Pritchett, and John Gunther subscribed to a lost-the-battle-but-won-the-war dictum. On the other hand, Edgar Robinson, Basil

Rauch, Rexford Tugwell, and Samuel Rosenman declared that Roosevelt lost. Merlo Pusey postulated that the attack was "the most serious mistake of President Roosevelt's brilliant political career," and Joseph Alsop allowed, "It was FDR's first serious miscalculation." The purpose in this chapter is to explicate this miscalculation from a rhetorical perspective.[2]

Some critics have assigned other reasons for FDR's defeat. One factor was the secrecy with which he literally sprung the plan on the Congress, the Court, and the people without prior warning. Raymond Moley and James Patterson decried Roosevelt's stealth in launching the plan. However, the secrecy was a rhetorical mistake. Second, the unexpected death of Senator Joseph Robinson, who led FDR's Court fight in the Senate, was a factor. Third, the plan itself was a factor. Simply put, it was a plan that allowed him to control the Court by appointing justices to his liking. However, the plan was a rhetorical mistake.[3]

President Roosevelt sent his controversial bill to reorganize the federal judiciary to the Congress on February 5, 1937. This bill was a rhetorical message to the Congress, and when more persuasion was needed, FDR took his case directly to the people over the airwaves in two speeches, the Victory Dinner Address, March 4, 1937, and his Fireside Chat on the Reorganization of the Judiciary, March 9, 1937. In order to explicate Roosevelt's rhetorical assault on the Court, the critic can undertake two tasks: (1) demonstrate why FDR lost the battle and war for rhetorical reasons, and (2) revise how he could have persuasively attacked the Court. One can take to its conclusion the premise of the argument that Rosenman stated in his oral history about the Court fight, which he thought "need not have been a disaster if it had been presented to the people correctly instead of the way it was. . . . I repeat that I think he was beaten not because of the merits of the cause, but because of the way it was presented." The point on which Gunther and Alsop were uncertain, but on which Samuel and Dorothy Rosenman decided negatively, is affirmed: Roosevelt would have been more successful with his rhetoric if he had enunciated in his Second Inaugural Address the political principles that impelled him to assail the Court while acknowledging the requirements and limitations of his executive function.[4]

THE SECOND INAUGURAL: A MISSED OPPORTUNITY

The reasons Roosevelt should have enunciated the political principles of his attack on the Court in his Second Inaugural Address are several. First, he would have obviated the charges of secrecy. Although he dealt with the Court issue in his Annual Message, January 6, 1937, no evidence suggested, except to Rauch who believed the message "prepared the way" for his proposals later, that this routine message did in fact lay the persuasive groundwork for the plan. Rosenman gave no rhetorical significance to the message, and Moley observed, "His quiet message to Congress asked cooperation from the Supreme Court in a manner to which even the sternest constitutionalist would not object." Moreover, although it is true contemporary reporters noted that "Chief Justice [Charles Evans Hughes] boomed" out the oath of office to FDR and that "Mr. Roosevelt threw back the challenge word for word, in tones which fairly cried aloud, 'My way, not yours, will save the Constitution!' " and that the "ring in his voice mounted as he shouted the words, each a separate challenge, 'Preserve' 'Protect' and 'Defend,' " no significant rhetorical impact has been assigned this anecdote. The secrecy charges would not have held if the Annual Message and the above exchange were efficacious, nor did Roosevelt ever refute the secrecy issue by alluding to either the message or his verbal sparring with the chief justice in any of his later speeches. Rather, the national prominence accorded an inauguration would seem to indicate that the inaugural address should be the vehicle to announce, if only in general terms, the political principles of a forthright attack on the Court at the very moment when national attention is focused upon the president to ascertain how he proposes to solve national problems, such as the Supreme Court in 1937. Second, critics have advanced that the president should have prepared the public for the Court attack, which supports the argument that the Annual Message had no rhetorical impact, although they did not mention how or when. Bernard Phelps noted that Roosevelt should have prepared the nation for the presentation of the plan, and Attorney General Homer Cummings, who was secretly working on the Court plan with the president, wrote in his diary in December 1936 that timing was important: "It occured to me that the only real problem would be one of timing; namely, when and how to manage such a program." The logical and efficacious time for FDR to have announced the political principles of executive action against the Court would have been his Second Inaugural Address. Although Campbell and Jamieson did not necessarily intend the generic inaugural elements to be prescriptive, FDR's Second Inaugural Address is proof enough that there is rhetorical wisdom in enunciating political principles as custom dictates. The justices, the press, and some of the people expected an indication from the president on how he would move against the Court. In his First Inaugural Address FDR did communicate, and successfully too, the broad political principles and specific actions of his New Deal against the moneyed interests and a laissez-faire economic order. The First Inaugural Address affirms the appropriateness of communicating political principles, and the omission of them in the Second Inaugural Address is telling. As the rhetorical situation of March 1933 demanded a statement about the political principles upon which he would meet the economic crisis, so did the *Zeitgeist* of January 1937 demand from the president an acknowledgment of the principles upon which he would meet the Supreme Court crisis.[5]

At least two possible objections may arise. First, what kind of accusation should FDR have made against the Court? One advocates the rhetoric FDR used when he finally turned to the real issue in his Victory Dinner Address. It will be treated later, but suffice it to say here that therein he stated the real problem: conservative justices ruled against a liberal government's attempts to solve a national Depression. Second, should FDR have attacked the Court in the 1936 campaign? The Rosenmans supported FDR's decision not to make the Court a divisive issue; moreover, Myles Martel observed that "candidates speak to please men—and win their votes." But once re-elected, FDR should have moved against the Court in his Second Inaugural. Even if he had couched his attack in the most general terms, the Congress and country would have been better prepared to receive his plan, and he would have preempted the secrecy charge.[6]

As a result of his assault, the record attests that FDR was attacked from many quarters, including even fellow Democrats. The packing charge precursed a dictatorship. Both FDR and the attorney general discussed the sensitivity of the packing image in late December: "I also discussed the general objection that there is to packing the Court, and said that while we were probably unduly terrified by a phrase, nevertheless, there was a substantial objection in the country to a deliberate addition to the S.C. bench for the purpose of meeting the present situation." By deliberate design, FDR did not deign to mention in his Second Inaugural his appreciation of the requirements and limitations of his office with respect to the Court.[7]

The president should have communicated this appreciation on January 20, 1937. In order to fulfill the requirements of his executive function vis-à-vis the problem of the Court's rulings, he needed to communicate why he was motivated to attack these rulings. In order to indicate his appreciation of the limits of his executive function, he needed to indicate his desire to work with the Congress and to inform it and the country about his strategy against the Court. A rhetorical model for this revisionism exists in his First Inaugural Address, wherein FDR paid lip-service to this appreciation of executive function. Although he marshalled military metaphors to persuade the Congress and the country, he took pains to assure his audience that they had little to fear of a nascent executive dictatorship in his New Deal. In 1937, FDR needed to avow the constitutional and situational requirements of the Court fight while concomitantly acknowledging his executive limits. This would have allayed many of the alarms raised by FDR's inept rhetorical handling of the Court battle, and it should have alleviated the apparent attempt to aggrandize executive power at the expense of the Court. James Burns said it another way: "His final presentation combined in a curious fashion two Rooseveltian traits—his instinct for the dramatic and his instinct for the adroit and circuitous stratagem rather than the frontal assault. Both instincts failed him."[8]

In summation, rhetorical revisionism can be a risky route. Yet, a reasonable case can be made for revising Franklin Roosevelt's Second Inaugural Address. In response to the rhetorical situation of January 1937 vis-à-vis the Court, FDR needed to communicate the political principles of his planned attack and his sensitivity to the requirements and limitations of his executive function. If Roosevelt would have paid attention to those two important topics, as inaugural custom dictates and as some contemporaries expected, he would have anticipated the secrecy charges and assuaged the nascent dictatorship diatribes. As he confronted the economic crisis in 1933 in his First Inaugural, so should he have confronted the judicial crisis in 1937 in his Second Inaugural. But Roosevelt followed his own political and rhetorical instincts in his judiciary message, the Victory Dinner Address, and the Fireside Chat on the judiciary. Since he changed the nature of his rhetoric in each speech, they must be treated separately.

THE JUDICIARY MESSAGE: INJUDICIOUS RHETORIC

In a press conference on February 5, 1937, two weeks after his inauguration, Roosevelt announced his bill to reorganize the federal judiciary. The bill contained a variety of measures. Not only did it allow the president to appoint a new Supreme Court justice for each one over seventy years old, with the proviso that the Court could not exceed fifteen members, but it also called for a proctor to monitor the calendars of all federal courts in order to keep them abreast of their cases, and it allowed the chief justice to assign circuit or district judges to any court in arrears. The reasons that impelled the president to propose the bill have been discussed, but the circumstances of its contrivance need to be clarified.

Attorney General Cummings's diary sheds light on the bill's birth. The diary demonstrates that on December 24, 1936, FDR and Cummings understood that the real issue was not the Court or the Constitution but the conservative justices on the bench: "The President thoroughly understands my attitude which is in substance that there is nothing the matter with the constitution but that the entire difficulty has grown out of a reactionary misinterpretation of it." The two men also realized that care must be taken to cast the issue in its true context by framing "it as an issue between Congress and the Court (usurpation of power) than Court and President." Two days later, on December 26, Cummings had a two-hour discussion with the president in which they both agreed that the real problem was: "not w/Const, but 'as we believed, misinterpreted.' I said this and much more to the same general effect and he seemed to be very interested and said, 'Go on, you are going good, I wish I had a stenographer present so that this could be taken down.' " At this meeting, Cummings presented to FDR the court plan he had been working on, and FDR liked it and accepted it: "This plan had evidently never been brought to the attention of the President before and he was very interested and, of course, caught the point immediately."[9]

The point that Roosevelt caught was that Cummings's plan was similar to one proposed by then Attorney General James McReynolds (now Justice McReynolds and one of Roosevelt's most conservative opponents on the Court) under President Woodrow Wilson. McReynolds had proposed a plan to revitalize the federal judiciary by appointing a new judge for every one over seventy years old. Although McReynolds's proposal did not pertain to the Supreme Court, Cummings's plan did, and FDR caught the irony of history returning to haunt McReynolds. Actually, the president's attempt to alter the Court was not new in American history. The Supreme Court was established with five justices and a chief justice by the Judiciary Act of 1789; the Court was raised to six justices in 1802, seven in 1807, and nine in 1837; the exigencies of the Civil War and

Reconstruction moved the Court to ten in 1864, back to eight in 1866, and to nine in 1869. Nine justices is not a Constitutionally mandated number, but FDR found it difficult to overturn a natural presumption of some sixty years for maintaining the Court at the sacrosanct number of nine in 1937.

It is also worth noting that Roosevelt was appraised of the possibility that the Court might change its judicial stance to pro–New Deal: "I told the President that the atmosphere of the Court had manifestly changed since the election returns to use the old phrase of Mr. Dooley. There is always the bare chance that we may begin to get some more enlightened opinions, though I have not much hope in that direction." Roosevelt also told Cummings that rumors had reached him to suggest that McReynolds, and probably George Sutherland and Willis Van Devanter, might resign after the present term, but that he could not rely on such information "as it did not come in the nature of any sort of promise." The irony is that the Court did change its rulings and Van Devanter did resign, but Roosevelt could not be expected to foresee the former and he had no guarantee of the latter. It now remains to explicate the crux of the interpretative problem: how did the president's and attorney general's clear understanding of the real problem of conservative justices' ruling against the New Deal evolve into a bogus misrepresentation of the problem in the message? A close examination of the drafts will illuminate that process.[10]

The judiciary message began with FDR's dictating some thoughts. This important dictation indicates FDR's analysis of the problem and how he wanted the speech writers to communicate it in the message. Consistent with his and Cummings's conception of the issue, Roosevelt addressed the real issue of the Court's usurpation of power at the expense of the Constitution:

What we are essentially trying to do is to save the Constitution. In saving it we are trying to restore legislative powers to the legislative branch of the government—the Congress of the United States. Today we believe that they have had legislative powers taken away from them by unconstitutional processes that have developed slowly over a long period of years in the Supreme Court. We, therefore, want the Supreme Court to revert to what the Constitution says it shall be—the Judicial arm of the government, not the legislative arm of the government, or the third house of the legislature.

In the following dictation, FDR inadvertently gave away his real purpose. The president really intended the bill to pressure the justices into either changing their rulings or resigning: "The Supreme Court may remain at nine; it may go to ten or eleven or twelve or thirteen or fourteen or fifteen—that determination will be made by the Justices of the Supreme Court themselves who are over seventy years of age."

The president was also aware that his message would cause some Americans to question why he did not propose some sort of amendment to the Constitution for redressing the problem. Roosevelt clearly communicated that he believed an amendment process was too time consuming: "And this applies—this purpose of saving the legislative power of the government to proposed amendments to the Constitution. No matter what amendment may be added to the Constitution, it will still be subject to legislative interpretation by the Supreme Court if the present temper of the Supreme Court or it successor remains as it is today.'' He added: ''Even if the Congress at this session were to take up seriously and *in extenso* all of the proposed Amendments, it is perfectly clear that this discussion could not and ought not to be rushed through at this session or even the next because of the very great difficulty on agreeing as to which course of amendment is best. After they have agreed, if it is possible in two or three sessions, you have the terrific problem of ratification. Meanwhile, where is the Nation?'' FDR presented good enough reasons for eschewing the amendment route. He also recognized that powerful economic forces would (and did) oppose any amendment and by extension his plan, because either an amendment or his plan would effectively curtail their incomes:

No amendment has ever passed with the opposition of a major party and that, incidentally, the leadership of the Republican party today is unquestionably opposed to amendment, but also that a very large percentage, not all, of newspaper publishers, Chambers of Commerce, Bar Associations, Manufacturers Associations, who are giving out the impression that problems can be solved by the amendment method and that, therefore, they would be for an amendment, when as a matter of practical fact they would be the first people, if an amendment were passed, to say Oh! that was not the kind of amendment that I was thinking of and, therefore, I am going to spend my time, my effort and my money to block ratification.

In other words, what lies really at the back of the minds of a very large proportion of those who are talking about amendment is simply this—that in their fundamental thinking they object to social and economic legislation along modern lines. They are, for example, stock brokers and security dealers—men, for the greater part, decent citizens, law-abiding and respectable within their communities—they know that the Securities Exchange Act has curtailed the volume of sales of new securities because it has prevented the continued issuance of many of the types of unsound securities sold in the old days to an innocent public. These people's incomes have been cut down by these Federal laws. Fundamentally they do not want any more Federal laws that would cut down their income and we cannot wholly blame them for taking a selfish position. Take, for example, the bankers, especially larger bankers, who fundamentally resent any extension of supervisory Federal laws over the national banking system. They are not making as much money as they did before this Administration came into office. We can understand and perhaps excuse their selfishness. Take the great lawyers of the Nation, men who are making what the average of us would call very large incomes in handling corporate cases—quite aside from the fact that the more cases they can get their corporate clients to take into court the more money they will make, they have so long been associated with efforts to save their clients from any kind of legal supervision that they oppose not only my plan but any plan of amendment which would hurt their legal business. We can understand and perhaps excuse their attitude.

For the speech writer, FDR stressed three themes for his message: the problem was the Court and not the Constitution, the Court could avoid enlargement by changing its judicial stance, and his plan overcame the obstacles to a prolonged amendment process.[11]

The authorship of the first draft is unknown because there are no identifying initials on it and no one has taken credit for composing it. Roosevelt made no emendations on this first draft, but Rosenman's handwritten changes are quite evident. The gist of the first draft intimated that the problem with the Court was tired, old men. Examples of this line of attack are: "Mental and physical decrepitude lead men to avoid an examination of complicated and changing conditions. Little by little new facts become blurred through old glasses, fitted for the needs of another generation; and men, resting upon the complacent assumption that the scene is the same as it was in the past, cease to explore or inquire into the present and the future"; "Constantly and systemically, new blood must be added to the judicial personnel, lest for lack of vigor, it cease to carry its burden in the work of the government. Younger judges of ability and energy, coming freshly to the bench, would enable the courts to make headway against an unwieldly docket; and the whole judicial machinery would take on new life"; and "Under the plan proposed, those who have passed the age of seventy and desire to continue their judicial work, would be able to do so under less physical and mental strain. . . . If, on the other hand, any judge eligible for retirement should feel that his court would suffer because of an increase in its membership, he may resign or retire and prevent such an increase. It would thus be left to the judges themselves to determine whether or not their numbers should be increased." The last quotation can be taken as evidence that the speech writer saw FDR's dictated thoughts and chose to include the veiled threat to the justices to change their rulings or to resign. Given that the authorship of the first draft is indeterminable, the critic can only note, without explaining why, that this draft veered away from the clear statement of the problem with conservative justices, as Cummings and Roosevelt had agreed, and as the president had dictated, and moved toward the bogus old age argument.[12]

On the second draft, FDR made some emendations that further stressed old age. In the following sentence, Roosevelt added specific kinds of materials to imply that old men were not up to their task: "Records and briefs must be read; [studies] *statutes*, decisions [and pertinent literature], *technical, scientific, statistical and economic material* must be searched and studied; opinions must be formulated and written. The modern tasks of judges call for the use of full energies." In two other instances, FDR again stressed age: "[Mental or] *Lessening mental or* physical [decrepitude] *vigor* leads men to avoid an examination of complicated and changed conditions" and "A constant and systematic [infusion of new] *addition of younger* blood will vitalize the courts and better equip them to recognize and apply the essential concepts of justice in the light of the needs and facts of an ever-changing world."

In the third draft, from which the reading copy was typed, FDR continued to bolster the age argument. Not content with his change in draft two, he further implied that old justices were unable to keep abreast of modern court work:

"Records and briefs must be read; statutes, decisions, *and extensive material of a* technical, statistical and economic [material] *nature* must be searched and studied." As the final draft emerged, it stressed the inability of the Supreme Court to adjudicate its cases on modern grounds because of the tired old justices on the bench. Rosenman and Richberg objected to this thrust of the speech, but the president wanted the old age argument. He even strengthened that issue in his handwritten revisions. Whereas the original plan was Cummings's, the textual evidence from the various drafts demonstrates that the bent and flavor of the message was primarily Franklin Delano Roosevelt's.[13]

THE JUDICIARY MESSAGE

As indicated earlier, the bill dealt with more than just the Supreme Court, but national attention focused quickly on the bill as a Court "packing" scheme. The historical record attests that the judiciary message was attacked from many quarters. Moley complained of the "half-baked scheme which commended itself chiefly because of its disingenuousness"; Wecter saw the plan as "flippant and evasive"; and Tugwell wrote that the plan "had to be described as tricky."[14]

The president made a rhetorical mistake in describing aged justices who were overburdened with judicial work. The Congress and the country were told: "The simple fact is that today a new need for legislative action arises because the personnel of the Federal Judiciary is insufficient to meet the business before them"; "Even at the present time the Supreme Court is laboring under a heavy burden"; "Modern complexities call also for a constant infusion of new blood in the courts"; "A constant and systematic addition of younger blood will vitalize the courts and better equip them to recognize and apply the essential concepts of justice in the light of the needs and facts of an ever-changing world."

FDR made two serious mistakes. First, he should have charged that the Court made, and probably would continue to make, harmful anti–New Deal rulings. This was an incontrovertible fact upon which both Cummings and Roosevelt had originally agreed. Roosevelt could then have defined those rulings as contravening the demonstrated votes of the Congress and the desires of the American people. This strategy would support the kind of rhetoric he should have used in the Second Inaugural. Unfortunately, FDR did not present the real exigency. Second, he wrongfully alleged that old and overburdened justices were the problem. As for age, it was true that several conservative justices, such as Willis Van Devanter, James McReynolds, George Sutherland, and Pierce Butler were over seventy, but so were liberals Louis Brandeis and Benjamin Cardozo. Age per se was not the real issue. As for an overburdened Court, opponents easily demonstrated it was fully abreast of its work. Rather than presenting an oblique argument, FDR should have presented the real accusation directly to the Congress and the people.

FDR did later admit he had affirmed the wrong issue in his first message: "I made one major mistake when I first presented the plan. I did not place enough emphasis upon the real mischief—the kind of decisions which, as a studied and continued policy, had been coming down from the Supreme Court. I soon corrected that mistake—in the speeches which I later made about the plan.'' But his problem was not one of emphasis but of kind. The point is that he rejected the advice of Rosenman and Richberg, who counselled a forthright approach, and rather connived with Cummings to be circuitous. If he had surfaced the Court accusation in his Second Inaugural and sustained the real issue in his judiciary message, then a reasonable chance exists that he would have had more success than he did have. Yet, he did neither. What he did do, and admirably well, was to plant in his audiences' minds a misrepresented fact and an ill-defined issue that would be difficult to dislodge rhetorically. He tried to adjust a bogus argument to the nation, but it would not be so easily persuaded by phony reasons. Having made a rhetorical blunder in the judiciary message, FDR tried belatedly to rectify his rhetorical mistake in his next two speeches.[15]

THE VICTORY DINNER ADDRESS

President Roosevelt delivered this speech to a Democratic Victory Dinner at the Mayflower Hotel in Washington on March 4, 1937, in commemoration of the old inaugural date in 1933. The speech was simultaneously broadcast by radio to about eleven hundred other victory dinners across the nation. James Farley saw this speech as a partisan appeal for the Democratic party to support the president. Roosevelt delivered this follow-up speech because he realized his first message had not worked.[16]

In the Victory Dinner speech, he avoided the artificial accusation in favor of a forthright charge about the Court's adverse rulings. He juxtaposed the favorability of his New Deal to the disadvantages of the Supreme Court's nullifying it. He selected materials that were designed to appeal to the Democratic party's strong support from farmers, workers, and others who materially benefited from the New Deal.

''When it became obvious that the bill would have to be 'sold' to the country,'' Senator Burton Wheeler observed, ''FDR himself opened up on the airwaves.'' Roosevelt practiced a tenet of the rhetorical presidency, but it would not work for him this time. About a third of the way into his speech, Roosevelt metaphorically stated the real issue in his fight with the Court: ''For as yet there is no definite assurance that the three horse team of the American system of government will pull together. . . . If one horse lies down in the traces or plunges off in another direction, the field will not be ploughed.'' He directly appealed to the farmers by reminding them that the Court had nullified the Agricultural Adjustment Act. In the following passage, FDR's emendations clearly indicate that he and the Congress believed that they could help the farmer on a national scale but that the Court did not: ''the Congress of the United States had full constitutional authority to solve *national* economic problems of the Nation's agriculture. *By overwhelming votes the Congress thought so too!* You know who assumed the power[s of] *to* veto [over] *and did veto* that program." To garner support from labor, FDR recited the legislation that he had proposed and that the Congress had disposed to help industrial workers. Having noted that the Court nullified the Railroad Retirement Act, the National Recovery Act, and the Guffey Coal Act, Roosevelt strengthened the speech draft to make certain that labor understood the enormity of the Court's adverse rulings: "Soon thereafter the Nation was told by a judicial [ukase] *pronunciamento* that although the Federal Government was powerless to touch the problem of hours and wages, the States were equally helpless and that we had to [go on pretending to be intelligent] *live* in a Nation where there was no legal power *anywhere* to deal with its most difficult problems—*a No man's land of final futility.*" Roosevelt must have believed that *ukase*, a term denoting an imperial Russian decree, would be lost on most of his listeners, and that *pronunciamento* better communicated the Court's legal pronouncements against the New Deal. The president challenged anyone to "tell us exactly what, if anything, we *can* do for the industrial worker in this session of the Congress with [even] *any* reasonable certainty that what we do will not be nullified as unconstitutional" (FDR underlined *can* for emphasis). President Roosevelt then appealed to many Americans who directly benefited from the federal government's efforts to control flood and drought in the Ohio River Valley and in the Dust Bowl. Again, he defied anyone to read the opinions in the T.V.A. case, the Duke Power case, and the A.A.A. case to determine if the government could do anything to alleviate flood and drought, and then he penned a new sentence: "*You and I owe it to ourselves and to our country to remove that cloud of doubt.*" FDR stressed in his emendations the unblinking fact that the Court had nullified the core legislation of the New Deal and hence, by definition, there was nothing that he or the Congress could do to rectify the Depression.

President Roosevelt also made other changes on the drafts to demonstrate that the Court's policy of nullifying the New Deal acts had caused him to fight back for the good of the entire country: "We gave warning last November that we had only just begun to fight. Did [anyone think] *some people really believe* we did not mean it? *Well—I meant it, and you meant it.*" The old age argument had backfired on Roosevelt in his judiciary message, so he cleverly and accurately indicted those members of the Court who lived mentally in another generation without mentioning their ages: "the future which men who [still] live *mentally* in another generation can least understand—the ever accelerating speed [in] *with* which [human movements] *social forces* now [gather] *gain head* way." Indeed, FDR was correct to charge that it was not the justices' ages but their negative mental attitude toward the New Deal that had caused their adverse rulings. The president also indicated that he believed his fight against the Court would save American democracy: "If we would keep faith with those who had faith in us, *if we would make democracy succeed*, I say we must act—NOW!" In regard to the Second Inaugural Address, this is the kind of frontal assault against the justices' negative rulings that FDR should have employed.[17]

The reaction to the Victory Dinner speech was varied. From both sides of the aisle, senators were willing to grant that the president had delivered a great speech, but they doubted that it would significantly change the battle lines already drawn; likewise, the press often favorably received Roosevelt's factual accusation against the Court, but they doubted the wisdom of the packing scheme. Two representative letters from the public reaction file indicate a negative reaction: a physician from New York City wrote "I think the President's outburst of last Thursday was disgraceful . . . [and others who voted for FDR] have quite voluntarily expressed to me their emphatic condemnation of the President's proposals concerning the Supreme Court,'' and from Williamsburg, Virginia, a supporter wrote: ''Would you please apologize for the manner and indirection of introducing the Court Bill—Please, you are so brave personally. It was your glee at fooling, or surprising your opponents that stunned us and frightened us.'' On the other hand, many writers supported FDR's attack on the Court. An unemployed steel worker from Canton, Ohio, complained, ''They can stay in the Supreme Court till 80 but we are kicked out at 45 making laws that does not help us but kick us out to Big Steel or die from worry''; a person from Los Angeles, California, related a conversation to the president, ''Speaking to an old man, nearly 80, on the street yesterday about the President's talk last Thursday evening, that old man said: 'For sixty years I have been waiting for a declaration like that from a President of the United States' ''; a writer from Dallas, Texas, declared, ''The Supreme Court is the 'unruly' member of the three-horse team now handling the politico-economic plow, and you have it just where you want it''; and from Oakland, California, came the statement that the ''opposition to the President's attempt to correct the long existing evils of the Supreme Court is being fought with all the power of the 'economic royalists,' who have controlled our government.''[18]

However one might assess FDR's eloquent Victory Dinner Address, the speech did not persuade those senators who were against the packing scheme to change, nor did it persuade enough Americans to pressure those senators to support the measure. Roosevelt's lack of rhetorical success in lining up the Democratic party behind his Court plan can be explained by two factors. First, FDR had to overcome several rhetorical disadvantages: from not having used his Second Inaugural Address to announce the political principles of the Court fight and his appreciation of executive limitations; from having affirmed a bogus argument in his judiciary message to the Congress, which backfired; and from having to switch to the real issue in the Victory Dinner Address, which did not work. Second, the President probably waited too long to deliver his follow-up attacks. Joseph Alsop and Turner Catledge reasoned that he might have been more persuasive if he had not waited a month to deliver his second major speech: ''In the first weeks of the court fight, when the present excitements of the struggle had not yet dimmed the memory of the election, members of Congress greatly feared the effects the President's talks to the nation might have on their constituents. Had he followed up his surprise attack with a couple of hard-hitting speeches the opposition might not have been able to recruit its numbers, organize its ranks and harden its spirit. As it was, it had been allowed ample time to do all of these things." FDR's frank and forthright affirmation against the Supreme Court was too little and came too late.[19]

THE FIRESIDE CHAT ON THE JUDICIARY

Whereas he waited a month to deliver his second attack, Roosevelt waited only five days for a third try. The president delivered his last attack on the Court as a Fireside Chat on March 9, 1937. The speech developed from a group of thoughts that Roosevelt had dictated and from which Rosenman had composed the speech.

FDR's dictation clearly indicates his rhetorical thoughts. He believed that the Court had ceased to be a judicial body by becoming a legislative body; that he sought in his plan only to solve the judicial problem; that his plan in no way sought to alter the Constitution but in fact to restore, as the Constitution had intended, the legislative function to the Congress; and that he wanted the people to back him up by forcing the Congress to pass the Court bill:

I have pointed out the need for some kind of action. I have pointed out my belief that the country cannot proceed over an indefinite term of years wrangling over what should be done, as it did in another great issue—Slavery. Therefore, I feel confident that the Nation will back me up in insisting that the Congress shall proceed to give the Nation action so that as quickly as may be possible the Government of the United States can function in curing the social and economic ills and in providing a social and economic policy without waiting until it may perhaps be too late. . . . I think the Constitution is a social and economic document. This is the real crux of the thing as I see it. Five people control the decision about what is in the Constitution and they have our democracy stymied. They do not interpret—they legislate. They tell Congress what it can do and what it cannot do. Government is responsible to the people. Congress has the constitutional power to act. . . . Therefore, all you do is to add additional men who can interpret the Constitution. This is a judicial not a constitutional question. Essentially this proposal is to restore to the Congress legislative power which has unconstitutionally been taken away from an elective legislature.

Roosevelt's themes were expanded and woven into the final address.[20]

Taking it for granted that by now Americans were fully aware of the fact of the Supreme Court's rulings against the New Deal (he only briefly alluded to three Court rulings that overturned New Deal acts), Roosevelt focused on the Court's policy. He charged that the Court's rulings had caused a crisis in the government's ability to act: "The Courts, however, have cast doubt on the ability of the elected Congress to protect us against catastrophe by meeting squarely our modern social and economic conditions. We are at a crisis in our ability to proceed with that protection." In summarizing a short history of the Court, he said: "In the last four years the sound rule of giving statutes the benefit of all reasonable doubt has been cast aside. The Court has been acting not as a judicial body, but as a policy-making body.'' Finally, he asserted how the Court was destroying itself and the Constitution: "We have, therefore, reached the point as a Nation where we must take action to save the Constitution from the Court and the Court from itself. We must find a way to take an appeal from the Supreme Court to the Constitution itself. We want a Supreme Court which will do justice under the Constitution—not over it. In our Courts we want a government of laws and not of men.''

However, FDR lapsed into the old age argument that he had mistakenly used in his judiciary message and wisely avoided in the Victory Dinner speech. By abandoning the justices' mental attitude argument in favor of their old age, he shunted aside the real issue and reintroduced the sham one. As in the message, he practically invited an easy refutation of his old age argument. Roosevelt had demonstrated the link between the Court's rulings and its negative mental attitude toward the New Deal in the Victory Dinner Address—which he should have continued in this Fireside Chat—but he never bothered to demonstrate the link between the justices' old age and their negative rulings in this speech. Rather, he merely asserted it in the following examples: "This plan will save our national Constitution from hardening of the judicial arteries''; "There is nothing novel or radical about this idea. It seeks to maintain the Federal bench in full vigor''; "It is the clear intention of our public policy to provide for a constant flow of new and younger blood into the Judiciary''; "But chance and the disinclination of individuals to leave the Supreme bench have now given us a Court in which five justices will be over seventy-five years of age before next June and one over seventy.'' But age, per se, was not the real issue.[21]

Given the president was on the offensive in his judiciary message and in the Victory Dinner speech, the rhetorical critic cannot overlook certain apologetic elements in his Fireside Chat. Although FDR's primary purpose in this speech was accusatory, it is not unusual to find defensive language in such an address. President Roosevelt apologized for both his policy and his character in the Fireside Chat. First, the President attempted to purify the image of his Court bill by clarifying his plan. He told his audience he "came by a process of elimination'' to the conclusion that, short of amendments, his legislation was the only solution to the problem. He defined the amendment process as too time-consuming to meet the immediate problem and besides, he wisely reminded his audience, "An amendment, like the rest of the Constitution, is what the Justices say it is rather than what its framers or you might hope it is.'' He also defined his policy as congruent with accepted past presidential practice: "The number of Justices has been changed several times before, in the Administrations of John Adams and Thomas Jefferson—both signers of the Declaration of Independence—Andrew Jackson, Abraham Lincoln, and Ulysses S. Grant.'' Second, FDR attempted to purify his character, or his motives behind the Court proposal. Indeed, Louis Filler noted that Roosevelt "defended himself with his usual energy'' in the speech. The president defined what his plan was and what it was not. FDR avowed that he was not "packing" the Court: "If by that phrase 'packing the Court' it is charged that I wish to place on the bench spineless puppets who would disregard the law and would decide specific cases as I wished them to be decided, I make this answer: that no President fit for his office would appoint, and no Senate of honorable men fit for their office would confirm, that kind of appointees to the Supreme Court." He was finally at pains to assuage Americans' fears of a nascent presidential dictatorship over the judiciary. This finally indicated his political sensitivity to the limits of his executive action. He predicated his present motive on his past political record, so that there would be no question of his character: "This proposal of mine will not infringe in the slightest upon the civil or religious liberties so dear to every American. My record as Governor and as President proves my devotion to those liberties. You who know me can have no fear that I would tolerate the destruction by any branch of government of any part of our heritage of freedom." He added: "You who know me will accept my solemn assurance that in a world in which democracy is under attack, I seek to make American democracy succeed."[22]

Although Roosevelt rode out the protests against his Court plan in his first two accusations by not responding to them, the existence of apologetic elements in the Fireside Chat indicates that he perceived the political pressures in early March warranted a response. Indeed, an answer to the change that he was "packing" the Court was necessary. If he remained silent on his policy and motives in the battle, that silence could be construed as tacit admission that the charges were true. But rather than waiting until his third speech to respond, FDR should have defended his policy and personal motives in the Victory Dinner speech. This rhetorical strategy could have made that speech even stronger and very well could have refuted at that earlier date the "packing" charge. Of course, if he had affirmed the real issue in the Second Inaugural, and then followed through in the judiciary message, then he could have preempted the packing charge and remained on the offensive in his accusations against the Court.

The results of the president's Fireside Chat were similar to his other attempts. Moley believed FDR's "fireside talk was one of the most moving public statements he ever made," yet Moley still disagreed with the president's proposed bill. Pritchett noted that "he put the real issue directly, but by that time his cause had been irreparably damaged." The public reaction file materials suggest that the president communicated his persuasive message to a polarized American audience. He received positive responses from the following typical letters and telegrams: from Philadelphia, Pennsylvania, "finest most lucid logical courageous statement"; from Lena Station, Louisiana, "this is the best speech for the nation I ever heard"; from a lawyer in Battle Creek, Michigan, "well presented from a legal standpoint"; and from another lawyer in New York City, who agreed with FDR's eschewing of the amendment process, "an amendment to the constitution, as you aptly described, will require a long time and by then, it may be too late." Yet, the con mail was often virulent. On the amendment process, a man from Philadelphia, Pennsylvania, contradicted the pro views given above, "the orderly process of amendment is the national safeguard, even at the cost of time"; from Jamaica, New York, "did not give you any mandate to take any such ill-advised action"; and from an anonymous writer: "I wonder if everyone who trusted you is in such a daze as I after the message regarding the Supreme Court. . . . and this curious play of words doesn't enlighten anybody." A man from Lancaster, Pennsylvania, asked what many other historians and critics have asked: "I cannot see how a man as politically wise and intelligent as you are can be so mis-advised." That question demands an answer from a rhetorical perspective.[23]

SUMMARY

Franklin Roosevelt made a rhetorical choice to attack the court in the manner he did, and the record attests that he did it unsuccessfully. One would like to be able to specify why he did it that way, but evidentiary proof—from both the FDR Library materials and from the secondary sources—does not warrant a definitive answer. One suspects that FDR changed from his normal rhetorical routine, of carefully preparing the Congress and the country, to the unusual surprise attack format because he believed he had just received an electoral mandate from the voters to act against the Court and, therefore, he had the political power to push the bill through the Congress.

By choice, FDR did not attack the Court in his Second Inaugural Address. With hindsight, one may reasonably infer that he chose not to do so because he wanted to dramatically surprise the Congress, the country, and most of all, the Supreme Court with his judiciary message. Yet, this choice was damaging to a successful rhetorical strategy because FDR did not communicate the political principles of his attack on the Court or his appreciation of the limits of his executive function at the inaugural *kairos*, when custom and expectation demand that the President do so. This rhetorical approach would have allowed him to preempt the secrecy charges and to defuse any dictatorship charges.

By choice, President Roosevelt did not affirm the real issue of an anti–New Deal Court in the judiciary message, but chose the old age and overburdened argument. Exactly why he did so is indeterminable. Yet, it was demonstrated that the president and the attorney general discussed the real issue, that they were cognizant of the pitfalls of a "packing" plan, but that for some inexplicable reason, they decided on the devious stratagem. FDR remained adamant on that approach even though Rosenman and Richberg protested it. This is yet another case that indicates presidents might be better served by following the rhetorical advice of their speech writers.[24]

By choice, FDR affirmed the real issue with the Court in his Victory Dinner Address. His choice was predicated, as he later admitted, on the fact that the bogus argumentation had failed and he realized that he finally had to tell the truth. Though it is noteworthy that FDR finally affirmed the real issue in the Victory Dinner speech, it was too late to be efficacious; moreover, the shift nicely confirmed that he had been devious, which confirmed in many listeners' minds the doubts of his real motives.

By choice, FDR must have been motivated to continue the attack on the Court in the Fireside Chat, and he obviously felt motivated to respond to the charges against his plan and against his character motives in proposing it. But when the rhetorical dust had settled, the president was unsuccessful: "But the plea failed. A few letters and telegrams came in to senators of the opposition; there was the usual deluge of mail at the White House, but there were no signs that the speeches had changed the situation in any important fashion." The speeches had some success with the American people, moving from a pro/con ratio in February 1937 of 47 percent to 53 percent, to a 49 percent to 51 percent ratio in the middle of March. But the Congress was the mediating audience with the real power to enact the change, and the Senate would not budge. Since FDR took his case to the people in order to urge them to pressure the Congress, with the people acting their role in the rhetorical presidency, he could have taken his case directly to the people in the very beginning in his Second Inaugural, wherein he could have used the carrot-and-stick technique on the Congress that he had used successfully in his First Inaugural. The rhetorical strategy of Roosevelt's speaking as the vox populi might have had more effect on the Congress if used from the very beginning, rather than trying belatedly to assume the role *ex post facto*.[25]

A presidential persuader's insistence on affirming bogus reasons for a legitimate problem should cause alarm and suspicion, and in FDR's case it did. The secrecy and dramatic announcement were rhetorical miscalculations because they did not give FDR an opportunity to adjust his plan to the Congress and the country by preparing them, in the Second Inaugural or even in the judiciary message. A take-it-or-leave-it stance is not necessarily persuasive in a democracy, and the Senate left it. FDR also found it difficult to adjust his audience to his plan because he changed his rationale in midstream and he did not preempt the packing charge early enough. It was too late to purify the images of his proposal and of his motives that had impelled him to attack the Court, both of which should have been defended in the Victory Dinner Address.

As for a plan, Roosevelt could have asked the Congress to increase the Court to eleven or thirteen justices. Granted, his plan would still have been perceived, and attacked by his critics, as packing the Court. He could have argued the same Senate that passed the bill would also confirm the justices. This would have been consistent with the powers and limitations of the executive function. For this frontal solution, his historical argument would have been a bona fide warrant without being tied to the bogus old age argument. Thus, the plan would have been consistent with the necessity to make the Court responsive to the national agenda in 1937, which even his critics generally agreed was a need.

This rhetorical revisionism would not have guaranteed success to FDR in his Court fight. But he could have been more persuasive than he was. He could not have done it much worse than he did, and a reasonable case exists that he could have done it much better than he did. The point is that effective presidential rhetoric should not facilitate an easy refutation of its claims on peoples' beliefs. Indeed, one person made the point thusly: "Tell the boss he may think he is some swell horse, but he sounds more like the wooden horse of Troy with a bellyful of opportunistic buccaneers and crackpots. . . . Every time I hear him on the radio he reminds me more and more of old Kaiser Bill, Big ME, and god." And another agreed: "Dear 'Frank': I heard your arguments last night on the Courts, politics, etc. Good rabble-rousing stuff; but they did not ring the bell. . . . I do not think your attacks on the Court are warranted; and I am neither a 'defeatist' nor a 'lawyer.' "[26]

JUDICIOUS RHETORIC: THE SUPREME COURT'S APOLOGIA

As the theory of accusation and apology would predict, Chief Justice Charles Evans Hughes was personally motivated to write a letter, which was the Court's apology, because he sought to purify the image that Roosevelt had affirmed against the Supreme Court. Although the chief justice was responsible for the Court's apology, Senator Burton K. Wheeler had a role in the letter's production. Justice Louis Brandeis had told Wheeler that the chief justice would give him a letter to be used against the Court bill. Hughes wrote the letter and gave it to Wheeler on Sunday, March 21, 1937, and the senator then read the chief justice's letter to the Senate Judiciary Committee on March 22. The letter was not Wheeler's but the chief justice's rhetoric: "Hughes was determined to see Roosevelt's Court bill fail. At just the right moment, therefore, the Chief Justice submitted a letter proving, coldly and in deadly detail, the complete falsity of Roosevelt's charge that the Court had fallen far behind in its proper work." Hughes aimed the letter to the Senate Judiciary Committee that had the power to approve or disapprove FDR's bill, but the letter was not unnoticed by the bill's other supporters and foes. The Court's apology is interesting with respect to what issues it addressed and to what ones it acquiesced.[27]

The chief justice apologized by denying the president's affirmation that the Court was behind in its case load. He contended: "The Supreme Court is fully abreast of its work." He added: "We shall be able to hear all these cases, and such others as may come up for argument, before our adjournment for the term. There is no congestion of cases upon our calendar." Peter Irons agreed with the chief justice's rhetoric: "There was no evidence that the Supreme Court docket was clogged with a backlog of cases." Hughes then provided statistical information to substantiate his argument. He demonstrated that the Court had actually been more productive—while the justices were getting older—during FDR's first term than during Hoover's last three years in office.

	1930	1931	1932	1933	1934	1935
Cases Disposed:	900	884	910	1,029	931	990

Although the chief justice did not directly address the president's old age argument, the facts clearly refuted it. Hughes also denied FDR's charge that more justices would somehow decrease the work load and would make the Court more efficient. He argued that just the opposite would accrue: "An increase in the number of justices of the Supreme Court, apart from any question of policy, which I do not discuss, would not promote the efficiency of the court. It is believed that it would impair that efficiency so long as the court acts as a unit. There would be more judges to hear, more judges to confer, more judges to discuss, more judges to be convinced and to decide. The present number of justices is thought to be large enough so far as the prompt, adequate and efficient conduct of the work of the court is concerned." The chief justice's factual purification clearly refuted the president's bogus arguments on old age and overwork.[28]

Yet, Hughes acquiesced in one important issue. He did not deny FDR's affirmation that the Court was wrecking the New Deal. In two instances, Hughes took pains to avoid answering the charge: "apart from any question of policy, which I do not discuss" and "As I have said, I do not speak of any other considerations in view of the appropriate attitude of the court in relation to questions of policy." Two points arise from Hughes's refusal to purify the Court's anti–New Deal image and rulings. First, by following the admonition that the rhetorical critic should compare an accusation and apology as analog in order "to evaluate the relative merits of both speaker's arguments, and to make an assessment of the relative failure or success of both speakers," one can realize why Hughes did not bother to refute the veracity of FDR's affirmation against the Court's rulings and image: Hughes could not because the affirmations were true and based on fact. Second, Hughes' refusal to purify the Court's anti–New Deal rulings and image offers additional support that FDR should have consistently argued only the genuine issues of fact and definition on the Court's rulings (as he did in the Victory Dinner Address but not in his judiciary message or Fireside Chat). The chief justice rather easily and successfully denied the president's underhanded accusations where he could. But his avoiding the issue of the Court's ruling was telling. If Roosevelt had consistently affirmed only the exigency of the anti–New Deal pronouncements, he would have narrowed the rhetorical field for Hughes's response. Hughes could not have denied the fact of the Court's rulings—and indeed he did not in his actual apology—so he would have been compelled either to argue some mitigating factor for the Court's rulings or to remain silent in a tacit admission that FDR was correct. Roosevelt certainly could have strengthened his accusations against the Court on the sole fact of its rulings, but he practically invited the chief justice to beat him on his own ill-conceived old age and overworked arguments, and Hughes clearly won there.[29]

The chief justice's letter was a successful rhetorical apology. Hughes's letter was not the sole factor in the bill's eventual defeat (other factors are discussed in the next section), but it was a significant contributing factor. Robert Allen allowed that the letter enabled Hughes "to get in some hefty blows at the

President's proposal.'' Leonard Baker believed the letter was successful in its aims: ''The extent of the letter's impact was significant. It also influenced many other citizens who accepted the letter in good faith to oppose FDR's plan. . . . The Hughes letter strengthened the doubts and fears of a great number of people, confirmed their feelings that the plan was a phony and that the real reasons had not been given.'' Edgar Robinson remarked, ''Subsequently it was agreed by the closest adherents of the President that the testimony of the Chief Justice more than anything else brought victory to the opponents of the bill.'' William Manchester opined that the letter ''crippled Court reform.'' James Patterson observed, ''The letter artfully demolished Roosevelt's spurious arguments concerning old age and inefficiency: it was one of the sharpest blows to the administration.'' Senator Wheeler recounted, ''Assistant Attorney General Jackson's opinion afterward was that the Hughes letter 'did more than any one thing to turn the tide in the Court struggle.' ''[30]

THE PRESIDENT VS. THE COURT

As a kind of presidential prosecuting attorney, FDR called the Supreme Court to the bar before the Congress and the country. Acting as a kind of defense attorney, Chief Justice Hughes defended the Court in order to keep it unpacked. Now, a verdict in the case is to be rendered.

When the rhetorical critic follows Noreen Kruse's advice ''to evaluate the success or failure of the discourse in terms of the speaker's perspective,'' one can ascertain how and why President Roosevelt lost both the battle and the war. On the face of the outcome, appearances suggested that the Supreme Court changed to a pro–New Deal stance as a result of FDR's accusations. On March 29, 1937, the Supreme Court did dramatically reverse itself by upholding a Washington state minimum wage case that six months earlier it had denied in a similar New York case, and it also upheld a slightly revised Frazier-Lemke farm bill whose overturning FDR had excoriated in the Victory Dinner Address. In early April, the Court also upheld the vital National Labor Relations Act. These reversals prompted the president to conclude that his accusations against the Court were successful: ''I feel convinced, however, that the change would have never come, unless this frontal attack had been made upon the philosophy of the Court'' and ''It would be a little naive to refuse to recognize some connection between these 1937 decisions and the Supreme Court fight.'' Other sympathetic writers have agreed with FDR's assessment. Stefan Lorant wrote, ''During the controversy the Court gradually committed itself to the New Deal policies, and this had been Roosevelt's aim all along.'' Grace Tully agreed: ''The real objective of having the judicial branch of the Government look upon the functioning of the legislative and executive branches with realistic twentieth century eyes was accomplished. No more was sought.'' However, FDR's and these writers' assessments are unwarranted.[31]

As a matter of fact, the Supreme Court had voted to reverse itself by upholding the Washington case *before* Roosevelt sent his message to the Congress. Rosenman noted that Justice Roberts switched his vote in conference in December 1936, and Baker stated, "Technically, it is true that the switch was made before Roosevelt's specific plan was announced." The point is that the Court had decided to change its philosophy before Roosevelt's attack, and if Roberts were "persuaded" by anything, it was probably FDR's landslide victory at the polls. But, there exists no evidence to suggest that FDR knew about the switch before he made his accusations. The Court's total capitulation came on May 18, 1937, when Justice Van Devanter announced his retirement, thus assuring a Roosevelt court by allowing the president to appoint Senator Hugo Black to the bench.[32]

It is now apparent why Chief Justice Hughes delivered the kind of apology he did. He did not seek to justify the Court's anti–New Deal rulings because he knew from the conference vote in late December that the Court would change: there was no reason to apologize for the political rulings because the Court would reverse itself. Although two other factors contributed to the bill's defeat—Senator Joseph Robinson, Roosevelt's leader of the bill in the Senate, died suddenly of a heart attack and no one was left to lead the fight, and the Supreme Court's reversal also detracted from the bill's urgency—from Hughes's perspective, his letter had its rhetorical effect of maintaining the Court at nine members.

From Roosevelt's perspective, his accusations against the Court were unsuccessful. He did not obtain an enlarged Court from the Congress, he did not persuade enough Americans to pressure their senators to back him, and the Court had even decided to change before he began his rhetorical attacks. Although it is true that FDR signed into law on August 26, 1937, a judicial reform bill, which contained most of the suggestions in his February 5 message, the Congress did not give him more Supreme Court justices. Perhaps Roosevelt can best summarize his encounter with the Court: "The net result is that we have obtained certain objectives, talking in the large."[33]

CONCLUSION

This chapter has dealt with how and why Roosevelt erred in his rhetorical attack against the Supreme Court. Based on generic theories of inaugural addresses and accusations and apologies, FDR should have initiated frontally and forthrightly the attack against the Court in his Second Inaugural Address, offered the real reasons in the judiciary message, and consistently affirmed these reasons in the Victory Dinner Address and the Fireside Chat on the judiciary. Rather than conceiving his plan in relationship to the justices' old age, he could have argued the merits of a plan to enlarge the Court by a set figure, thereby stressing a liberal Court, not an aged one. But Roosevelt chose injudicious rhetoric, and he paid a precious price. By handing his opponents a bogus issue, he invited conservative Democrats to join forces with conservative Republicans, thus breaking the New Deal coalition. The foray also proved that Roosevelt's rhetoric could be weathered and refuted. Roosevelt's injudicious language did not persuade the Senate or the country, it easily invited a successful apology from Chief Justice Hughes for the Court, it angered and divided the president's own party, and it played a role in the purge.

7

A War of Words and Words of War: The Purge and the Isolationists

In the later half of the 1930s, Franklin Roosevelt addressed two persuasive problems. One he initiated, the other he reacted to. On his own impetus, he conceived and executed the purge of 1938. The preparation-for-war rhetoric was his response to foreign events and domestic isolationists. The purge, contrived for good reasons but conducted in a maladroit manner, was the second of a one-two self-inflicted wound that he dealt his rhetorical presidency—the other was the ill-fated Court fight. His war rhetoric, although often characterized by advance-retreat, was vindicated on December 8, 1941. As the purge was petty, so the war rhetoric was a prime accomplishment in Roosevelt's rhetorical presidency. Both persuasive campaigns, against domestic and foreign infidels, illustrate the possibilities and limitations of presidential rhetoric.

A WAR OF WORDS: THE PURGE

On the face of it, the purge addressed a genuine need, as the Court-packing scheme had in 1937. Elected as ostensible New Dealers, many Democrats—closet conservatives, often from the South—bolted Roosevelt's coalition in the Court fight and found comfortable quarters with their Republican brethren in obstructing the president's liberal political agenda in 1937–38. At issue were Roosevelt's executive reorganization bill and the wages and hours measure. With the early victory of Senator Lister Hill in the Alabama primary in January 1938, Roosevelt and his cabal of purgers—his son James Roosevelt, Harry Hopkins, Tom Corcoran, and Harold Ickes—concluded that they should help Claude Pepper in his senatorial primary race in Florida. When Pepper won handily over his conservative opponent, two important inferences were made. Reading the early returns, the House Rules Committee, chaired by Representative John O'Connor, who was the only successfully purged candidate of the lot, discharged the Fair Labor Standards Act, which passed the Congress after a struggle. Roosevelt concluded that since administration support for Pepper had been successful and that since Hill's and Pepper's early primary victories had pried the wages and hours bill from committee, he could, and perhaps should, move against other conservative enemies. The purgers tried their untested hands on Senator Guy Gillette of Iowa; although son Jimmie had campaigned for "My friend Otha Wearin" against Gillette, the purgers were rebuked by the Iowan voters. Senators Alva Adams of Colorado, Pat McCarran of Nevada, Frederick Van Nuys of Indiana, and Bennet "Champ" Clark from Missouri were prime targets, but these foes were too formidable. Roosevelt attacked Senators Harry Byrd and Carter Glass of Virginia, who could not be purged because they would not run until 1940 and 1942 respectively, by withholding federal patronage; countering on the issue of senatorial courtesy, the Senate supported Glass and Byrd by roundly defeating Roosevelt's nominee, Floyd Roberts, for a federal District Court seat by 72 to 9. Perusing the easier pickings, the purgers targeted three purgees for the full wrath of Roosevelt's rhetoric.[1]

FDR announced the rationale for the purge in his Fireside Chat on June 24, 1938. The word *purge* was not Roosevelt's—he detested it for obvious reasons—nor, with its negative associations of purges by Mussolini, Hitler, and Stalin, did it help the president's image. Having scored the Tory press in the 1936 election, he might have reasoned that the royalist press would characterize the effort as it did: "Roosevelt the Dictator," "Marching through Georgia," and "Eliminating the States." His talk was an admixture of contradictions. Within it were two flaws that contributed to the purge's ultimate failure.[2]

Except for a sideswipe at the Seventy-fifth-Congress for not passing his executive reorganization bill, Roosevelt detailed and praised eight liberal measures the Congress had passed. To be sure, the wages and hours bill was a bitter battle, but despite its many loopholes, Roosevelt did have a measure of success. Therefore, the question logically arises, "What was the extraordinary need?" Roosevelt even later admitted that "most of the liberal measures had already been passed." Unlike the Supreme Court issue in 1937, FDR faced no compelling urgency in June 1938. At stake, rather, were two schools of thought, the conservative vs. the liberal. He told his listeners that he was concerned with a Democrat's "general attitude," "inward desire," and a "yes, but" position on the New Deal that voters had overwhelmingly reaffirmed in 1936. Although his descriptions doubtless left verbal leeway to apply these characterizations however and to whomever he wished, they also had the disadvantage of being vague. Lacking specific attacks on matters of policy, the president did not clearly nor cleanly demarcate liberals from conservatives. Thus, FDR's failure in this speech to specify legislation as the liberal litmus test, relying instead on "attitudes," invited charges that he was purging his conservative nemeses for the Court defeat. It was a reasonable inference, which he never purged from the public mind.[3]

His second persuasive problem was a fine distinction, too fine by half. In language that called attention to his disingenuous disclaimer, FDR averred that as president he would not ask Americans to vote a certain ticket nor would he take part in Democratic primaries (he would let his surrogates do that for him). However, as head of the Democratic party, he allowed that he had the right to address those instances involving "principles" or a "clear misuse of my own name." Although the pedantic mind might appreciate the chief executive's separate theoretical roles, the average person perceived that the man who played legerdemain with titles was still Franklin D. Roosevelt, president of the United States. The distinction was also lost on the Tory press.[4]

As president, and not as head of the party, Roosevelt publicly attacked the senior Senator from Georgia, Walter George, in a speech at Barnesville, Georgia, August 11, 1938, before an audience of fifty thousand. The occasion was a dedication of a Rural Electrification Administration project. In impromptu remarks at Warm Springs, Georgia, on the previous day, Roosevelt had recognized in an offhand manner Lawrence Camp, U. S. attorney, as the next senator from Georgia. But the Barnesville speech was FDR's frontal assault on George. The president told his audience that he felt "no hesitation in telling you what I would do if I could vote here next month." Although George was "a gentleman and a scholar" and FDR's personal friend, the president told the senator to his face that George did not believe in "his heart, deep down in his heart," the objectives of the Democratic party or of Roosevelt's New Deal. FDR then praised Camp as a man who believed in the necessary "objectives." Unfortunately, whereas the president did not specifically indict George's voting record, neither did he mention Camp's stand of any of the issues. Envisioning a "cooperation between members of my own party and myself," Roosevelt came perilously close to constructing a one-way political street that ran only from the Capitol to the White House. Indicative of the amateurism that plagued the purge, Raymond Clapper noted that Camp's supporters failed to arrange "for adequate radio broadcasting throughout Georgia."[5]

Senator George responded to Roosevelt's attack by wisely skirting the issue of the New Deal. Instead, he appealed to Georgian interests at Waycross on August 15. Emotionally and tearfully allowing to his audience of fifteen hundred in one-hundred-degree heat that "I'm a Georgian, bred and born, I'm a fulltime Georgian," the senator stocked his speech with basic Southern oratorical staples: appeals against John L. Lewis's Communist following, allusions to carpetbaggers, Negro-baiting by mentioning white Democrats, and state's rights. He defended his role in the Supreme Court fight, and brought the crowd to its feet when he said, "I'm a Democrat, but the Democratic party is not a one-man party." Since the senator was not constrained by Roosevelt's accusatory speech to address specific policies, George was able to reply widely, as he did. In fact, he tellingly turned FDR's speech against him: "In the indictment against my record of public service, there are no specifications—no bill of particulars."[6]

Roosevelt's rhetorical strategy allowed George to transcend the issue of vague "principles" to one of state sovereignty, a potent value in southern oratory with its many implications. (Senator Ellison "Cotton Ed" Smith of South Carolina, although not dignified by a frontal assault, was the object of an unsuccessful purge because the voters of South Carolina liked "his old-time oratory, his Negro-baiting"—the similarities in degree between Smith and George were not coincidental.) Reacting to the second march through Georgia, the *Atlanta Constitution*, normally Roosevelt's supporter, editorialized: "He would turn the United States Senate into a gathering of ninety-six Charley McCarthys with himself as the sole Edgar Bergen to pull the strings and supply the vocalisms"; likewise, the *New York Times* caught the efficacy of the separation of powers doctrine in an editorial when, of George's primary victory, it stated that the voters of Georgia did not subscribe to the theory "that the test of Senatorial fitness must be undividing loyalty to Mr. Roosevelt's own personal interpretation of the pledges of the Democratic party."[7]

In studying other reasons for Roosevelt's defeat and George's victory, Luther Zeigler found that the president was too heavy-handed with federal aid—George stated in his speech that Georgians could not be bought, that the firing of RFC attorney Edgar Dunlap for refusing to resign from George's campaign backfired, that Georgian newspapers could not tolerate presidential interference because their power to help choose and elect candidates would be nullified, that FDR's campaign tactics offended Georgians, that the administration grossly underestimated George's considerable local appeal and solid support from the business community, and that Camp was simply outclassed by the senator.[8]

Varying the medium for no discernible reason, except perhaps because FDR sensed the frontal assault on George had been too bold, Roosevelt attacked Representative John J. O'Connor and Senator Millard Tydings in two press conferences, the first on August 16 in Washington and the second on August 23 at Hyde Park. The president purged O'Connor and Tydings by reading from an editorial in the *New York Post*. Evidently better than Roosevelt could, its editorial department had put the issue succinctly: "The voter could take his choice between the New Deal and Tydings record of consistent opposition to it. . . . Fay is running against Representative John J. O'Connor, one of the most effective obstructionists in the lower house." FDR made the editorial his own statement. On August 23, FDR complained about Republicans crossing over in the primaries in Maryland to vote for Tydings and condemned O'Connor for entering the Republican primary. He also needled the Tory press for not printing that story. Roosevelt did not campaign against O'Connor or for James Fay, the representative's opponent, in New York.[9]

O'Connor took to the airwaves to defend himself only three days after being attacked. On August 19, he delivered a speech that was bereft of logic and reason, but full of maxims and rhetorical questions. After warming to his subject by charging Communism on the part of the *New York Post* and likening the purge to Hitler, he discharged a fusillade of cliches: "It is an escalator to a dictatorship"; "Which shall it be—democracy or monocracy?"; "The peoples liberties cannot be taken away except through euthanasia"; "do we now stand at Thermopylae?"; and "A Representative has no responsibility to the President." Sandwiched among these representative slogans, which suggested a man distinctly on the defensive, was the separation of powers doctrine, used by O'Connor so that his audience would not miss that critical appeal.[10]

Taking a cue from Roosevelt, Senator Tydings delivered a statewide radio broadcast on a prime-time Fireside Chat day, a Sunday, August 21. The senator must have read George's speech, and to a much lesser degree O'Connor's, and then adapted these to his Maryland audience. Themes borrowed from George's speech included the following: allusions to "fixed bayonets" from the Reconstruction era and to those (read Roosevelt) who could not vote, did not live, and did not pay taxes in Maryland; a defense of the Supreme Court battle against the president; and a heavy dose of state sovereignty appeals. Additionally, Tydings scored FDR's sophistical distinction in playing presidential roles by stating the "president is the same man . . . no matter what other titles he may assume." Unlike George, who sensed the battle was between himself and FDR, Tydings attacked his opponent, David J. Lewis. The senator cleverly used guilt by association to argue that Lewis would not vote as Marylanders wanted but as FDR dictated—Lewis was, after all, his candidate. Thus, a vote for Lewis was an affirmation of federal ascendancy in state matters; a vote for Tydings would stay the usurper's hand. In a rousing peroration, Tydings coalesced his themes: "Maryland will not permit her star in the flag to be 'purged' from the constellation of the states."[11]

Realizing a good defense is a good offense, Tydings, like George, transcended the issue of the New Deal to appeal to local concerns. A campaign placard direly warned "Citizens of Maryland Defend Your State Against Federal Invasion," warned about "The CIO, John L. Lewis and Communists," and urged "Keep the Free State Free." Raymond Moley and Arthur Krock both noted the appeal George and Tydings made to state sovereignty—that a congressman's responsibility was to constituents and not to the national party leader and that the people had a right to choose their own representatives and senators in an independent Congress—was an argument that FDR could not easily refute.[12]

Although try he did. At Denton, Maryland, on September 5, 1938, FDR invaded the Eastern Shore. Mindful of Tyding's speech, FDR was at pains in his introduction to allude to the "Free State of Maryland" three times and allowed how Maryland was "happily a part of the Union" and that "the Flag, the Constitution and the President are still as welcome as in all of the other forty-seven States of the Union." Those expecting purgative rhetoric of the George genre were disappointed. Instead, Roosevelt revealed that he came to campaign for a "Mr. A" versus a "Mr. B," who was the liberal. After coyly listing "B's" legislative accomplishments, FDR finally identified "B" as Representative Lewis. Cleverly describing Lewis as a "Good Samaritan—and he has never passed by on the other side," Roosevelt let the audience infer that "Mr. A," the conservative, was Tydings. The Denton speech was perhaps the least objectionable purge speech because it was constructive for Lewis and not destructive against Tydings.[13]

"Cotton Ed" Smith, Walter George, and Millard Tydings all won their primary elections and were subsequently re-elected to the U. S. Senate. The Roosevelt forces claimed victory in O'Connor's case because he was defeated by Fay. This claim, as in the Court "victory," was the fallacy of *post hoc, ergo propter hoc*. According to Richard Polenberg, the representative was defeated for a variety of reasons, none of which had much to do with Roosevelt's purge: O'Connor could not rely on Tammany Hall, which was disorganized and lacked money; Mayor Fiorello LaGuardia campaigned for Fay and against O'Connor; Fay appealed to the poorer people in the Sixteenth Congressional District, whereas O'Connor courted the "silk stocking" constituents; Fay scored O'Connor's living out of the district; and O'Connor ran as a Republican, at last showing his true colors. Local politics and alignments, concluded Polenberg, proved more important in the primary and election.[14]

SUMMARY

The purge failed for a variety of reasons. The lack of a concerted effort against all conservative Democrats, the early amateurism of FDR's aides, the fact that more flagrant violators of Roosevelt's "principles" were not attacked, the fact that the strategy and tactics varied so, and the fact that the word *purge* conjured connotations of Communist and Nazi murders, combined to present a formidable front to the president.

In terms of the persuasive presidency, Roosevelt made several serious mistakes. First, unlike the Court fight, there was no compelling urgency, hence FDR was hard pressed to present a prima facie case that went beyond vague "principles." Second, as in the Court fight, he handed the opposition an issue to use against him. Just as the nine-old-men argument never caught on, neither did the "principles" ploy succeed. By attacking frontally only a few men— George with a weak attack on "attitude" toward the New Deal, O'Connor with a petulant press conference, and Tydings by benign neglect in a major speech— Roosevelt opened the door to charges of vindictiveness over the Court fight and practically invited the senators to rehearse their Court arguments all over again. O'Connor analogously obliged by defending his stand against the executive reorganization bill as the last bulwark against Roosevelt's nascent dictatorship. The *Christian Century* noted that Roosevelt gave "a well-nigh irresistible impulse to those of his opponents who are about to be purged to combine in an organization of a compact, fighting opposition," and Marquis Childs sympathized with the president but pragmatically noted: "Senator Tydings might run more logically as a Republican than a Democrat. But that is not important. What has happened is a sufficient excuse to set the whole pack to baying again." Indeed, both George and Tydings turned their votes on the Court issue to their advantage, and O'Connor was proud to be on the roll of honor against the reorganization bill. Third, as Jack Gravlee demonstrated, FDR missed the opportunity to constrain the purgees' range of responses, by making attacks against their characters more than their policies. George and Tydings responded to FDR by relying on potent appeals to racism, bigotry, radical Reconstructionism, Communism, anti-unionism, and so forth; O'Connor lashed out at FDR's attempt to dictate to New York from Washington. If FDR had rhetorically forced these candidates to confront the real issue of the New Deal, he might have constrained them to defend their voting records rather than allowing them leeway to choose their own aggressive stance, hence their ability to muddle the issue. On the liberal-conservative litmus test, Roosevelt was "hampered by the fact that in no case so far has he been able to make that a clear-cut issue. The chief purge targets fought not as anti-New Dealers but on such issues as 'white supremacy' and 'stop outside meddling.' " Fourth, Roosevelt mistakenly assumed he was not only the vox populi but also the voice of the Democratic party. Raymond Moley cogently argued, "This bit of mysticism, however, did not sit well with the country—largely, it seems, because such a conception of dualism not only affronted the logic of the intelligent, but strained the credulity of the ignorant." Fifth, in terms of the construct of the rhetorical presidency, Roosevelt miscalculated, as he did in the Court fight, that his personal popularity transcended the separation of powers doctrine. In his oral history, Samuel Rosenman, who was not for or a part of the purge, put his finger on the vital persuasive point:

You see, he tried to justify it on the ground that these men whom he was attempting to purge had been elected on a national platform, and that they were riders on his coat tails who had no right to do that. Well, I think it's only partially true that they were running on the national platform. The fact is that Senator George of Georgia, for example, who was perhaps the strongest target of the purge attempt, could have been elected Senator from Georgia whether we'd had a platform or didn't—whether it was Roosevelt or whether it was Coolidge. And while theoretically in running for the United States Senate he was running on the national platform, this was only a theory. I'm sure that the people of Georgia, if they had ever read the platform—particularly some of the planks—would never realize that they were voting for a man who would have to vote for some of these things. They would have been considerably astonished to learn that Senator George was bound by the national platform.

Although the New Deal remained popular in the South, J. B. Shannon showed that Roosevelt was unable "to confer upon another[a candidate] he favored his personal popularity."[15]

Ironically, the conservative southern Democrats that outflanked the president's war of words became his ally against the midwestern isolationists in his words of war.

WORDS OF WAR: THE ISOLATIONISTS

President Roosevelt's rhetorical transaction on the preparation-for-war rhetoric went from Chautauqua, New York, in 1936 to Pearl Harbor in 1941. During this critical interval, he delivered some of his most memorable, though not always successful, orations. Part of his inability to persuade was because of his audience: "A strong case can be made that his failure to convince Americans of the dangers of isolationism lay with their unwillingness to be persuaded rather than with their president's earnestness or rhetorical talent."[16]

The speeches that figured prominently in the war rhetoric were the "Quarantine" address on October 5, 1937; the message to Hitler and Mussolini on April 14, 1939; the speech to the extraordinary session of the Congress for the repeal of the arms embargo, September 21, 1939; the "hand that held the dagger" address at the University of Virginia, June 10, 1940; the "Arsenal of Democracy" address on December 29, 1940; the Annual Message or "Four Freedoms" speech, January 6, 1941; the "Freedom of the Seas" Chat, September 11, 1941; and the War Message, December 8, 1941.

"QUARANTINE" ADDRESS, OCTOBER 5, 1937

Roosevelt's apparent purpose and the speech's supposed effects have baffled critics. Robert Divine believed that "Roosevelt's intentions in delivering his Chicago address remain mysterious today as they were to contemporary observers in 1937," and *Newsweek* noted that "the President left his audience puzzled as to what form the 'quarantine' should take." Dorothy Borg, investigating the speech a generation ago, made some valuable findings. First, notwithstanding Samuel Rosenman's assessment, which was seconded by later critics, that the president's speech met with condemnation almost immediately, thus forcing him to moderate his position, Borg demonstrated that a surprising number of newspapers rushed to praise the president's address; second, the speech was not, as had generally been thought, a shift in foreign policy; and third, FDR was motivated to be more sensitive to the isolationist press than contemporary reaction warranted. Following in Borg's footsteps, the rhetorical critic should contend that the quarantine speech was a continuation of Roosevelt's basic noninterventionist rhetoric; that the address, his subsequent press conference, and Fireside Chat on October 12, when conceived as noninterventionist persuasions, were thematically consistent; and that FDR's meaning was unintentionally obfuscated by the metaphor of the quarantine, which was received by the press and public as indicating more than the president intended or was prepared to say.[17]

The press hailed the address as a new foreign policy initiative. True enough, FDR's high drama and surprise tactics, reminiscent of his attack on the Supreme Court, may have facilitated the press's inference. But a close examination of Roosevelt's rhetoric reveals an alternative reading. At first glance, the quarantine address was an apparent shift from Roosevelt's position enunciated in the "I hate war'' speech at Chautauqua, New York, August 14, 1936. In that address, constrained by the Neutrality Act of 1936, which was the Congress's reaction to Nazi occupation of the Rhineland in March, Italy's annexation of Ethiopia in May, and the Spanish civil war in July, Roosevelt affirmed noninterventionism to placate the isolationists and to preempt the war issue in the 1936 campaign. A year later, the situation was worse.[18]

In July 1937, war broke out between China and Japan over an incident at the Marco Polo bridge. Acting on a suggestion by Secretary of State Cordell Hull that he deliver a major address in the heartland, FDR asked Hull and Norman Davis—a kind of ambassador-at-large with close ties to Roosevelt—to prepare such a speech. In a draft dated September 18, 1937, Davis wrote the idea that may have prompted the quarantine image: ''War is a contagion.'' Deprecating ''international lawlessness'' that ran counter to the Covenant of the League of Nations, the Kellogg-Briand Pact, and the Nine Power Treaty, Roosevelt delivered his medical metaphor in measured meter (slashes delineate his vocal phrasing and italics his ad-libbed words):

It seems to be unfortunately true / that the epidemic of world lawlessness is spreading / *And mark this well* / When an epidemic of physical disease starts to spread / the community approves and joins in / a quarantine / of the patients / in order to protect the health of the community / against the spread of the disease / [applause] It is my determination / to pursue a policy of peace.

Moreover, he thematically grounded his idea in the conclusion, which echoed the language of the Chautauqua speech, by stressing peace:

America / hates / war / America / hopes for peace / Therefore / America actively engages / in the search / for peace.[19]

Borg's belief that Roosevelt at the time of the quarantine speech had in mind the concept of ''collective non-belligerency,'' or collective noninterventionism, is supported by his subsequent utterances on the subject that showed a consistent pattern. (In terms of conception and execution, the quarantine speech was similar to the ''bold experimentation'' speech, in which candidate Roosevelt urged the nation in 1932 to try something under his leadership, and to the 1936 campaign, wherein Roosevelt ran for the New Deal by running against Hooverism. That is, FDR had a clear conception of what the quarantine *was not*, but was unclear in his mind on what it *was*.) Against the perception that Roosevelt backtracked in his press conference the next day, October 6, Borg countered, ''It seems quite possible that the President's replies were meant to be taken at face value.'' To repeated parries from the press, FDR consistently stressed the speech's conclusion ''the lead is in the last line, 'America actively engages in the search for peace,' '' admitted that he had not moved beyond the speech, admitted that it ''is an attitude, and it does not outline a program; but it says we are looking for a program,'' and asserted that his idea might even be a stronger neutrality. Given the fact that Robert Dallek and Wayne Cole observed the strong initial reaction for the address, there was no particular reason for Roosevelt to back away from his speech one day later.[20]

In his Fireside Chat on October 12, FDR addressed his executive reorganization bill and the quarantine speech. The fact that he raised the subject at the end of his talk, thus employing the recency effect, suggests the importance Roosevelt gave the quarantine idea. As a logical consequence of his Chicago speech, FDR announced in the chat his willingness to attend the Brussels conference that had been called to discuss sanctions against Japan. As an example of *post hoc, ergo propter hoc*, Borg demonstrated that the Nine Power Treaty conference, called by the League the day after FDR's quarantine speech, was not related directly to the speech, although the League powers evidently thought Roosevelt's message signaled a change in American policy. If FDR had been responding to isolationist attacks, he could have scotched the conference by not following his words with action. Rather, the conclusion of his chat attests that he was indeed acting on his rhetoric:

Meanwhile, remember that from 1913 to 1921, I personally was fairly close to world events, and in that period, while I learned much of what to do, I also learned much of what *not* to do [italics in original].

The common sense, the intelligence of America agree with my statement that ''America hates war. America hopes for peace. Therefore, America actively engages in the search for peace.''

Note that in his own words, FDR emphasized what not to do over what to do.[21]

Lastly, this speech demonstrates a finding of the rhetorical presidency that speaking is not necessarily governing. The Chicago speech was a problem-solution address whose solution was a metaphor that was misread. Carefully analyzing the president's purpose, *Time* observed that ''Franklin Roosevelt had correctly gauged public psychology in giving a cue that all moral indignation need not be repressed any longer.'' Arthur Krock also caught the rhetorical essence of the speech: ''It seems sufficient to view the speech as an expression of public opinion. . . . This alone is considered in Washington ample explanation of and justification for the Chicago speech.'' Moreover, *The Times* of London praised the speech for what it was and was not: ''It detracts nothing from the great importance of his declaration to remind overeager interpreters that Mr. Roosevelt was defining an attitude and not a program.''[22]

The denouement of the Chicago address was played out in Brussels. Due to a number of factors, among them the fact that at his October 6 press conference Roosevelt rejected sanctions, which he declared were ''out of the window,'' the conference failed. Thus, some of the media that supported Roosevelt's initiative felt betrayed. *Newsweek* opined that ''Mr. Roosevelt appeared to have strategically retreated from the forthright attitude of his Chicago speech two months ago,'' and the *Milwaukee Journal* complained, ''There wasn't any bright new dream when the President spoke at Chicago . . . only rhetoric.'' This discontent is consistent with the interpretation that the quarantine speech was not a program, but a signal that FDR was searching for a viable solution. Although many observers thought so, FDR did not deliver a deliberative speech that advocated an immediate policy; however, if properly conceived as an instance of epideictic rhetoric, in this case, a speech of blame, then the president fulfilled his goal of preparing the way for subsequent action. True, his end was not obtained totally until December 8, 1941, but the quarantine speech did signal the beginning of his rhetorical campaign to adjust the American people to war and the war to the American people.[23]

The attitude-without-a-program that was reflected in Roosevelt's speech was also evident in the public's reactions. They supported the president's stand as long as it did not involve belligerency. A letter signed by thirty-eight members of the College of Liberal Arts at Northwestern University declared their ''desire to commend the principles of co-operation for obedience to international law.'' A writer from Boston stated, ''We want peace but we also want justice''; from Pasadena, California, ''We believe that strength of character and courage must be expressed by nations''; and from Bangor, Maine, ''The war should be stopped before we have another world war, but I don't believe we should go to the extent to get into war ourselves.'' The people's approach for Roosevelt's rhetoric but their avoidance of any action to implement it was basically his persuasive problem until the day of infamy.[24]

APPEAL TO HITLER AND MUSSOLINI, APRIL 14, 1939

Sensing the coming of World War II, Roosevelt sent a public message to the Duce and to the Fuehrer. The latter, having just pocketed Czechoslovakia, was in no mood to be lectured by the President. Under no illusions that his message could influence the dictators, Roosevelt targeted the American people. He cleverly asked Hitler a rhetorical question, ''Are you willing to give assurance that your armed forces will not attack or invade . . . the following independent nations?'' Then he named the thirty-one countries that were threatened. Although his message did not in the least menace Hitler, and both men knew it, it did place the president on high moral ground and enunciated for the isolationists the countries that could fall to Hitler. The national and international responses to FDR's rhetorical ploy were positive.[25]

Stung by the international sympathy and criticism that FDR's message evoked, Hitler responded on April 28 in the Kroll Opera House. Robert Payne found that Hitler, as a self-encomiast, surpassed even Mussolini ''with such avidity, and such fearful disregard for the facts.'' Hitler explained away his recent conquests by asserting his and Germany's destiny, and turning to Roosevelt in the last half of his speech, Hitler played the debater by giving a point-by-point refutation that consisted of half-truths, turning-the-tables, *tu quoque* appeals, scapegoating of the Jewish and international presses, and in his *tour de force*, a sarcastic enumeration of the countries that Roosevelt had listed. This appeal brought derisive laughter from his Reichstag audience. In terms of invective and abuse, Hitler's rambling discourse should have made anyone pause, but not California's senior Senator and isolationist Hiram Johnson, who opined: "Roosevelt put his chin out and got a resounding whack. I have reached the conclusion that there will be no war. . . . " Contrastingly, John Toland believed the Fuehrer's speech "was designed more to satisfy Hitler's people than to persuade his enemies."[26]

SPEECH ON REPEAL OF THE EMBARGO PROVISIONS, SEPTEMBER 21, 1939

Notwithstanding Senator Borah's belief that there would be no war in Europe, Hitler invaded Poland on September 1, 1939. The irony in the war of words and the words of war was that conservative and southern Democrats who had stymied Roosevelt's domestic policies after 1935, and thus were to be purged, became supporters of aid-short-of-war; whereas midwestern and western Democrats, who were members of the liberal New Deal coalition, were also the isolationists whom FDR had to fight in Congress. In his Fireside Chat on war, September 3, he told the American people: "This nation will remain a neutral in thought as well. . . . Even a neutral cannot be asked to close his mind or his conscience." Having taken the moral ground with the people, FDR endeavored to change the legal situation with the Congress.

Had George Orwell's concept of political Newspeak been current, isolationists would surely have countered that Roosevelt's speech was a prime example. FDR constructed a clever strategem in the speech: the embargo provisions of the Neutrality Act should be repealed because, if left unchanged, they could lead the United States to war. Arguing that uncompleted implements of war could still be sold to belligerents and shipped in American flag ships, he allowed that repeal would keep American citizens and ships "away from the immediate perils of the actual zones of conflict." The same reasoning also applied to the principle of "cash and carry" when selling goods to belligerents. After each of these issues, FDR refuted objections that isolationists might have, contending that "by the repeal of the embargo the United States will more probably remain at peace than if the law remains as it stands today" and "There lies the road to peace!"[27]

In late October, the Senate approved the bill and the House sustained the measure in early November. Although the isolationists staged a bitter fight, FDR gave the Congress good reasons to vote for repeal. Dallek determined that the war was the major factor that persuaded the Congress, but that the cash-and-carry policy stilled fears that the United States would get into the war.[28]

THE "DAGGER" SPEECH, JUNE 10, 1940

Following the "phony" war during the winter of 1939–40, Hitler unleashed his blitzkrieg in April 1940. Faltering, France looked to the south as Mussolini attacked under the terms of the Pact of Steel with Hitler. Rhetorical bluster was Roosevelt's public response to his unsuccessful private efforts to persuade the Duce to stay out of the war. The speech served two presidential purposes: it communicated FDR's and the country's moral indignation and it avowed open aid to France and Great Britain. Moreover, the drafts demonstrate FDR's sensitivity to language at a watershed in U. S. history.

Notwithstanding Rosenman's interpretation, and those who followed his lead, Archibald MacLeish, and not the State Department, composed the first draft. FDR made two noteworthy changes on MacLeish's draft. Mindful of the national and immediate southern audience at Charlottesville, Virginia, and perhaps of conservative senators such as Carter Glass and Harry Byrd, who two years earlier would have been purged if they had been running but who were now solidly enlisted in Roosevelt's internationalist coalition, FDR changed a reference to the "Civil War" to the more palatable, for Southern sensibilities, "War Between the States"; he also strengthened the text to indict personally the dictators: "belief in force [a belief in obedience, a belief in discipline]—*force directed by self-chosen leaders.*"[29]

Draft 1, which actually ensued from MacLeish's text, displays Roosevelt's linguistic disparagement of the Duce and the Fuehrer. Although Robert Ivie revealed that FDR used "decivilized language" and metaphors of force in his pre-war discourse, Ivie did not treat this speech or show what language was Roosevelt's or a speechwriter's. FDR penned a long insert that portrayed both a mechanized state and warfare in stern terms:

We see today in stark reality some of the consequences of the machine age. Where control of machines has been retained in the hands of mankind, untold benefits have accrued to mankind. For mankind was then the master, the machine was the servant. But . . . The machine in the hands of irresponsible conquerors becomes the master; mankind is not only the servant but the victim.

He also refuted a metaphor in which the isolationists erroneously found succor: "Some indeed still hold to the now obvious delusion that we of the United States can safely permit the United States to become a lone island in a world dominated by the philosophy of force." Since Roosevelt usually corrected his drafts with pencil, it is interesting to note that he pressed down hard on "contemptuous" in the following emendation: "day by the [supercilious] *contemptuous* unpitying masters of [the philosophy of force] *other continents.*" Not only was "contemptuous" a more demeaning word and more common than "supercilious," but the addition of "other continents" avoided the redundancy of "the philosophy of force" in the previous paragraph and bore witness to Mussolini's mastery of Ethiopia in Africa.[30]

Although not in FDR's hand, two inserts were appended to Draft 1. One was directed to the French, whom words could not help at this late date:

On this 10th day of June, 1940, in this University founded by the first great American teacher of democracy, we send forth our prayers and our hopes to those beyond the seas who are maintaining with magnificent valor their battle for freedom.

The other emendation told the American people of Roosevelt's program that would eventually help the British:

That is a component part of national defense itself. The program unfolds and into it will fit the responsibility and the opportunity of every man and woman to preserve our heritage in days of peril.[31]

The origins of the famous reference to the Italian stiletto—"the hand that held the dagger has plunged it into the back of its neighbor"—must be revised. Textual evidence in the various drafts does not support the view that the phrase was in a draft, was removed at Sumner Welles's request, and was then reinserted by Roosevelt. The phrase appears in none of the drafts, and unfortunately the reading copy is lost; however the stenographic shorthand report, which was given as a press release, does have the phrase in it as an addition. Moreover, a close examination of the address as FDR delivered it suggests that he inserted the line at the time of utterance in an impromptu fashion.[32]

For this speech, as for no other before it, the letters and telegrams urged specific actions in sending arms and material to Britain and France. Doubtless, FDR's speech in part motivated these responses, but the messages seemed to indicate that the objective reality to which Roosevelt spoke was beginning to dawn on people. To be sure, a writer from Arlington, Virginia, sent "a respectful protest against the bitterness and hysteria in your speech last evening." However, the *Christian Century* caught the essence of Roosevelt's speech that gave "vent to feelings held by the overwhelming majority of his countrymen," two examples of which follow: "Only a fearless man would have had the courage to speak as you did. Be assured that the true American is unconditionally behind you" and "Isolationists are helping Hitler and the WHOP conquer America."[33]

"ARSENAL OF DEMOCRACY," DECEMBER 29, 1940

Elected for a third term and with his "neighbor's garden hose" press conference behind him and a congressional battle on Lend-Lease, H. R. 1776, before him, Roosevelt typically took his presidency to the people in a Fireside Chat that he disingenuously described as "not a fireside chat on war."

Prefacing his remarks with an allusion to the banking crisis of 1933, Roosevelt stated the urgency with a sentence he dictated for the third draft: "Never before since Jamestown and Plymouth Rock has our American civilization been in such danger as now." The rhetorical devices he used to seek the assent of the American people and ultimately the Congress on sending guns, ships, and planes to the British were masterfully conceived. His strategy was two-pronged: fear appeals to intensify allegiance from his partisans and to move those less committed toward his position, and the scapegoat technique in a guilt-by-association application to denigrate the isolationists, which concomitantly reinforced why one should patriotically support President Roosevelt.[34]

The address was laced with fear appeals. He quoted Hitler, who proclaimed he could beat any power in the world; told how the range of modern bombers "is ever being increased"; quoted Nazi doublespeak on "restoring order" and "protecting" conquered countries from "aggression"; for the Irish-American vote, asked rhetorically if Ireland could hold out if Britain fell, and for the Italian-American vote, predicted Italians would soon "be embraced to death by their allies"; and in brutally realistic language, declared, "The history of recent years proves that shootings and chains and concentration camps are not simply the transient tools but the very altars of modern dictatorships."[35]

Roosevelt set up the isolationists and America Firsters by quoting a telegram: "Please, Mr. President, don't frighten us by telling us the facts." Immediately thereafter he used an insert prepared by Adolph Berle that characterized opponents as fearful children: "Frankly and definitely there is danger ahead—danger against which we must prepare. But we well know that we cannot escape danger, or the fear of it, by crawling into bed and pulling the covers over our heads." FDR then debunked Hitler's nonaggression pacts, colloquially reminded his audience that the American hemisphere had the "most tempting loot," and then frontally attacked his adversaries. Allowing that many important Americans were "aiding and abetting" the work of foreign agents bent on sapping the homeland, he used affirmation by denial to denigrate them: "I do not charge these American citizens with being foreign agents. But I do charge them with doing exactly the kind of work that the dictators want done in the United States." He deprecated the appeasers by showing that peace with the Nazis came only at the price of total surrender. Dismissing cowards who championed a negotiated peace, Roosevelt dispatched them with a metaphor that identified them with those who would cravenly submit to a "gang of outlaws." Having culled the chaff from the wheat, Roosevelt rhetorically assured that patriotic Americans would be loath to associate with those thusly scapegoated.[36]

In the latter part of his address, he buttressed his proposed aid to Britain. FDR changed the nature of the draft to support his pleas for these materials and to preempt a charge from the isolationists that the United States would be dragged somehow into the war by his proposal: "to support the [fight against the Axis] nations *defending themselves against attack by the Axis than if we acquiesce in their defeat*, submit tamely to an Axis victory, and wait our turn to be [dragged into] *the object of attack in* another war later on." He strengthened the text to show how vital the armaments were: "[If we can only] *Emphatically we must* get these weapons to them." Additionally, he used an insert prepared by Berle to assuage audience reservations: "If we are to be completely honest with ourselves, we must admit there is risk in any course we may take. But I deeply believe that the great majority of our people agree that the course that I advocate involves the least risk and the greatest hope for world peace.'' Thus, Roosevelt consistently affirmed the theme he had used in urging the repeal of the embargo provisions on September 21, 1939: Lend-Lease, rather than leading to war, would in fact keep the United States out of war. Lest anyone miss the point, he declared they could ''nail any talk about sending armies to Europe as deliberate untruths.''[37]

Unfortunately, it is unclear exactly where or how the ''arsenal of democracy'' phrase was worked into the speech. Rosenman took credit for inserting it without stating in what draft; however, Robert Sherwood claimed it was from Harry Hopkins, but he did not indicate in what draft Hopkins inserted it. Both Rosenman and Sherwood agreed that it came originally from Jean Monnet, a Frenchman. Either version of the insertion could be correct because both men, in addition to Berle, worked on the speech. The drafts are no help. The phrase is not in the first two drafts but appears in the fourth one. Obviously, the phrase was placed in the third draft, but it is incomplete and so the genesis of the phrase remains a mystery.[38]

The responses to Roosevelt's rhetorical appeal were important. Typical of the unpersuaded was the letter from Muskogee, Oklahoma: ''Deliberation convinces me your words getting supplies to England means convoying, that means ships sunk, that means war. Don't! A father of six sons.'' A man of German descent from Elgin, Illinois, wrote, ''What did Britain ever do for us?'' However, others responded favorably: Schenectady, New York; ''Agree completely with your speech tonight keep going but much faster''; Brooklyn, New York; ''I am with you 100% in your program to defend America as you outlined it''; Baltimore, Maryland, ''We have been sitting on the fence but we now have the go sign with you as an inspiration''; and Louisville, Kentucky, ''This *is* an emergency [italics in original].'' Most important, however, were the national polls.

Of those who heard or read the address, 61 percent agreed with FDR's views while 9 percent disagreed. Approximately the same amount of respondents, about 50 percent in early 1940 and rising to 70 percent by late 1940, believed the United States should aid France and Britain short-of-war. Moreover, the public opinion polls from 1937 to Pearl Harbor demonstrated that consistently over 60 percent, sometimes as high as 80 percent, of those polled favored increased spending on the army, navy, and air force even if it meant paying more taxes. Thus, there was clear support for Roosevelt's short-of-war policies. However, such measures were open to differing interpretations. The Fireside Chat was his opening salvo to begin the battle for an expanded Lend-Lease, and he brought more rhetorical guns to bear in his Annual Message of 1941.[39]

THE "FOUR FREEDOMS" ADDRESS, JANUARY 6, 1941

For Lend-Lease, as in the Court fight, FDR delivered two eloquent speeches, one on the heels of the other. The significant difference is that Roosevelt succeeded in 1941. Although the talk was his Annual Message, to which Constitutional requirement he made reference at the beginning of the speech, it was delivered to the people as well as to the Congress. This speech has been investigated thoroughly by Laura Crowell, so there is no compelling reason to reduplicate her work. Rather, the focus here is to illuminate the rhetorical techniques FDR used.[40]

For the isolationists, he designed appeals not so much to change their minds but to convey to his wider and wiser audience the folly and danger of their ostrich-like logic. Whereas the America Firsters espoused a passive isolation on the part of the United States, Roosevelt inverted their policy to show its dark underside. Adroitly turning the tables on them, he demonstrated that isolationist policy actually enabled the Axis to operate actively on the United States and "to lock us in behind an ancient Chinese wall. . . . we oppose enforced isolation." "Every realist," he said, knows democracy is "being directly assailed"; therefore, isolationists must not be "realists." Moreover, he caricatured their stand: "In times like these it is immature—and incidentally, untrue—for anybody to brag that an unprepared America, singlehanded, and with one hand tied behind its back, can hold off the whole world." And he implied the isolationists were "soft-headed." These aspersions probably would not win over the minority of isolationist Americans, but they were nevertheless good arguments to reinforce the majority who favored increased aid to Britain short-of-war.

Roosevelt evidently read the opinion polls and spoke as the majority's vox populi:

We know that enduring peace cannot be bought at the cost of other people's freedom.

In the recent national election there was no substantial difference between the two great parties in respect to that national policy. No issue was fought out on this line before the American electorate. Today it is abundantly evident that American citizens everywhere are demanding and supporting speedy and complete action in recognition of obvious danger.

In an appeal to self-interest without going to war, he said: "Our most useful and immediate role is to act as an arsenal for them as well as for ourselves. They do not need manpower. . . . " He also cleverly refuted an isolationist argument, that Lend-Lease was an act of war against the dictators, with an argument based on stark examples: "Such aid is not an act of war. . . . When the dictators, if the dictators, are ready to make war on us, they will not wait for an act of war on our part. They did not wait for Norway or Belgium or the Netherlands to commit an act of war."

The rhetorical coup in this speech was to make the war issue subservient to domestic policy. This was consistent with his campaign rhetoric in 1940 and helped to defuse charges that he was a warmonger. He accomplished this masking in a brilliantly conceived transition: "Certainly this is no time for any of us to stop thinking about the social and economic problems which are the root cause of the social revolution which is today a supreme factor in the world." After

Table 4
Aid or War

		Aid England Short of War	Declare War
March 8,	1940	51%	10%
April 17,	1940	27%	5%
May 23,	1940	65%	4%
June 11,	1940	73%	5%
June 25,	1940	67%	5%
September 17,	1940	76%	5%
December 11,	1940	78%	3%
March 29,	1941	73%	7%
April 25,	1941	67%	9%

listing his domestic goals for various constituents, he hinted at a progressive income tax and softened the need for higher taxes by declaring no one would "get rich out of this program." (In an earlier part of his speech, he used a much better metaphor to express the same thought: "We must especially beware of that small group of selfish men who would clip the wings of the American eagle in order to feather their own nests.")

The famous "four essential human freedoms," listed in the peroration, elevated the speech's purpose. In contrast to Hitler, who made domestic policy the slave of foreign conquest, Roosevelt proclaimed domestic values that subsumed Lend-Lease. Indeed, the speech is known more for its lofty "four freedoms" than for its appeal for guns, tanks, and planes. After enumerating the liberties FDR championed—freedom of speech and expression, worship of God, from want, and from fear—he used three epistrophes of "everywhere in the world" to conclude the first three clauses, for variety changed to "anywhere in the world" after the fourth freedom.[41]

In early March, the Senate passed an amended but not gutted Lend-Lease Act by 60–31 and the House by 317–71.[42] Tables 4 and 5 show why.

It is quite clear that public opinion moved in support for aiding Great Britain short-of-war and for the United States to enter the war, although neither shifts could be termed dramatic, except for entering the war a month before Pearl Harbor. Therefore, it is true, as Ralph Towne suggested, that FDR can be credited with some success:

Over and over, there was a shift in public opinion (as measured by the polls) in favor of Roosevelt's position after one or more speeches had been given—a definite positive correlation. Also interesting was an occasional situation where no speeches were given

Table 5
Whether to Fight

		Go In	Stay Out
June 11,	1940	19%	81%
June 25,	1940	14%	86%
July 3,	1940	15%	85%
September 26,	1940	17%	83%
November 30,	1940	12%	88%
December 31,	1940	15%	85%
January 28,	1941	14%	86%
February 27,	1941	7%	83%
February 28,	1941	14%	86%
April 8,	1941	19%	81%
April 25,	1941	21%	79%
June 7,	1941	24%	76%
June 24,	1941	21%	79%
July 9,	1941	26%	67%
July 29,	1941	20%	75%
August 5,	1941	20%	75%
August 19,	1941	74%	20%
August 27,	1941	21%	74%
September 9,	1941	26%	69%
November 5,	1941	47%	46%

by Roosevelt for an extended period of time and where results of polls show a shift against the position held by the President—a negative trend in time.

On the debit side, however, were those obstinate figures, holding in the 80–70 percent range until very late 1941, that indicates an overwhelming majority of the respondents did not want to go to war. The isolationists read the same polls Roosevelt did and fought him, with tacit support from their constituents, every inch of the legislative battle. The converse of that argument also applies: the congressmen who voted for Lend-Lease obviously read the polls that favored aid short-of-war. Therefore, one can say FDR had a qualified success in Lend-Lease. Whether he, and the Congress, was abreast of public opinion or followed it closely is unclear; it is quite clear that Roosevelt was not ahead of it.[43]

FIRESIDE CHAT ON "FREEDOM OF THE SEAS," SEPTEMBER 11, 1941

This radio address has not been, but can be, conceived as an instance of presidential crisis rhetoric. Theodore Windt determined that the Commander-in-Chief uses the genre to ensure support from the people and the Congress by creating a *rhetorical* crisis. In a speech, the president enunciates New Facts that produce, according to the chief executive, a New Situation for which the president presents his policy, often *fait accompli*, and then argues for its acceptance by appealing to Americans' sense of patriotism and manliness and by depicting the aggressor-U. S. relationship in devil/angel, good/bad, black/white dichotomies in language.[44]

Roosevelt wasted no time in reporting the New Facts. The destroyer *Greer* was attacked by a German submarine: "She was then and there attacked by a submarine. Germany admits that it was a German submarine. The submarine deliberately fired a torpedo at the *Greer*, followed by another torpedo attack." He condemned the attack by defining it as "piracy—piracy legally and morally." Moreover, he compounded Nazi perfidy by listing other acts of naval violence: the merchant ship *Robin Moor* sunk, a battleship dogged by a German submarine, and the sinking of the *Sesa* and *Steel Seafarer*.

Cleverly, Roosevelt at first assured his audience he would react to the New Situation with "feet on the ground." He said he was concerned not so much about an "incident" but about "a general plan" of Nazi actions. He described in devil/angel dichotomies Hitler's plots, machinations, and sabotage in the New World. Intertwined with these characterizations of the Nazis, Roosevelt subtlely attacked the isolationists in asides: "It is time for all Americans . . . to stop being deluded by the romantic notion that the Americas can go on living happily and peacefully in a Nazi-dominated world" and "Normal practices of diplomacy—note writing—are of no possible use in dealing with international outlaws who sink our ships and kill our citizens." Concluding the New Situation, he compared the Nazis to rattlesnakes and metaphorically stated that words would not work: "We cannot bring about the downfall of Nazism by the use of long-range invective."

Rather than enunciating the policy and then justifying it, as later presidents such as John Kennedy and Richard Nixon would do, Roosevelt reversed the process. Twice, he declared we could not be hairsplitters and twice he claimed the time for action was now. A final justification was the bandwagon effect argued by analogy: John Adams had ordered the Navy to "clean out" European ships that "infested" American waters, and Thomas Jefferson had ordered the Navy "to end the attacks" on American ships. In that verbal context, FDR finally revealed his plan. (Although this speech is often known as the "shoot on sight" speech, FDR did not actually use those words until the Navy Day address, October 27, 1941.) Notice the circumlocuted language:

It is no act of war on our part when we decide to protect the seas that are vital to American defense. The aggression is not ours. Ours is solely defense.

But let this warning be clear. From now on, if German or Italian vessels of war enter the waters, the protection of which is necessary for American defense, they do so at their own peril.

The order which I have given as Commander in Chief of the United States Army and Navy are to carry out that policy—at once.

The sole responsibility rests upon Germany. There will be no shooting unless Germany continues to seek it.

In order to seek assent, FDR called on the people to face the crisis with "courage," "resolution," "clear heads and fearless hearts," and "duty."[45]

This speech illustrates several of the complaints that Windt lodged against presidential crisis rhetoric. First, the policy is often enacted as the president announces it, thus bypassing democratic debate. Second, the president often lies about/or misrepresents the New Facts. In truth, Roosevelt used the *Greer* episode to announce a policy that had been quietly enacted in mid-August at Argentia, Newfoundland. Notwithstanding what Roosevelt said about "Hitler's propaganda bureau," Hitler had studiously avoided an "incident" with the United States. Actually, Roosevelt was looking for one. His policy to shoot at any German submarine led to the *Greer*'s chasing the submarine. After it was depth-charged by a British airplane, the sub fired in self-defense. Although it was technically a "blunt fact" that the German submarine fired first, FDR neglected to inform the country that he was looking for a casus belli and that the German sub had been goaded into firing first.

Joseph Lash found FDR's account of the *Greer* episode "troublesome," and Robert Dallek observed that he "created a precedent for manipulation of public opinion." Indeed, Senator J. William Fullbright seconded Windt's condemnation of presidential crisis rhetoric: "FDR's deviousness in a good cause made it much easier for LBJ to practice the same kind of deviousness in a bad cause."[46]

WAR MESSAGE, DECEMBER 8, 1941

At 12:30 P. M., December 8, 1941, President Franklin D. Roosevelt delivered the best speech he ever composed. Although he received very slight help on it, the address is essentially FDR's diction. Hermann Stelzner has already investigated the language of the speech from a microscopic perspective, a focus on how "the speech *is*, not how it came to be" (his italics); therefore, the aim here is to unfold the speech and, in that laying out, demonstrate how FDR composed a speech that is illustrative of presidential crisis rhetoric. Whereas Roosevelt had in effect circumvented the war-making powers of the Congress by ordering an undeclared naval war with Germany, which he sought to justify *ex post facto* in the "Freedom of the Seas" Fireside Chat, he did in the War Message ask the Congress to declare war. That blunts the negative connotations about deviousness and circumvention inherent in crisis rhetoric. As the techniques of rhetoric are amoral, the War Message also demonstrates that crisis rhetoric can urge good ends through valid persuasive means. For, the vital difference between the War Message and the "Freedom of the Seas" speech is that Roosevelt did not misrepresent the facts.[47]

FDR dictated the speech to his secretary, Grace Tully. Her typed dictation became the first draft. A second draft exists. It contains his emendations from draft one. Curiously, however, he did not make changes on draft two but went back to draft one and made corrections on it. That is, draft one has words on it that are not in draft two but are in draft three; therefore, draft three is actually a compilation of changes on draft one. Evidence in the form of different handwriting suggests that he went over the third draft at least twice: he added the anaphora of several "Last night" sentences on page two in a large and bold hand, whereas changes on pages three and four were made in smaller and narrower penmanship, presumably at a different sitting. FDR's dictation and emendations were a culmination and vindication of his war rhetoric since the late 1930s. In this speech, he naturally continued expressing his thoughts, as he had in his earlier talks, to demarcate dichotomies between the aggressors and the United States. In order to demonstrate how he created these polarities within the context of the New Facts and New Situation, the procedure is to give a paragraph-by-paragraph analysis of the speech. Each paragraph, or sometimes a group of related paragraphs, will be quoted as he delivered them and then analyzed. Unfortunately, the reading copy has been lost. An extant stenographic copy of the address, with deletions and additions, suggests the nature of the final manuscript. What follows, then, is a probable reconstruction of Roosevelt's reading copy. His oral deletions are bracketed, his ad libitum words italicized (the paragraphs are grouped for clarity of discussion).[48]

[To the Congress of the United States:] *Mr. Vice President, Mr. Speaker, and Members of the Senate and the House of Representatives*:
    Yesterday, December seventh, 1941—a date which will live in infamy—the United States of America was suddenly and deliberately attacked by naval and air forces of the Empire of Japan.

The New Facts were delivered gravely and announced in the blackest manner. On draft one, he inserted dashes, to replace the original commas, in order to stress the phrase in apposition, which he did orally by pausing slightly; but note also that the dashes featured the appositive for the reading audience. Other significant emendations reveal his efforts to portray Japanese perfidy. On draft one, he had written: "a date which will live in [world history] *infamy*—the United States of America was [simultaneously] *suddenly* and deliberately attacked by naval and air forces of the Empire of Japan *without warning*." But then he crossed out "without warning." It may be that he noticed "without warning" and "suddenly" were redundant, but more likely he added "suddenly" and then crossed out "without warning" to keep the force of parallelism with the adverbs. At any rate, "infamy" and "suddenly," in conjunction with his dictated "deliberately," communicated the moral outrage he had so long expressed. In juxtaposition, the next paragraph stressed the purity of U. S. motives and actions.

The United States was at peace with that nation and, at the solicitation of Japan, was still in conversation with its Government and its Emperor looking toward the maintenance of peace in the Pacific. Indeed, one hour after Japanese air squadrons had commenced bombing in *the American island of* Oahu, the Japanese Ambassador to the United States and his colleague delivered to [the] *our* Secretary of State a formal reply to a recent American message. *And* [W]while this reply stated that it seemed useless to continue the existing diplomatic negotiations, it contained no threat or hint of war or *of* armed attack.

Cognizant at the time of utterance that many Americans might not know what or where Oahu was, he ad-libbed "the American island of" to establish it was U. S. territory. Changing "the" to "our" had the effect of clarifying whose secretary of state it was and also intensified the polarities between Japan and the United States. Doubtless, he added the second "of" for vocal parallelism.

A deconstruction of the speech as delivered demonstrates that he built the devil/angel images into the address: "The United States was at the moment at peace with that nation and *at the solicitation of Japan* was [continuing the] *still in* conversation[s] with its Government and its Emperor. . . . Japanese air squadrons had commenced bombing in [Hawaii and the Philippines] *Oahu . . .* a formal reply to a [former] *recent American* message [from the Secretary]. *While* [T]this reply [contained a statement] *stated* that *it seemed useless to continue the existing* diplomatic negotiations [must be considered at an end, it] *it* contained no threat [and no] *or* hint of [a] *war or* armed attack." It is not remarkable that Roosevelt excised "must be considered at an end": if he had let it stand, Americans could easily infer that he knew war was imminent. Rather, "it seemed useless" does not quite close the door on negotiations, hence there was no signal of impending hostilities. Words such as "at the solicitation of Japan," "still in," "one hour after," and "While" reinforced the image that Japan had caused the New Facts, that the United States was trusting and was duped. A small change on the third draft continued that train of thought: "The United States was [at the moment] at peace"; the deletion of "at the moment," a qualifier, communicated categorically that the United States was at peace with Japan. In the next paragraph, he narrated more New Facts that revealed additional Japanese duplicity.

It will be recorded that the distance of Hawaii from Japan makes it obvious that the attack was deliberately planned many days or even weeks ago. During the intervening time the Japanese Government has deliberately sought to deceive the United States by false statements and expressions of hope for continued peace.

Interestingly, FDR spoke only of Hawaii in this paragraph, as he did in paragraph two. He emended his dictation in this manner: "It will be recorded that the distance[s of Manila and especially] of Hawaii from Japan makes it obvious that the[ese] attack[s] [were] *was* deliberately planned many days *or even weeks* ago.'' In the popular mind, Hawaii was probably more associated with the United States than were the Philippines, hence was more vital to U. S. security. Moreover, the stressing of ''distance'' was more telling with Japan to Hawaii than with Japan to the Philippines, and ''distance'' reinforced the images of ''deliberately planned'' and ''deliberately sought to deceive'' (note that this is the third time FDR used a form of the word *deliberate*) that denigrated the Japanese. In the next paragraph, he gave the crux of the New Facts, but these were attenuated by general language.

The attack yesterday on the Hawaiian Islands has caused severe damage to American naval and military forces. *I regret to tell you that* [V]very many American lives have been lost. In addition American ships have been reported torpedoed on the high seas between San Francisco and Honolulu.

For the third time, he excised Manila as he had in previous paragraphs: ''The attack[s] yesterday on [Manila and on the island of Oahu have] *the Hawaiian Islands has. . . .* '' Mindful that isolationists charged that he wanted to get the United States into the war, he may have inserted the ''regret'' phrase to communicate his sorrow. Indeed, it is perhaps a measure of the man that although his diction does not imply he is finally getting his wish, neither does it express any sorrow that the war has come, and this from a man who hated war.

Yesterday the Japanese Government also launched an attack against Malaya.
    Last night Japanese forces attacked Hong Kong.
    Last night Japanese forces attacked Guam.
    Last night Japanese forces attacked the Philippine Islands.
    Last night the Japanese attacked Wake Island.
    And [T]this morning the Japanese attacked Midway Island.

The accumulation of New Facts in anaphora were added to the drafts as the cables came to the White House. On the first draft he added:

Last night Japanese forces attacked Guam.
"   "   "   "   "   the Philippine Islands [sic].

On the third draft, he added more attacks:

Yesterday the Japanese Government also launched an attack against Malaya.
Last night Japanese forces attacked Hong Kong.
Last night Japanese forces attacked Guam.
Last night Japanese forces attacked the Philippine Islands.
Last night the Japanese attacked Wake Island.
This morning the Japanese attacked Midway Island.

These New Facts led inexorably to the New Situation that he characterized in summary fashion:

Japan has, therefore, undertaken a surprise offensive extending throughout the Pacific area. The facts of yesterday *and today* speak for themselves. The people of the United States have already formed their opinions and well understand the implications to the very life and safety of our nation.

The vox populi let the facts figuratively speak for themselves and enunciated the people's will because they "have already formed their opinions" and "understand" the "facts." In this vein, he made an improvement in diction that intensified the "implications": "understand the implications [these attacks bear on] *to* the *very* safety of our nation." The New Facts led inexorably to the President's perception of the New Situation.

As Commander-in-Chief of the Army and Navy I have directed that all measures be taken for our defense.
  But always will [we] *our whole nation* remember the character of the onslaught against us.
  No matter how long it may take us to overcome this premeditated invasion, the American people in their righteous might will win through to absolute victory.
  I believe *that* I interpret the will of the Congress and of the people when I assert that we will not only defend ourselves to the uttermost but will make *it* very certain that this form of treachery shall never *again* [endanger us] *endanger us* [again].

In the first sentence, FDR emended his original dictation by striking "of course": "As Commander-in-Chief of the Army and Navy I have [, of course,] directed that all measures be taken for our defense." A competent president would "of course" act, so by deleting these words, he removed any doubt that he might have contemplated waiting to act or would have acted otherwise.

In the second sentence, he made two ad libitum adjustments. He inserted orally the adverb "But" to modify the verb phrase "always will . . . remember." Its genesis is interesting. He originally dictated "Long will we remember"; on draft three he substituted "[Long] *Always* will we remember." Thus, his diction progressed increasingly categorically from "Long" to "Always" and finally to "But always." At the very time of utterance, it might have seemed to him that the unconditional nature of "But always" logically demanded diction more demonstrative than the pronoun "we" so he said "our whole nation," which is more concrete. The impact of his unqualified language, in conjunction with his climaxing delivery, motivated the first congressional applause.

The third sentence, "No matter how long," was an insert that Roosevelt composed on the first draft. This emendation is proof that FDR went back to the first draft to make additional changes because the so-called second draft does not have the insert typed on it. That sentence was surely one of FDR's most eloquent inventions—notice the polarities between "premeditated invasion" and "religious might," "absolute victory"—and his rousing cadence and superb phrasing prompted loud and prolonged cheers and applause from the Congress.

Paradoxically, Roosevelt diluted his presidential role in the opening part of the fourth sentence. He said he believed he interpreted the will of the Congress and people. This bespoke hesitancy. In his original dictation, he was unconditional: "I speak the will of the Congress and of the people [of this country]." (He doubtlessly deleted "of this country" because it was redundant.) On the third draft, he made the correction he actually delivered: "I [speak] *believe I interpret* the will." Without putting too fine a point upon it, this small emendation supports the thesis that FDR was abreast of public opinion, but was not ahead of it: "I speak" suggests an assured leader in the vanguard; "I believe I interpret" implies uncertainty, a sounding out of the ranks before ordering the charge. This kind of analysis is supported in the next paragraph, but first an interesting point can be illustrated concerning FDR's aural memory.

Roosevelt dictated: "but will see to it that this form of treachery." On draft three, he made a change and left out the "it": "but will [see to it] *make very certain* that this form of treachery." However, when he delivered the speech the same day, he probably remembered subconsciously the "it" he had excised and spoke accordingly: "but will make it very certain that this form of treachery."

Hostilities exist. There is no blinking at the fact that our people, our territory and our interests are in grave danger.

With confidence in our armed forces—with the unbounding determination of our people—we will gain the inevitable triumph—so help us God.

I ask that the Congress declare that since the unprovoked and dastardly attack by Japan on Sunday, December seventh, *1941*, a state of war has existed between the United States and the Japanese Empire.

As originally dictated, the "Hostilities exist" paragraph concluded the "I speak" paragraph. On the first draft, FDR sectioned it to stand separately as he delivered it. This sectioning made sense. Since hostilities existed, since American interests were threatened, he therefore asked the Congress to declare war in his next and final paragraph. There matters stood until Harry Hopkins entered the process. He noticed there was no reference in the third draft to the Deity, so he composed the "With confidence" sentence and inserted it after the "Hostilities exist" paragraph and before the formal declaration. Although Robert Sherwood thought this sentence "the most platitudinous line in the speech," Stelzner correctly observed its eloquence: "Once underway the line cannot be turned nor resisted. Its sweep catches all."[49]

However, not all of Hopkins's advice was helpful. On his draft, Hopkins underlined "mincing" and placed a question mark above it. In consultation with Hopkins, FDR was evidently motivated to make this change: "There is no [mincing] *blinking* the fact." Stelzner made a convoluted explanation of why "blinking" was more appropriate than "mincing." As originally dictated, "mincing" was fitting because it was an analogous verb to "speak" and "assert": "no mincing" means not to soften ones spoken words, whereas "no blinking" has the sense of not evading the issue. Had not FDR minced his words in his previous rhetoric because the people had blinked at the facts?[50]

With Hopkins's insert, the "Hostilities" paragraph became rhetorical overkill. In FDR's original dictation, the New Facts led to the New Situation, hence to FDR's and Americans' response through his rhetoric to the Japanese attack. He was consubstantial with his audience; his rhetoric assumed the nation's assent. Then why rehearse that hostilities existed, that the United States was in grave danger?

Two reasons may explain FDR's motivation. The first one relates to the flow of the original dictation. There, he made a logical link between the hostilities and his formal request for a declaration of war: "Hostilities exist. . . . I, therefore, ask that the Congress declare." The "therefore" was warranted in that context. The second reason, and by far the more revealing one, is that Roosevelt was so accustomed to repeating over and over in his previous speeches the danger of Axis aggression that he recapitulated that theme even in this address. His habit illustrates Windt's thesis that presidents repeat the rhetorical past, and in this case, Roosevelt reiterated his own past persuasive practices.[51]

But the "therefore" was not delivered. Stelzner noted, "The formal, logical sign is unnecessary." With Hopkins's insert, Stelzner is correct. But he misread the third draft, contending that the "therefore" was in all three drafts. It was not, as the third draft illustrates: "I [, therefore,] ask that." On this draft, FDR inserted a caret for Hopkins's "With confidence" sentence. Then, he must have realized that the insert obviated the "therefore" and he crossed it out. Hence, Hopkins's insert divided the logical progression in FDR's first draft from cause to effect, but demarcated a cleaner formal request for war. The point is the original dictation, more than the final speech as helped by Hopkins, was a truer reflection of Roosevelt's rhetorical habits.[52]

Surprisingly, there was very little public reaction mail, about one-third of a box, to this address. Two examples testify to Roosevelt's eloquence. A man from Columbus, Ohio, was finally persuaded: "I have always been a Republican and have opposed many of your policies . . . but now I realize that you have been right in your analysis of the situation ever since Hitler began his overrunning of the various European states." A newspaper man from New York City appreciated the President's written and oral style: "I think it was the finest bit of writing—and speaking—I have ever seen or heard."[53]

SUMMARY

Rather than recapitulating the various points from the section on the preparation-for-war rhetoric, I will let Roosevelt speak for himself. Finally vindicated, he spoke two famous lines in his Fireside Chat two days after Pearl Harbor. These intimately reveal his persuasive motives and responses. To borrow author

James MacGregor Burns's famous metaphor, the first quotation is FDR the fox, "We don't like it—we didn't want to get in it—but we are in it and we're going to fight it with everything we've got"; the second is Roosevelt the lion, "We are going to win the war and we are going to win the peace that follows."[54]

CONCLUSION

This chapter on Franklin D. Roosevelt's purge and war rhetoric ends with uncertainty regarding the rhetorical presidency. If rhetorical critics base a study of presidential persuasions on public opinion polls, it seems they run the risk of committing the fallacy of *post hoc, ergo propter hoc*, or appropriately translated, "after the speech therefore because of the speech." At the other extreme, except for *ex cathedra* pronouncements about effect, how can one warrant that FDR's rhetoric was successful? Critics continually confront the difficulty in separating stimuli from responses and causes from effects when Roosevelt addressed the American audience.

He did not persuade the people or the Congress to go to war. The Japanese did that on December 7, 1941, and on December 8 FDR acknowledged the people had "already formed their opinions." He did not persuade on the proposition that the people purge Democratic candidates politically distasteful to their president.

What is not so easily discerned is the proposition of aid to Great Britain short-of-war. Ostensibly, he had a measure of success at the public opinion polling places and at the ballot box in 1940. But President Roosevelt and congressmen, both pro and con members, read the same polls. A similar "yes, but" argument applies to the issues of arming the United States and preparing psychologically the country for war. The problem is did Roosevelt persuade, or did other stimuli such as Axis aggression do it, or did he capitalize on these events with responsive rhetorical techniques?

In fact, this problem is pervasive throughout this study. On the proposition that the federal government should solve national problems with national legislation, FDR won assent in 1932 and overwhelmingly in 1936. Yet the Depression, Hoover, and Landon surely helped his cause by enabling him to marshall the kind of rhetorical techniques he used in those campaigns. On the questions should the New Deal continue for a third term and should the United States arm for defense in 1940, Roosevelt won by a slimmer margin, but he certainly made the most of Willkie's kind of campaign. Although Dewey was his toughest competitor, Roosevelt's rhetorical response, aided by the luck of the governor's fumbling the United Nation's armed forces issue, contributed to a winning campaign.

In fine, this study implodes to the nexus of public opinion and persuasive technique. To eschew either obviates the usefulness of both. Whatever the relationship, it should be clear that the public's reaction was motivated in part by

FDR's rhetoric, just as his persuasive devices were a response to his audiences' attitudes. By combining opinion polls with the practice of rhetoric, which in Roosevelt's case sometimes persuaded, sometimes reinforced, and sometimes failed, one can pronounce FDR a preeminent presidential persuader.

8

Writing the Rhetoric

This chapter is the counterpart of the one on delivery. There, the focus was on how Roosevelt used voice and gestures to communicate his speeches; here, the inquiry is how he composed the words. To the extent possible, this chapter attempts to shape FDR's theory of presidential rhetoric.

As a point of departure, it is illuminating to compare contemporary speakers of FDR's era. On the newsreels and radio and in person, Father Charles Coughlin, Senator Huey Long, and Fuehrer Adolph Hitler had in common with President Roosevelt the ability to electrify their audiences primarily with their forceful deliveries. Devoid of a live dynamism, however, Coughlin's, Long's, and Hitler's speeches lost considerable voltage on the printed page. Roosevelt's did not. Neither did the speaker's whose oratorical career was similar to FDR's—the Reverend Harry Emerson Fosdick. As a famed preacher at Riverside Church in New York City, whose National Vespers radio program reached millions from 1927 to 1946, Fosdick composed his sermons to be delivered from the pulpit and to be read, with little or no editing, in his nineteen books of collected sermons published during this era. At the highest pinnacle of artistic achievement, which Fosdick and FDR attained, good written and oral style meld. Thus, Fosdick's books of sermons and FDR's texts of speeches in the newspapers were not dependent for effect only on delivery. David Halberstam observed that FDR's "speeches were scripted not to be read in the newspapers but to be heard aloud." He is correct by half.[1]

First, Roosevelt recognized the requirements of a president to be distant but not detached, apart but not aloof. Verbally, he achieved that posture by selecting language that was a cut above ordinary parlance but not *haute couture*. Time and again it has been illustrated throughout this study that he took care to excise language that speech writers thought elegant or tasteful but that FDR believed inappropriate. One instance from his Syracuse, New York, speech, 1936, in which he sarcastically scored the silk-hatted economic royalist who fell into the water only to be rescued by a New Dealer, reiterates the point: "After the old gentleman had been [resuscitated] *revived*." On the other hand, FDR's favorite stylistic techniques elevated his talks. Alliteration, anaphora, and metaphor were the hallmarks of FDR's diction.[2]

The convergence of alliteration and anaphora for a written-oral communication was purposeful. On the printed page, the reader's eye delights in successive words beginning with the same sounds, and anaphora is easily spotted in texts (it is not coincidental that three noted addresses, the Second Inaugural, the 1937 Victory Dinner Address, and the War Message, structurally abounded with anaphora). Moreover, Roosevelt delivered these passages of anaphora so that they achieved their rhetorical end of repetition and restatement, the dinning of "I see millions," "Here are . . . NOW!" and "Last night. . . . " Everyman probably could not speak nor write with such eloquence but could take vicarious pride in having voted for a president who could articulate such compelling images.

As a coiner of figurative language, FDR had an affinity for metaphor. In fact, metaphor not only established his reading-listening eloquence but also and more important served his political aims. The litany of famous phrases with which this book began helped actuate Roosevelt's presidency and are well established in U. S. political lexicon. More than mere purple patches of prose, he used metaphors for changing ends as his presidency progressed. On the moral plain, which he usually tried to attain in his speeches and addresses, the word images that conjured traditional mores and values identified the Roosevelt administration with higher, yet elusive, goals. That is, if the New Deal was not at the moment solving the Depression or if the war was going badly, Roosevelt could nevertheless claim credit for advancing the nation morally and spiritually. At the pragmatic level, metaphors—such as the Tory press, economic royalists, Republican fiction writers, and the neighbor's garden hose—had a capacity for ambiguity. Each auditor or reader could interpret the image to suit him or herself. Conversely, for much the same reasons, FDR generally eschewed statistics. He used them widely only in the 1940 campaign when actual numbers of bombers and battleships were more concrete than air power or sea power. Numbers can be refuted, whereas images, being equivocal, are hard to controvert (as Roosevelt learned when he was unable to disengage from the "Court packing" and "purge" metaphors that his enemies used to sully his schemes).

As the war approached, Roosevelt's metaphors became balefully bellicose. Constrained by law and the public opinion polls that he and also the isolationist senators and congressmen read, he only could counter foreign menaces with images that represented Hitler's and Mussolini's malignant plans for mankind. Even when the dictators' militarism became the reality to which FDR figuratively referred, American belief led only to painfully slow incremental action. Roosevelt cannot be faulted for speaking forthrightly. For the Fireside Chat on war, September 3, 1939, he pledged "no black-out of peace in the United States." For his Fireside of May 26, 1940, he made several changes on the drafts in order to strengthen the impact of his words: "to escape [the ruthlessness of war] *bombs and shells and fire.*" On the reading copy he added "*and machine gunning*"; [Give] *Please—I beg you—give* [to your nearest] *according to your means to your nearest* Red Cross chapter"; and on draft 2, he pledged help "from across the seas *from those who are still free to give it.*" In the arsenal of democracy Chat, he portrayed how Americans could "be living at the point of a gun" under "Nazi masters," and he confuted appeasers with "No man can tame a tiger into a kitten by stroking it." In his Fireside Chat on September 11, 1941, he warned graphically, "One peaceful Nation after another has met disaster because each refused to look Nazi danger squarely in the eye until it actually had them by the throat." These and other such images figuratively supported FDR's thesis that the United States had to arm itself, supply Britain, and although never openly stated, prepare for war.[3]

Second, although FDR appealed to diverse spiritual and political needs of the American people, he and his speech staff seldom seem to have paid much attention to organizational patterns to convey his thoughts. Textbooks on speech communication often include famous examples of his style, but his addresses are not models of structure. Traditionally, speeches are divided into an introduction, body, and conclusion. All of FDR's addresses have an introduction insofar as he had to start his speech, but most of them were not rousing beginnings, save for exceptions such as "This is not a fireside chat on war" and "Yesterday, December 7, 1941." It may be that Roosevelt reasoned he already had his audience's attention by the fact that he was president. Neither did he or the staff make the mainheads of his speech's body march in any methodical manner. Structure tends to compartmentalize thoughts. It may be that an organizational pattern of the first-second-third variety was purposefully avoided on the ground that the ambiguity so carefully built into an address would be clarified by baldly stated issues. This point can be illustrated best in the 1940 campaign speeches wherein FDR had to weave appeals to war and peace into the same talk. This tactic might have failed if FDR had said something to the effect of "on the one hand, but on the other." As it was, his isolationist critics saw through the obfuscation, but he did not have to do their work for them. Those who voted for FDR in 1940 were evidently comfortable enough with the inconsistency in their minds, which Roosevelt reinforced, by maintaining peace by preparing for war.

However, many of his conclusions could be classified as classical perorations—summary appeals of exceptional elegance and force. The following come immediately to mind: the New Deal convention speech in 1932; the "rendezvous with destiny" speech at Franklin Field in 1936; the Chautauqua speech, 1936, that closed with eight clauses of anaphora; the Victory Dinner Address, 1937, with seven clauses of anaphora and eight epistrophes; the "Four Freedoms" speech in 1941 that was one of Roosevelt's clearest characterizations of the essence of democratic government; and certainly the War Message, with the closing paragraph, "With confidence in . . . ," that Harry Hopkins had composed. These, and FDR's other endings, when coupled with his dynamism in delivery, produced state speeches of the highest order for his listeners and readers.

Although Roosevelt and the speech staff invested considerable time and energy in writing the rhetoric for maximum effect and diction, he was famous for ad-libbing. There were no ad libitum remarks that changed the course of history, but the practice does reveal something of the orator-writer. The cadences and phrasings that read well on paper sometimes were delivered differently. Two examples from the War Message illustrate the point. Roosevelt wrote, "the American people will in their righteous might win through to absolute victory," and dictated, "that this form of treachery shall never endanger us again." The close eye will note that he split the verb "will win" with the adverbial prepositional phrase "in their righteous might." Similarly, he dangled the adverb "again" at the end of the sentence. These went unchanged through all the drafts. Upon delivering the speech, however, FDR spoke in correct English grammar: "people in their righteous might will win" and "never again endanger us." On the other hand, the terseness that he built into the Fourth Inaugural Address was not amenable to oral delivery. For instance, he inserted a two-word verbal transition to move his train of thought from one paragraph to another: "*And so* today." In the courage from conviction thought that Sherwood composed, FDR added a "the" before "understanding," and that rendition was in the final reading copy; however, in delivering the speech, FDR inserted a "the" before "confidence" and before "courage" to maintain parallelism: "We can gain it only if we proceed with the understanding and *the* confidence and *the* courage which flow from conviction."[4]

One last significant exception to the rule that Roosevelt prepared his speeches seriously and delivered them as composed is his address to a joint session of the Congress on the Yalta conference, March 1, 1945. Both Sherwood and Rosenman noted that FDR ad-libbed considerably for this speech—Rosenman thought some of the remarks were "irrelevant" and some bordered on the "ridiculous"—and the reference to his leg braces was ad libitum. The Yalta speech was also an example that the text read better than it was delivered, which was in halting phrasings often punctuated with pauses and coughs. Overall, though, Roosevelt and his staff composed his speeches to be both heard and read. Generally, he excelled in both media.[5]

Third, although the motto of the United States is *E pluribus unum* [from many, one], Roosevelt, as the vox populi, conceived the people as many, not one. That is why, for instance, his Fireside Chats, usually thought to be limited to one subject, were in fact multi-topical. In order to maximize air time, he used these opportunities to appeal to the diverse needs of the American people, who were laborers, farmers, factory workers, housewives, shop owners, and so forth. The something-for-everyone (except the economic royalists) tactic, which he did not originate but did perfect, usually worked with his varied constituents. On occasion, however, the tactic could backfire, as it did in the first Pittsburgh campaign speech, the neutrality revision effort, and the 1940 campaign where peace was war and war was peace.

Of course, Roosevelt waved the bloody shirt every four years, and the motivated could see thereon the pound of flesh the Republicans had extracted prior to 1933, and would therefore vote Democratic. But in a sense, FDR campaigned continuously. Responding to the what-have-you-done-for-me-recently question that resides in most voters' minds, Roosevelt usually used a speech occasion to remind the audience, and the greater newspaper audience, of federal largess under Franklin D. Roosevelt's New Deal. In his first Fireside Chat of 1934, he asked the people, "Are you better off than you were last year?"; before getting to the quarantine part of his address, he reminded Chicagoans about the Outer Link Bridge, a federal project; and in a representative humorous vein, he told an Alabama Polytechnic Institute audience at Auburn, March 30, 1939, that some P. W. A. money, which was supposed to be used only for buildings that had burned or fallen down, had been allocated to the University in Alabama, at its president's pleading, to build a new library because General Sherman had burned theirs down in 1864.[6]

Fourth, the cadences of FDR's vocal phrasing also made good reading. His tendency to place important verbs and nouns at the end of phrases or sentences—"the only thing we have to fear is fear itself," "No matter how long it may take us to overcome this premeditated invasion, the American people in their righteous might will win through to absolute victory"—and to divide his clauses in thirds, not only made listeners await the completion of the idea but also arrested readers' attention until the fulfillment of the thought. An excellent example of FDR's craftsmanship with words is his handwritten first draft for the 1935 Annual Message, wherein he executed his typical style:

We have undertaken a new order of things: yet we progress towards it under the framework and in the spirit and intent of the American Constitution. We have proceeded throughout the nation a measurable distance on that road towards the new order of things. Materially, I can report to you substantial benefits to our agricultural population, increased industrial activity, and profits to our merchants. Of equal moment we rejoice in an evident restoration of that spirit of confidence and faith which marks the American character. Let him who for speculative profit or partisan purpose without just warrant would seek to disturb or dispel this assurance, take heed before he assumes responsibility for any act which slows our upward step.

Throughout the world change is the order of the day. In every nation economic problems long in the making have brought crises of many kinds for which the masters of our practice and theory were unprepared. In most nations social justice has become no longer a distant ideal but a definite goal, and ancient governments are beginning to heed the call.

This passage also demonstrates FDR's ability to co-opt other orators' metaphors, in this case Father Coughlin's Union for Social Justice.[7]

Although Roosevelt personally made many of the word choices quoted throughout this book, most of his speeches were composed by speech writers. Strictly, then, how can one conceive of a Rooseveltian style, a Rooseveltian theory of presidential rhetoric? When FDR delivered a speech, he gestured and he modulated his voice; however, the words, or most of them, were the product of one or more advisers. Kenneth Davis confronted this issue by condemning FDR's copying of Raymond Moley's draft of the First Inaugural Address, contending it "was done with deliberate *intent* to deceive posterity [italics in original]." If so, Roosevelt might have deceived better by not leaving spaces at the bottom of some pages and by making some interlinear corrections here and there; too, to have assumed that the hired help would remain eternally silent on such matters strains one's credulity in view of Roosevelt's practical politics.[8]

To be sure, it was not general public knowledge who contributed what to a presidential address, but neither was it a secret that men such as Moley, Archibald MacLeish, Harry Hopkins, Robert Sherwood, Thomas Corcoran, Stanley High, and the equal among equals, Samuel Rosenman, helped the president with his speeches. Yet, there are those who cavil at the practice of ghostwritten presidential addresses. Most objections seem to have at their epicenter the concern that since citizens elect a person to be president, the people have a right to hear or read the president's words and not some shadowy figures' rhetoric composed behind the throne.[9]

The most serious concern is that writers may produce policy. One will recall that Roosevelt tried to blame Attorney General Cummings for the Court packing fiasco. In his oral history, Rosenman faced the problem directly. He stated, "The point I want to make is that speech-writers do prepare policy—if no statement of policy is given to them before the speech or message is written." However, one sentence later, he balanced that observation: "Scores of times the President would tell us what policy he wanted put into his speech. In that event, we certainly didn't originate policy." In fine, Rosenman placed the ultimate responsibility for Roosevelt's rhetoric on the president, and there is nothing in this study that contravenes his finding:

Very frequently we did literally make policy in putting down things which we had not previously touched on in discussion with him. But these were of course always submitted to him, because he went very carefully over every draft of a speech. And although we would make policy in the sense that we would suggest that this is something he might want to say, it was always up to him, of course, to cross it out—which he did very frequently.[10]

Another concern is deception. On that point, FDR stood on something less solid than granite. True, Rosenman complained when Roosevelt acknowledged his speech staff, but one could infer that FDR misled in the 1936 volume of his *Public Papers and Addresses*, depending, as Earnest Brandenburg stated, on the "definition of the word *write* [italics in original]." Roosevelt liberally recognized his help and openly, although flatteringly to himself, sketched the compositional process. However, it was not poetic license when he averred that he read all submissions and then dictated "my own draft" and that the final speech would naturally contain "some thoughts" and even "some of the sentences" submitted to him. Although the War Message was primarily his, and such notable addresses as the Third Inaugural and the Fourth more or less his, these speeches are the exception and not the rule, for the extant drafts simply do not support his contention. In FDR was a curious admixture of honesty and hubris: truthfulness that he had help, pridefulness that he, and not his speech staff, was president.[11]

Rhetorical style is also the subject of this chapter. Ernest Bormann stated the issue, "Style may be the man, but when style is five men it ceases to be any style at all." His observation might apply to other presidents, but it will not hold in FDR's case. A close examination of the drafts revealed enough Rooseveltian emendations and dictations, enough famous phrases that were his inventions, and enough consistency over time with relationship to alliteration, anaphora, and metaphor (often nautical in nature) that one could reasonably conclude Roosevelt's speeches had style and it was his.[12]

Shortly after his election in 1932, Roosevelt presciently stated the goals of his presidential oratory. He said:

All our great Presidents were leaders of thought at times when certain ideas in the life of the nation had to be clarified. . . . That is what the office is—a superb opportunity for reapplying, applying in new conditions the simple rules of human conduct to which we always go back. Without leadership alert and sensitive to change, we are bogged up or lose our way.

By word and delivery for thirteen years, he prodded and oftentimes persuaded the American people to take his path. The concluding words of his last speech, to have been delivered for the Jefferson Day Dinner, April 13, 1945, on the day after his death, are an eloquent epitaph for Franklin Delano Roosevelt's rhetorical presidency. He wrote: "The only limits to our realization of tomorrow will be our doubts of today. Let us move forward with strong and active faith."[13]

APPENDIX: Chronology of Fireside Chats

1. On the Banking Crisis, Sunday, March 12, 1933
2. On the New Deal, Sunday, May 7, 1933
3. On Recovery, Monday, July 24, 1933
4. On Our Way, Sunday, October 22, 1933
5. On Economic Progress, Thursday, June 28, 1934
6. On the NRA, Sunday, September 30, 1934
7. On Fear, Confidence, and Faith, Sunday, April 28, 1935
8. On Conservation, Sunday, September 6, 1936
9. On the Judiciary, Tuesday, March 9, 1937
10. On the Extraordinary Session of Congress, Tuesday, October 12, 1937
11. On the Unemployment Census, Sunday, November 14, 1937
12. On Economic Conditions, Tuesday, April 14, 1938
13. On the Purge, Tuesday, June 24, 1938
14. On the War in Europe, Sunday, September 3, 1939
15. On National Defense, Sunday, May 26, 1940
16. On "The Great Arsenal of Democracy," Sunday, December 29, 1940
17. On the Unlimited National Emergency, Friday, May 27, 1941
18. On "Freedom of the Seas," Thursday, September 11, 1941
19. On War with Japan and Germany, Tuesday, December 9, 1941
20. On the Progress of the War, Monday, February 23, 1942

21. On National Economic Policy, Tuesday, April 28, 1942
22. On Inflation and War, Monday, September 7, 1942
23. On the Home Front, Monday, October 12, 1942
24. On the Coal Crisis, Sunday, May 2, 1943
25. On War and Peace, Wednesday, July 28, 1943
26. On the Third War Loan Drive, Wednesday, September 8, 1943
27. On the Teheran and Cairo Conferences, Friday, December 24, 1943
28. On the Fall of Rome, Monday, June 5, 1944
29. On the Fifth War Loan Drive, Monday, June 12, 1944
30. On the Sixth War Loan Drive, Sunday, November 19, 1944

Notes

CHAPTER 1

1. James W. Ceaser, Glen E. Thurow, Jeffrey Tulis, and Joseph Bessette, "The Rise of the Rhetorical Presidency," *Presidential Studies Quarterly* 11 (1981): 159, 161.

2. "Roosevelt on the Presidency," *New York Times*, November 13, 1932, Sec. 8, p. 1.

3. Donald L. Wolfarth, "John Kennedy in the Tradition of Inaugural Speeches," *Quarterly Journal of Speech* 47 (1961): 125.

4. Richard E. Neustadt, *Presidential Power: The Politics of Leadership* (New York: John Wiley and Sons, 1960), p. 10; Theodore Windt, with Beth Ingold, *Essays in Presidential Rhetoric* (Dubuque: Kendall/Hunt Publishing Co., 1983), p. xiii, and Theodore Windt, *Presidential Rhetoric (1961–1980)*, 2nd ed. (Dubuque: Kendall/Hunt Publishing Co., 1980), p. 1; Harry Bailey, "Neustadt's Thesis Revisited: Toward the Two Faces of Presidential Power," *Presidential Studies Quarterly* 11 (1981): 352, 354; Windt, *Presidential Rhetoric (1961–1980)*, p. 2.

5. Aristotle, *Rhetoric*, trans. W. Rhys Roberts (New York: Modern Library, 1954), 1355b9–13.

6. See Robert Underhill, *The Truman Persuasions* (Ames: Iowa State University Press, 1981).

7. Aristotle, *Rhetoric*, 1355b26.

8. James R. Andrews, *The Practice of Rhetorical Criticism* (New York: Macmillan Publishing Co., 1983), p. 11. Italics in original.

9. John F. Wilson and Carroll C. Arnold, *Public Speaking as a Liberal Art*, 5th ed. (Boston: Allyn and Bacon, 1983), p. 99.

10. Public Reaction File, PPF 200-B, Box 8, Franklin D. Roosevelt Library, Hyde Park, New York. Hereafter cited as FDRL.

CHAPTER 2

1. Earnest Brandenburg and Waldo W. Braden, "Franklin D. Roosevelt's Voice and Pronunciation," *Quarterly Journal of Speech* 38 (1952): 23–30; Gail W. Compton, "Franklin D. Roosevelt: An Annotated Bibliography of His Speaking" (Ph. D. diss., University of Wisconsin, 1966), p. liii.

2. I stressed the need to conduct rhetorical research in the presidential libraries in "Franklin D. Roosevelt's Second Inaugural Address" (Paper presented at the Speech Communication Association Convention, Washington, D. C., 1983).

3. Donald Richberg, *My Hero* (New York: G. P. Putnam's Sons, 1954), p. 270; *PPA (The Public Papers and Addresses of Franklin D. Roosevelt) 1941*, p. 515.

4. Motion Picture (MP) 79–21, Fall 1937, Boise, Idaho; MP 201–14, August 1936, Chautauqua, New York, FDRL. For a photograph of the podium device on an observation car, see Otis L. Graham, Jr., and Meghan Robinson Wander, eds., *Franklin D. Roosevelt: His Life and Times* (Boston: G. K. Hall, 1985), p. 120.

5. MP 78–3, May 1, 1939, Rhinebeck, New York; MP 79–21 also shows FDR walking, actually sliding, down a ramp from his railroad car to the ground by leaning forward and letting gravity help to slide-pull himself down.

6. For Truman's distaste of speaking, see Robert Underhill, *The Truman Persuasions* (Ames: Iowa State University Press, 1981), pp. 334–37.

7. MP 201–14; MP 201–148, September 29, 1936, Syracuse, New York; *PPA 1936*, pp. 388–89; MP 201–165, December 5, 1938, Chapel Hill, North Carolina; *PPA 1938*, p. 615.

8. MP 77–5, March 4, 1933, Washington, D. C.; MP 201–154, January 20, 1937, Washington, D. C.; MP 201–161, October 5, 1937, Chicago, Illinois; MP 201–511–2, June 6, 1940, Charlottesville, Virginia; MP 201–2747–14–1, January 20, 1945, Washington, D. C.; MP 201–2757–14–4, September 23, 1944, Washington, D. C.; *PPA 1944–45*, p. 290.

9. Earnest Brandenburg and Waldo W. Braden, "Franklin Delano Roosevelt," in *History and Criticism of American Public Address*, ed. Marie Kathryn Hochmuth, 3 vols. (New York: Russell and Russell, 1955), 3: 516; MP 201, March 12, 1933, Washington, D. C.; *PPA 1933*, p. 64; *PPA 1937*, p. 410; MP 201–148; MP 201–1122–5–6, December 8, 1941, Washington, D. C.

10. Brandenburg and Braden, "Franklin Delano Roosevelt," p. 516.

11. MP 201–9, July 2, 1932, Chicago, Illinois; MP 201–141, June 27, 1936, Philadelphia, Pennsylvania; *PPA 1936*, p. 236.

12. James MacGregor Burns, *Roosevelt: The Lion and the Fox* (New York: Harcourt, Brace and Company, 1956), p. 273.

13. John B. Voor and Rev. Joseph W. Miller, "The Effect of Practice Upon the Comprehension of Time-Compressed Speech," *Speech Monographs* 32 (1965): 452; Charles F. Diehl, Richard C. White, and Kenneth W. Burke, "Rate and Communication," *Speech Monographs* 26 (1959): 229; Charles M. Rossiter, Jr., "Some Implications of Compressed Speech for Broadcasters," *Journal of Broadcasting* 15 (1971): 303–4.

14. The wpm were obtained by timing at least 15 minutes of speaking time (except for the banking crisis and European war at 13:15 minutes and 11:55 minutes respectively, which were timed for the entire broadcasts) and then dividing the number of words in that time span by the time.

15. Robert E. Sherwood, *Roosevelt and Hopkins: An Intimate History* (New York: Harper and Brothers, 1948), p. 217; Grace Tully, *F. D. R. My Boss* (New York: Charles Scribner's Sons, 1949), p. 98.

16. *PPA 1944–45*, p. 284.

17. *PPA 1937*, p. 410, the italicized words indicate FDR's ad libitum words that are not in the printed text; *PPA 1940*, p. 263; *PPA 1937*, p. 115.

18. John H. Sharon, "Roosevelt and Truman: The Fireside Technique," *Daily Princetonian*, March 22, 1950, p. 4; Thomas H. Greer, *What Roosevelt Thought* (East Lansing: Michigan State University Press, 1958), p. 111.

19. *PPF 1820*, Madison Square Garden, New York City, October 31, 1936, Box 1007, Reading Copy, pp. 3, 5, 7, FDRL.

20. PPF 200-B, Box 8, Box 78, FDRL.

21. Robert Littell, "Hard on Heroes," *Reader's Digest*, July 1936, p. 90.

22. Lew Sarett and William Trufant Foster, *Basic Principles of Speech* (New York: Houghton-Mifflin Company, 1936), pp. 193–94; PPF 200-B, Boxes 16, 69, 118, and PPF 200-T, Box 519, FDRL.

CHAPTER 3

1. Quoted in Richard Grunberger, *The 12-Year Reich* (New York: Holt, Rinehart and Winston, 1971), p. 401.

2. David Naylor, *American Picture Palaces* (New York: Van Nostrand Reinhold Co., 1981), p. 14; Margaret Farrand Thorp, *America at the Movies* (New Haven: Yale University Press, 1939), p. 21, *PPA 1941*, p. 515.

3. Robert Littell, "A Glance at the Newsreels," *American Mercury* 30 (1933): 264, 270; Littell, "Hard on Heroes," *Reader's Digest*, July 1936, p. 90.

4. Thomas Sugrue, "The Newsreels," *Scribners'* 101 (April 1937): 11.

5. Leif Furhammar and Folke Isaksson, *Politics and Film*, trans. Kersti French (New York: Praeger Publishers, 1971), p. 152, italics in original; Sugrue, "The Newsreels," p. 10.

6. Arthur P. Molella, *FDR The Intimate Presidency* (Washington, D. C.: Smithsonian Institution, 1982), p. 52; Lewis Jacobs, *The Rise of the American Film* (New York: Harcourt, Brace and Co., 1939), p. 538.

7. Littell, "A Glance at the Newsreels," p. 270.

8. John H. Sharon, "The Fireside Chat," *Franklin D. Roosevelt Collector* 2 (November 1949): 3; Waldo W. Braden and Earnest Brandenburg, "Roosevelt's Fireside Chats," *Speech Monographs* 22 (1955): 293.

9. Sharon, "The Fireside Chat," p. 3; Braden and Brandenburg, "Roosevelt's Fireside Chats," p. 290; Thomas Conley, "The Linnaean Blues: Thoughts on the Genre Approach," in *Form, Genre, and the Study of Political Discourse*, ed. Herbert W. Simons and Aram A. Aghazarian (Columbia: University of South Carolina Press, 1986), pp. 59–78.

10. *PPA 1934*, p. 314; *PPA 1941*, p. 390

11. *PPA 1933*, pp. 302, 427; *PPA 1938*, pp. 248, 397; *PPA 1942*, pp. 227–38, 368–77.

12. *Complete Presidential Press Conferences of Franklin D. Roosevelt*, 12 vols. (New York: De Capo Press, 1972); 12:60.

13. The Reminiscences of Samuel I. Rosenman, (1959), p. 25, in the Oral History

Collection of Columbia University, hereafter Rosenman, COHO; Sharon, "The Fireside Chat," p. 3; Richard Lee Strout, "The President and the Press," in *The Making of the New Deal: The Insiders Speak*, ed. Katie Loucheim (Cambridge: Harvard University Press, 1983), p. 13.

14. PPF 200-B, Boxes 16, Con Box 104, 116, 129, 145, 170, FDRL.

15. *PPA 1938*, p. 39; B. H. Winfield, "Franklin D. Roosevelt's Efforts to Influence the News During His First Term Press Conferences," *Presidential Studies Quarterly* 11 (1981): 189–99; Jill McMillan and Sandra Ragan, "The Presidential Press Conference: A Study in Escalating Institutionalization," *Presidential Studies Quarterly* 13 (1983): 231–41.

16. *PPA 1938*, p. 38; Graham J. White, *FDR and the Press* (Chicago: University of Chicago Press, 1979), p. 70; for texts of Agnew's and Stanton's speeches, see Halford Ross Ryan, ed., *American Rhetoric from Roosevelt to Reagan: A Collection of Speeches and Critical Essays* (Prospect Heights, Ill.: Waveland Press, 1983), pp. 206–21; George Wolfskill and John A. Hudson, *All But the People: Franklin D. Roosevelt and His Critics 1933–39* (Toronto: Collier-Macmillan Canada, 1969), p. 184.

17. Maury Maverick, "The Next Four Years," *New Republic*, November 25, 1936, p. 99.

18. *PPA 1938*, p. 295.

19. *Press Conferences of Franklin D. Roosevelt*, 12:37, 53.

20. Ibid., p. 76.

21. *PPA 1941*, p. 31.

22. David Halberstam, *The Powers That Be* (New York: Alfred A. Knopf, 1979), p. 16.

23. James E. Pollard, *The Presidents and the Press* (New York: Macmillan Co., 1947), p. 840.

CHAPTER 4

1. *PPA 1928–32*, pp. 624–27.

2. "Roosevelt's Soft Answer to Smith's Wrath," *Literary Digest*, April 30, 1932, pp. 3–4; editorial, "The 'Bottom' Man," *New York Times*, April 9, 1932, p. 14; "Demagogues and Plutogogues," *New Republic*, April 27, 1932, p. 286.

3. *PPA 1928–32*, p. 639.

4. Ibid., p. 646.

5. Ibid., pp. 647–59; PPF 1820, Acceptance Speech, July 2, 1932, Box 483, p. 4, FDRL.

6. Kenneth S. Davis, *FDR: The New York Years 1928–1933* (New York: Random House, 1985), p. 368; Berle Papers, Box 18, FDRL.

7. Wil A. Linkugel, "FDR: Master Campaigner" (Paper presented at annual meeting of Central States Speech Association, Cincinnati, Ohio, 1986).

8. Craig Allen Smith, "The Audiences of the 'Rhetorical Presidency': An Analysis of President-Constituent Interaction, 1963–81," *Presidential Studies Quarterly* 13 (1983): 620; *PPA 1928–32*, pp. 742–56; Compton Mackenzie, *Mr. Roosevelt* (New York: E. P. Dutton, 1944), p. 174.

9. Myles Martel, *Political Campaign Debates: Images, Strategies, and Tactics* (New York: Longman, 1983), pp. 63–70; *PPA 1928–32*, pp. 795–811.

10. *PPA 1928–32*, p. 837.

11. Alfred B. Rollins, Jr., *Roosevelt and Howe* (New York: Knopf, 1962), p. 362.

12. PPF 1820, Acceptance Speech, June 27, 1936, Box 879, pp. 3, 4, 6, 7, 11, FDRL.

13. Robert H. Ferrell, ed., *Dear Bess: The Letters from Harry Truman to Bess Truman 1910–1959* (New York: W. W. Norton, 1983), p. 389; PPF 200-B, Acceptance Speech, 1936, Box 69, FDRL.

14. Samuel I. Rosenman, *Working with Roosevelt* (New York: Harper and Brothers, 1952), p. 108.

15. John T. Flynn, "Other People's Money," *New Republic*, September 16, 1936, pp. 155–56; Oswald Garrison Villard, "Issues and Men," *Nation*, August 29, 1936, p. 242; PPF 200-B, Chautauqua Speech, Box 72, FDRL; *PPA 1936*, pp. 285–92.

16. PPF 200-B, Syracuse Speech, Box 74, FDRL.

17. Quoted in Alan Bullock, *Hitler: A Study in Tyranny* (New York: Bantam Books, 1961), p. 45.

18. *PPA 1936*, pp. 383–90.

19. PPF 200-B, Syracuse Speech, Box 74, FDRL.

20. *PPA 1936*, pp. 566–73; PPF 200-B, Madison Square Garden Speech, Box 77, FDRL.

21. "I Accept," *Time*, July 6, 1936, p. 9; E. T. Weir, "I Am What Mr. Roosevelt Calls an Economic Royalist," *Fortune*, October 1936, p. 118.

22. *PPA 1940*, pp. 293–303.

23. Ibid., pp. 359–64, 370–75.

24. Ibid., pp. 407–16.

25. Ibid., pp. 435–42.

26. Wayne S. Cole. *Roosevelt and the Isolationists 1932–45* (Lincoln: University of Nebraska Press, 1983), pp. 398–99; *PPA 1940*, pp. 461–62.

27. I. F. Stone, "The Press Loses the Election," *Nation*, November 16, 1940, pp. 467–68; Cole, *Roosevelt and the Isolationists 1932–45*, p. 405; Robert E. Sherwood, *Roosevelt and Hopkins: An Intimate History* (New York: Harper and Brothers, 1948), p. 192.

28. *PPA 1940*, pp. 485–510.

29. Ibid., pp. 499–510.

30. "Text of Willkie's Speech Before 25,000 in Chicago," *New York Times*, October 23, 1940, p. 16; "Text of Willkie's Baltimore Address Setting Forth a Six-Point Defense Program," *New York Times*, October 31, 1940, p. 18.

31. Rosenman, *Working with Roosevelt*, p. 242; Sherwood, *Roosevelt and Hopkins*, p. 191; Warren Moscow, *Roosevelt and Willkie*(Englewood Cliffs, N. J.: Prentice-Hall, 1968), p. 159.

32. Robert Divine, *Foreign Policy and U. S. Presidential Elections 1940–1948* (New York: New Viewpoints, 1974), pp. 71–72.

33. *PPA 1940*, pp. 514–24.

34. Ibid., pp. 530–39.

35. Ibid., pp. 539–41, 541–43.

36. Ibid., pp. 544–53.

37. "Why Roosevelt Won," *Nation*, November 9, 1940, p. 435.

38. "The Campaign in Essence," *New Republic*, November 4, 1940, p. 614.

39. Divine, *Foreign Policy and U. S. Presidential Elections 1940–1948*, p. 55; "Non-Political Campaign," *Time*, September 9, 1940, p. 11; "God Willing," *Time*, November

4, 1940, p. 12; "*Viva la Democracia!*" *Time*, October 21, 1940, p. 16; "President Assails 'Falsifications,' " *New York Times*, October 24, 1940, p. 15.

40. *PPA 1944–45*, pp. 197–98.

41. *PPA 1944–45*, pp. 201–6; PPF 1820, Acceptance Speech, July 20, 1944, draft 5, Box 1525, FDRL; PPF 200-B, Acceptance Speech, Box 250, FDRL; "Mr. Roosevelt Speaks from the Heart," *Christian Century*, July 26, 1944, p. 870.

42. Rosenman, *Working with Roosevelt*, p. 462; "The Campaign," *Time*, October 30, 1944, p. 11; "The Waikiki Conference," *Time*, August 21, 1944, p. 21; Hadley Cantril, ed., *Public Opinion 1935–46* (Princeton: Princeton University Press, 1951), pp. 636–38.

43. Dr. James F. Bender, "The Two Men: A Radio Analysis," *New York Times Magazine*, September 17, 1944, pp. 11, 36; "Say Dewey Rivals President on Radio," *New York Times*, June 29, 1944, p. 14.

44. "The Campaign," *Time*, p. 11.

45. *PPA 1944–45*, p. 286; "The Old Magic," *Time*, October 2, 1944, p. 21; "Back in the Groove," *New Republic*, October 2, 1944, p. 429; PPF 200-B, Teamsters' Union Speech, September 23, 1944, Box 25, FDRL.

46. *PPA 1944–45*, pp. 317–24.

47. "Why F. D. R.," *Nation*, October 28, 1944, p. 504; "Campaign Sidelights," *New Republic*, October 30, 1944, p. 567; *PPA 1944–45*, pp. 342–54.

48. *PPA 1944–45*, pp. 356–66.

49. Ibid., pp. 369–78.

50. Ibid., pp. 383–88.

51. Ibid., pp. 397–406.

CHAPTER 5

1. Karlyn Kohrs Campbell and Kathleen Hall Jamieson, "Inaugurating the Presidency," *Presidential Studies Quarterly* 15 (1985): 396.

2. David M. Potter, *The Impending Crisis 1848–1861*, ed. Don E. Fehrenbacher (New York: Harper and Row, 1979), p. 145.

3. Harry Hopkins, Foreword to *Nothing to Fear*, ed. B. D. Zevin (Boston: Houghton Mifflin, 1946), p. viii.

4. Inaugural Address, 1933, PPF 1820, Box 610, FDRL. The first draft is on legal paper. The second draft was typed on Tuesday, February 28. The third draft was retyped on Wednesday, March 1. The reading copy was typed on March 3 in Washington.

5. Raymond Moley, *The First New Deal* (New York: Harcourt, Brace & World, 1966), p. 114. In his *After Seven Years* (New York: Harper, 1939), Moley made only casual reference to the authorship of the first inaugural because his "function as a collaborator was well known" and everyone knew he was "involved in the preparation of this speech" (p. 116); Inaugural Address, PPF 1820, Box 610, pp. 1–10, FDRL.

6. Moley, *The First New Deal*, p. 115; Frank Freidel, *Franklin D. Roosevelt Launching the New Deal* (Boston: Little Brown, 1973), p. 203, complained that the source has eluded later researchers. My search of Howe's papers and contemporary magazines provided nothing.

7. Inaugural Address, first handwritten draft, PPF 1820, Box 610, p. 1, FDRL.

8. Ibid., third draft (typed), PPF 1820, Box 610 pp. 1–4, FDRL.

9. Ibid., pp. 10–11.

10. Inaugural Address, reading copy, PPF 1820, Box 610, pp. 1–2, FDRL.

11. *PPA, 1933*, p. 16.

12. Rexford G. Tugwell, *Roosevelt's Revolution* (New York: Macmillan, 1977), p. 6, and Finis Farr, *FDR* (New Rochelle: Arlington House, 1972), p. 182.

13. William E. Leuchtenburg, *Franklin D. Roosevelt and the New Deal: 1932–1940* (New York: Harper & Row, 1963), p. 41.

14. Universal Films, MP 77–5, Pathe News, 201–29–1, FDRL. Complete newsreel footage of FDR's First Inaugural is not extant; therefore, what the editors retained is significant; Rexford G. Tugwell, *In Search of Roosevelt* (Cambridge: Harvard University Press, 1972), p. 222; "The Inaugural Address," *Christian Century*, March 15, 1933, p. 351; "The Faith of Roosevelt," *Nation*, March 15, 1933, p. 278; "Roosevelt Takes Oath in Crisis," *News-Week*, March 11, 1933, p. 9; "The President's Speech," *The Times* (London), March 6, 1933, p. 13; Basil Rauch, *The History of the New Deal: 1933–1938* (New York: Creative Age Press, 1944), p. 61.

15. *PPA, 1928–32*, p. 658.

16. William E. Leuchtenburg, "The New Deal and the Analogue of War," in *Change and Continuity in Twentieth-Century America*, ed. John Braeman, Robert Bremmer, and Everett Walters (Columbus: Ohio State University Press, 1964), pp. 104–5.

17. Quoted in Cabell Phillips, *From the Crash to the Blitz: 1929–1939* (London: Macmillan, 1969), p. 107; "Leaders Here Praise Address as 'Strong,' " *New York Times*, March 5, 1933, p. 6; James A. Hagerty, "Roosevelt Address Stirs Great Crowd," *New York Times*, March 5, 1933, p. 2; "Comment of Press on Roosevelt's Inaugural Address," *New York Times*, March 5, 1933, p. 6; "The President's Speech," *The Times* (London), p. 13; Farr, *FDR*, p. 182.

18. Farr, *FDR*, p. 182.

19. Quoted in Farr, *FDR*, p. 191; quoted in John Toland, *Adolph Hitler*, 2 vols. (Garden City: Doubleday, 1976), 1:340–41; quoted in Freidel, *Franklin D. Roosevelt Launching the New Deal*, p. 208; quoted in Paul Preston, "The Burning of the Reichstag," in *Sunrise and Storm Clouds*, vol. 10 of *Milestones of History*, ed. Roger Morgan (New York: Newsweek Books, 1975), p. 137.

20. Quoted in James T. Patterson, *Congressional Conservatism and the New Deal* (Lexington: University of Kentucky Press, 1967), pp. 1–2.

21. Pathe News and Universal Films both included this important segment; Joseph P. Lash, *Eleanor and Franklin* (New York: Norton, 1971), p. 360; "Comment of Press on Roosevelt's Inaugural Address," p. 6; quoted in Phillips, *From the Crash to the Blitz: 1929–1939*, p. 107.

22. Alfred B. Rollins, Jr., *Roosevelt and Howe* (New York: Knopf, 1962), p. 366.

23. Cleveland Rodgers, *The Roosevelt Program* (New York: Putnam, 1933), p. 16.

24. For an authoritative text of the speech, see Franklin D. Roosevelt, "First Inaugural Address," in *American Rhetoric from Roosevelt to Reagan*, ed. Halford Ross Ryan, 2nd ed. (Prospect Heights, Ill.: Waveland Press, 1987), pp. 2–6.

25. PPF 1820, Second Inaugural Address, second draft, Box 1030, pp. 1, 3, 6, third draft, p. 7, FDRL.

26. Rauch, *History of the New Deal*, p. 268; Donald Richberg, *My Hero* (New York: G. P. Putnam's Sons, 1954), pp. 281–82; PPF 200-P, Second Inaugural Address, Box 449, FDRL; Lester W. Chandler, *America's Greatest Depression* (New York: Harper and Row, 1970), p. 5; U. S. Bureau of the Census, *Historical Statistics of the United States, Colonial Times to 1970*, Bicentennial edition, Part 2, Washington, D. C., 1975,

p. 299; Hadley Cantril, ed., *Public Opinion, 1935–46* (Princeton: Princeton University Press, 1951), p. 138.

27. PPF 1820, Second Inaugural Address, Insert F, third draft, Box 1030, FDRL. See also John F. Kennedy, "Inaugural Address," in Ryan, ed., *American Rhetoric from Roosevelt to Reagan*, p. 157.

28. See "Swearing in the Rain," *Time*, February 1, 1937, p. 10, and "Address is Praised," *New York Times*, January 22, 1937, p. 1; "Seven of 9 Justices Hear Roosevelt" and "The Second Inaugural," *New York Times*, January 22, 1937, pp. 15, 22; Nathan Miller, *FDR: An Intimate History* (Garden City: Doubleday, 1983), p. 392.

29. "Roosevelt Again President of the U. S.," *New York Times*, January 21, 1941, p. 3.

30. PPF 1820, Handwritten draft, Box 1355, pp. 1–3, FDRL.

31. The new introduction was an insert, marked as such on the third draft in Rosenman's handwriting. I could not locate the actual insert. See PPF 1820, Third Draft, Box 1355 p. 1, Fourth Draft, Box 1355, p. 1, FDRL.

32. PPF 1820, Fifth Draft, Box 1355, pp. 1–2, FDRL.

33. See Samuel I. Rosenman, *Working with Roosevelt* (New York: Harper and Brothers, 1952), p. 270; PPF 1820, Fourth Draft, Box 1355, p. 2, FDRL.

34. PPF 1820, Fifth Draft, Box 1355, p. 2, FDRL.

35. Ibid., Sixth Draft, p. 2, FDRL.

36. Ibid., Reading Copy, p. 1, FDRL; Franklin Delano Roosevelt, "Third Inaugural Address," The President Speaks Cassette Library, CXL 520–2, Side 4.

37. "Roosevelt Calls Upon America to Defend Faith in Democracy," *Newsweek*, January 27, 1941, p. 13; "Inaugural Strides Away from Past," *New York Times*, January 21, 1941, p. 2; Rosenman, *Working with Roosevelt*, p. 271.

38. PPF 200-T, Third Inaugural Address, Box 519, FDRL; "No Retreat Here," *New York Times*, January 21, 1941, p. 1; Rosenman, *Working with Roosevelt*, p. 271.

39. *PPA 1944–45*, p. 424; "Roosevelt Asks Simple Inaugural," *New York Times*, November 15, 1944, p. 18; "Roosevelt Takes Fourth-Term Oath," *New York Times*, January 21, 1945, p. 26; William D. Hassett, *Off the Record with F. D. R. 1942–1945* (New Brunswick: Rutgers University Press, 1958), p. 312; Arthur Krock, "The Fourth Inaugural," *New York Times*, January 21, 1945, sec. 4, p. 8.

40. Rosenman, *Working with Roosevelt*, p. 517; Grace Tully, *F. D. R. My Boss* (New York: Charles Scribner's Sons, 1949), p. 351.

41. "Some Thoughts for Inaugural Speech," January 6, 1945, PPF 1820, Box 1570, p. 1, FDRL. For an appraisal of Groton's and Dr. Endicott Peabody's influence on Roosevelt, see Laura Crowell, "Roosevelt the Grotonian," *Quarterly Journal of Speech* 38 (1952): 31–36; Edgar Eugene Robinson, *The Roosevelt Leadership 1933–1945* (Philadelphia: J. B. Lippincott, 1955), p. 342; "Other Thoughts For Inaugural Speech, January 13, 1945, PPF 1820, Box 1570, pp. 1–3, FDRL.

42. Robert Sherwood, handwritten draft for Fourth Inaugural, PPF 1820, Box 1570, p. 1, FDRL; Archibald MacLeish, draft for Fourth Inaugural, PPF 1820, Box 1570, p. 1, FDRL.

43. Samuel I. Rosenman, typewritten draft for Fourth Inaugural, PPF 1820, Box 1570, p. 1, FDRL; Hassett, *Off the Record with FDR*, p. 311; Rosenman, typewritten draft for Fourth Inaugural, pp. 1–4; Sherwood, handwritten draft for Fourth Inaugural, p. 3; Rosenman, typewritten draft for Fourth Inaugural, p. 4.

44. Sherwood, handwritten draft for Fourth Inaugural, pp. 1–3; Harold P. Zelko,

"Franklin D. Roosevelt's Rhythm in Rhetorical Style," *Quarterly Journal of Speech* 28 (1942): 138–41.

45. Robert E. Sherwood, *Roosevelt and Hopkins: An Intimate History* (New York: Harper and Brothers, 1948), p. 846.

46. "FIRST DRAFT," Fourth Inaugural, PPF 1820, Box 1570, pp. 1–3, FDRL; First Draft, January 20, 1945, PPF 1820, Box 1570, pp. 1–3, FDRL; Final Reading Copy, Fourth Inaugural Address of the President, January 20, 1945, PPF 1820, Box 1570, pp. 5, 2, FDRL. For a description of FDR's deteriorating health as seen at his Fourth Inauguration, see John Gunther, *Roosevelt in Retrospect* (New York: Harper, 1950), p. 364.

47. Film MP–78–1, no. 3, and Film MP 65–7–21, FDRL. For a verbatim transcript of the address, complete with FDR's additions and deletions from the reading copy, see Halford Ross Ryan, "Roosevelt's Fourth Inaugural Address: A Study of Its Composition," *Quarterly Journal of Speech* 67 (1981): 164–65.

48. Frances Perkins, *The Roosevelt I Knew* (New York: Viking Press, 1946), p. 394, and Tully, *F.D.R. My Boss*, p. 351; Denis W. Brogan, *The Era of Franklin D. Roosevelt*, in *The Chronicles of America Series*, edited by Allan Nevins (New York: Yale University Press, 1950), p. 354; "Hail to the Chief," *Newsweek*, January 29, 1945, p. 40; "For the Fourth Time," *Time*, January 29, 1945, pp. 18–19; Hassett, *Off the Record with FDR*, p. 312; Finis Farr, *FDR* (New Rochelle: Arlington House, 1972), p. 411.

49. Harry S Truman, "Broadcast to the American People Announcing the Surrender of Germany," May 8, 1945, *Public Papers of the Presidents of the United States: Harry S Truman, 1945* (Washington, D. C.: GPO, 1961), p. 48.

50. Richard A. Joslyn, "Keeping Politics in the Study of Political Discourse," in *Form, Genre, and the Study of Political Discourse*, ed. Herbert W. Simons and Aram A. Aghazarian (Columbia: University of South Carolina Press, 1986), p. 337; Bruce E. Gronbeck, "Ronald Reagan's Enactment of the Presidency in His 1981 Inaugural Address," in Simons and Aghazarian, eds., *Form, Genre, and the Study of Political Discourse*, pp. 226–45.

51. See Kennedy, "Inaugural Address," in Ryan, ed., *American Rhetoric from Roosevelt to Reagan*, pp. 156–59; Robert Ivie, "Reagan's First Inaugural Address: Emphasizing Contemplation and Action" (Paper presented at the annual meeting of the Speech Communication Association, Chicago, Illinois, 1986; Bert E. Bradley, "Jefferson and Reagan: The Rhetoric of Two Inaugurals," *Southern Speech Communication Journal* 48 (1983): 119–36; Gregg Phifer, "Two Inaugurals: A Second Look," *Southern Speech Communication Journal* 48 (1983): 378–85; Joslyn, "Keeping Politics in the Study of Political Discourse," p. 336.

CHAPTER 6

1. *PPA 1935*, p. 221; C. Herman Pritchett, *The Roosevelt Court* (New York: Macmillan, 1948), p. 22.

2. *PPA 1937*, p. lxvi; Leonard Baker, *Back to Back* (New York: Macmillan, 1967), p. 279; Dixon Wecter, *The Age of the Great Depression* (New York: Macmillan, 1948), p. 106 Pritchett, *The Roosevelt Court*, p. 9; John Gunther, *Roosevelt in Retrospect* (New York: Harper, 1950), pp. 296–97; Edgar Eugene Robinson, *The Roosevelt Leadership 1933–45* (Philadelphia: J. B. Lippincott, 1955), p. 210; Basil Rauch, *The History of the New Deal: 1933–1938* (New York: Creative Age Press, 1944), p. 283; Rexford G.

Tugwell, *FDR: Architect of an Era* (New York: Macmillan, 1967), p. 166; Rosenman, COHO, p. 154, FDRL; Merlo J. Pusey, *The Supreme Court Crisis* (New York: Macmillan, 1937), p. 9; Joseph Alsop, *FDR 1882–1945* (New York: Viking Press, 1982), p. 162.

3. Raymond Moley, *After Seven Years* (New York: Harper, 1939), p. 362; James T. Patterson, *Congressional Conservatism and the New Deal* (Lexington: University of Kentucky Press, 1967), p. 91.

4. Rosenman, COHO, p. 154, FDRL; Gunther, *Roosevelt in Retrospect*, p. 296; Alsop, *FDR 1882–1945*, p. 186; Samuel and Dorothy Rosenman, *Presidential Style: Some Giants and a Pygmy in the White House* (New York: Harper and Row, 1976), p. 353.

5. Rauch, *The History of the New Deal*, p. 266; Samuel I. Rosenman, *Working with Roosevelt* (New York: Harper and Brothers, 1952), pp. 141–42; Moley, *After Seven Years*, p. 356; "Swearing in the Rain," *Time*, February 1, 1937, p. 10; Bernard Fred Phelps, "A Rhetorical Analysis of the 1937 Addresses of Franklin D. Roosevelt in Support of Court Reform" (Ph.D. diss., Ohio State University, 1957), pp. 385–86; Homer S. Cummings Papers (#9973), Manuscripts Department, University of Virginia Library, December 26, 1936, p. 192.

6. Rosenman and Rosenman, *Presidential Style*, p. 352; Myles Martel, *Political Campaign Debates: Images, Strategies, and Tactics* (New York: Longman, 1983), p. 126.

7. Rosenman, *Working with Roosevelt*, p. 160; Rauch, *The History of the New Deal*, p. 273; Nicholas Halasz, *Roosevelt Through Foreign Eyes* (Princeton: D. Van Nostrand, 1961), p. 81; Cummings Papers (#9973), December 26, 1936, p. 190.

8. James MacGregor Burns, *Roosevelt: The Lion and the Fox* (New York: Harcourt, Brace, and Co., 1956), p. 297.

9. Cummings Papers (#9973), December 24, 26, 1936, pp. 165, 187, 191, FDRL.

10. Ibid., pp. 166, 188, FDRL.

11. Remarks, FDR Message to Congress on the Judiciary, February 5, 1937, Rosenman Papers, Box 20, p. 3, FDRL; Remarks, FDR (covered by dictation), Rosenman Papers, Box 20, pp. 1–3, FDRL.

12. First Draft, Rosenman Papers, Box 20, pp. 5, 6, 10, 11, FDRL.

13. FDR, Draft 1, Rosenman Papers, Box 20, p. 7, FDRL—although this draft is denoted a first draft, it is really the second draft of the judiciary message; FDR, Draft 2, Rosenman Papers, Box 20, p. 8, FDRL; Rosenman, *Working with Roosevelt*, p. 147; Donald Richberg, *My Hero* (New York: G. P. Putnam's Sons, 1954), p. 221.

14. Moley, *After Seven Years*, p. 362; Wecter, *The Age of the Great Depression*, p. 105; Rexford G. Tugwell, *The Democratic Roosevelt* (Garden City: Doubleday, 1957), p. 397.

15. *PPA 1937*, pp. 52, 53, 55, lxv.

16. James A. Farley, *Jim Farley's Story* (New York: McGraw-Hill, 1948), p. 75; William E. Leuchtenburg, "Franklin D. Roosevelt's Court 'Packing' Plan," in *Essays on the New Deal*, ed. Harold M. Hollingsworth and William F. Holmes (Austin: University of Texas Press, 1969), p. 86.

17. Burton K. Wheeler, "My Years with Roosevelt," in *As We Saw the Thirties*, ed. Rita James Simon (Urbana: University of Illinois Press, 1967), p. 201; *PPA 1937*, p. 116; Victory Dinner speech, Mayflower Hotel, Washington, D. C., March 4, 1937, draft 14, PPF 1820, Box 1040, p. 10, FDRL—I identified six drafts for this speech, which are strangely numbered: 1, 2, 4, 14, 21, and a final reading copy; draft 4, PPF 1820,

Box 1040, pp. 12, 13, 16, FDRL; draft 14, PPF 1820, Box 1040, pp. 4, 6, FDRL; draft 21, PPF 1820, Box 1040, p. 20, FDRL.

18. "Party Foes Score Roosevelt Speech; Go to the Country," *New York Times*, March 6, 1937, p. 2; "Press Comment on Roosevelt Court Speech," *New York Times*, March 6, 1937, p. 2; Victory Dinner speech, PPF 200-B, Boxes 70, 78, FDRL.

19. Joseph Alsop and Turner Catledge, *The 168 Days* (Garden City: Doubleday, Doran, and Co., 1938), p. 109.

20. Fireside Chat, March 9, 1937, Rosenman Papers, Box 20, FDRL. The drafts for this speech are evidently incomplete: drafts 2, 4, 5, 6, and 7 exist. There are a number of substantive changes on draft 7 that suggest an intermediate draft, but I was unable to account for it. FDR's typewritten remarks were typed in blue ink as was draft 2, and thereafter the drafts were in Rosenman's black ink; dictated remarks, pp. 1–4.

21. *PPA, 1937*, pp. 123, 125, 126, 128–30.

22. Louis Filler, ed., *The President Speaks* (New York: Capricorn Books, 1964), p. 224; *PPA 1937*, pp. 127–33.

23. Raymond Moley, "Today in America," *Newsweek*, March 20, 1937, p. 5; Pritchett, *The Roosevelt Court*, p. 8; OF–41, Judiciary Reorganization Act of 1937, Boxes 1, 39, FDRL.

24. For a study in which I argued that President Truman would have been more persuasive if he had followed his speech staff's advice, see "Harry S Truman: A Misdirected Defense for MacArthur's Dismissal," *Presidential Studies Quarterly* 11 (1981): 576–82; for a study in which I argued that President Johnson was more persuasive because he followed his speech staff's advice, see "President Lyndon Johnson's Voting Rights Address: Adjusting Civil Rights to the Congress and Congress to Civil Rights," in *American Rhetoric from Roosevelt to Reagan*, ed. Halford Ross Ryan, 2nd ed. (Prospect Heights, Ill.: Waveland Press, 1987), pp. 190–99.

25. Alsop and Catledge, *168 Days*, p. 113; Hadley Cantril, ed., *Public Opinion 1935–46* (Princeton: Princeton University Press, 1951), p. 149.

26. PPF 200-B, Victory Dinner Address, Box 70, FDRL.

27. Burton K. Wheeler, with Paul F. Healy, *Yankee from the West* (Garden City: Doubleday, 1962), pp. 328–29; Alsop, *FDR*, p. 187.

28. Peter H. Irons, *The New Deal Lawyers* (Princeton: Princeton University Press, 1982), p. 276.

29. "Text of Hughes Letter," *New York Times*, March 23, 1937, pp. 1, 19; Halford Ross Ryan, "*Kategoria* and *Apologia*: On Their Rhetorical Criticism as a Speech Set," *Quarterly Journal of Speech* 68 (1982): 254.

30. Robert S. Allen, "Hughes Checkmates the President," *Nation*, May 29, 1937, p. 610; Baker, *Back to Back*, pp. 159–60; Robinson, *The Roosevelt Leadership*, p. 202; William Manchester, *The Glory and the Dream* (Boston: Little, Brown and Co., 1973), p. 152; Patterson, *Congressional Conservatism and the New Deal*, p. 119; Wheeler, *Yankee from the West*, p. 333.

31. Noreen W. Kruse, "Motivational Factors in Non-Denial Apologia," *Central States Speech Journal* 28 (1977): 21; *PPA, 1937*, pp. lxvi, lxix; Stefan Lorant, *The Glorious Burden* (New York: Harper and Row, 1968), p. 629; Grace Tully, *F. D. R. My Boss* (New York: Charles Scribner's Sons, 1949), p. 223.

32. Rosenman, *Working with Roosevelt*, p. 161; Baker, *Back to Back*, p. 176.

33. *PPA, 1937*, p. 91.

CHAPTER 7

1. See J. B. Shannon, "Presidential Politics in the South: 1938, I," *Journal of Politics* 1 (1939): 151; Raymond Clapper, "Roosevelt Tries the Primaries," *Current History* 49 (October 1938): 16–19; "Roosevelt Tightening on Reins After Aides' Bungling in Iowa," *Newsweek*, June 20, 1938, pp. 7–8; and Alvin L. Hall, "Politics and Patronage: Virginia Senators and the Roosevelt Purge of 1938," *Virginia Magazine of History and Biography* 82 (1974): 331–50.

2. Clapper, "Roosevelt Tries the Primaries," p. 16.

3. *PPA 1938*, p. xxxii.

4. *PPA 1938*, pp. 391–400; George Wolfskill and John A. Hudson, *All But the People: Franklin D. Roosevelt and His Critics 1933–39* (Toronto: Collier-Macmillan Canada, 1969), pp. 288–91.

5. *PPA 1938*, pp. 463–71; Clapper, "Roosevelt Tries the Primaries," p. 18; Luther Harmon Zeigler, Jr., "Senator Walter George's 1938 Campaign," *Georgia Historical Quarterly* 43 (1959): 338.

6. For the text of George's speech, see "George Asks Fight on 'One-Man' Rule," *New York Times*, August 16, 1938, pp. 1–2.

7. "Mild Shocks," *Newsweek*, September 12, 1938, p. 11; quoted in "Roosevelt Now Seeks to 'Pack' the Senate With 'Yes Men,' Says Atlanta Constitution," *New York Times*, August 12, 1938, p. 1; editorial, "And Now Georgia," *New York Times*, September 16, 1938, p. 22.

8. Zeigler, "Senator Walter George's 1938 Campaign," pp. 344, 348, 351.

9. *Complete Presidential Press Conferences of Franklin D. Roosevelt*, 25 vols. (New York: Da Capo Press, 1972), 12:26, 37.

10. "Sees Purge as Step to Dictatorship," *New York Times*, August 19, 1938, pp. 1, 5.

11. "Senator Tydings' Appeal to the People of Maryland Against Roosevelt," *New York Times*, August 22, 1938, p. 2.

12. Raymond Moley, "He Did, and They Did," *Newsweek*, September 26, 1938, p. 40; Arthur Krock, "To Many Voters Washington Still Foreign," *New York Times*, September 1, 1938, p. 22.

13. *PPA 1938*, pp. 512–20.

14. Richard Polenberg, "Franklin Roosevelt and the Purge of John O'Connor: The Impact of Urban Change on Political Parties," *New York History* 49 (1968): 306–26.

15. "The President's Purge," *Christian Century*, July 13, 1938, p. 862; Marquis W. Childs, "They Still Hate Roosevelt," *New Republic*, September 14, 1938, p. 148; G. Jack Gravlee, "President Roosevelt and the 'Purge' of 1938," in *Oratorical Encounters: Selected Studies and Sources in Twentieth-Century Political Accusations and Apologies*, ed. Halford Ross Ryan (Westport: Greenwood Press, 1988), pp. 63–77; "Failure of the Purge Portends New Independence in Congress," *Newsweek*, September 26, 1938, p. 10; Raymond Moley, "Why the Purge Petered Out," *Newsweek*, July 25, 1938, p. 40; Rosenman, COHO, p. 158; J. B. Shannon, "Presidential Politics in the South: 1938, II," *Journal of Politics* 1 (1939): 296–97.

16. Halford R. Ryan, "Franklin Delano Roosevelt," in *American Orators of the Twentieth Century: Critical Studies and Sources*, ed. Bernard K. Duffy and Halford R. Ryan (Westport: Greenwood Press, 1987), p. 347.

17. Robert A. Divine, *The Illusion of Neutrality* (Chicago: University of Chicago Press, 1962), p. 212; "America Condemns Japan as an Aggressor," *Newsweek*, October 18, 1937, p. 10; Dorothy Borg, "Notes on Roosevelt's 'Quarantine' Speech," *Political Science Quarterly* 72 (1957): 405–33; "Quarantine," *Newsweek*, December 20, 1937, p. 11; John E. Wiltz, *From Isolationism to War, 1931–1941* (New York: Thomas Y. Crowell, 1968), pp. 62–63.

18. In addition to its support for Roosevelt's speech, the *New York Times* assayed the reactions of sixteen leading newspapers, four of which were against the speech—the *New York Herald Tribune* and the *Chicago Tribune* being the most prominent; see "The President's Address," *New York Times*, October 6, 1937, p. 24, and "Nation-Wide Press Comment on President Roosevelt's Address," *New York Times*, October 6, 1937, p. 24.

19. Letter of Norman K. Davis to President, September 18, 1937, PPF 1820, p. 1, FDRL; "Quarantine," 10/5/37, tape SRT 72–1:2, FDRL.

20. Borg, "Notes on Roosevelt's 'Quarantine' Speech," pp. 407, 423; Wayne S. Cole, *Roosevelt and the Isolationists 1932–45* (Lincoln: University of Nebraska Press, 1983), pp. 247–48; Robert Dallek, *Franklin D. Roosevelt and American Foreign Policy, 1932–45* (New York: Oxford University Press, 1979), pp. 150–52.

21. Borg, "Notes on Roosevelt's 'Quarantine' Speech," p. 417; *PPA 1937*, p. 438.

22. "The Presidency," *Time*, October 18, 1937, p. 19; Arthur Krock, "The 'Quarantine' Policy Must Await Definition," *New York Times*, October 6, 1937, p. 24; quoted in "Whom the Shoe Fits," *New York Times*, October 7, 1937, p. 26.

23. "Quarantine," *Newsweek*, p. 11; quoted in Borg, "Notes on Roosevelt's 'Quarantine' Speech," p. 429.

24. PPF 200-B, Box 82, FDRL.

25. *PPA 1939*, p. 203; "London and Paris Quickly Approve the President's Message to Dictators," *New York Times*, April 16, 1939, p. 40; "Roosevelt's Plea Hailed in Congress," *New York Times*, April 16, 1939, p. 41.

26. Robert Payne, *The Life and Death of Adolph Hitler* (New York: Praeger Publishers, 1973), p. 340; quoted in Dallek, *Franklin D. Roosevelt and American Foreign Policy, 1932–1945*, p. 187; John Toland, *Adolph Hitler*, 2 vols. (Garden City: Doubleday and Co., 1976), 2:618.

27. *PPA 1937*, pp., 463, 518, 520.

28. Dallek, *Franklin D. Roosevelt and American Foreign Policy, 1932–1945*, pp. 204–5.

29. Samuel I. Rosenman, *Working With Roosevelt* (New York: Harper and Brothers, 1952), p. 198; University of Virginia, June 10, 1940, PPF 1820, Box 1285, first draft by Archibald MacLeish, pp. 1–2, FDRL.

30. Draft 1, PPF 1820, Box 1285, pp. 2, 2–3, 4, FDRL; Robert L. Ivie, "The Metaphor of Force in Prowar Discourse: The Case of 1812," *Quarterly Journal of Speech* 68 (1982): 252.

31. Draft 1, PPF 1820, Box 1285, p. 6, FDRL.

32. See *Memoirs of Cordell Hull*, 2 vols. (New York: Macmillan Co., 1948), 1: 784–85; Draft 2 and press release, PPF 1820 Box 1285, FDRL; FDR, Address at the University of Virginia, June 10, 1940, SRT 72–1:13, FDRL.

33. "What Comes Next?" *Christian Century*, June 19, 1940, p. 790; PPF 200-B, Box 131, FDRL; for the belief that Roosevelt often gave expression to the groundswell of public opinion, see Henry Steele Commager, "Twelve Years of Roosevelt," *American Mercury* 55 (1945): 392.

34. Fireside #16, December 29, 1940, draft 3, Insert A, PPF 1820, Box 1351, FDRL. The drafts were curiously numbered: 1, 4, 5, 6, 7; I refer numerically to the progression of drafts, not their strangely assigned numbers.

35. *PPA 1940*, pp. 634–39.

36. Fireside #16, draft 3, Insert A, PPF 1820, Box 1351, p. 7, FDRL; *PPA 1940*, pp. 636–39.

37. Fireside #16, draft 4, p. 13, draft 5, p. 12, draft 3, insert, PPF 1820, Box 1351, p. 14, FDRL; *PPA 1940*, p. 640.

38. Rosenman, *Working with Roosevelt*, p. 260; Robert E. Sherwood, *Roosevelt and Hopkins: An Intimate History* (New York: Harper and Brothers, 1948), p. 226; a second draft of the speech can be found in SIR, Box 22, FDRL.

39. PPF 200-B, Box 145, FDRL; for additional reactions to this address, see chapter 3 n. 27; Hadley Cantril, ed., *Public Opinion 1935–1946* (Princeton: Princeton University Press, 1951), pp. 588, 940–43.

40. Laura Crowell, "Building the 'Four Freedoms' Speech," *Speech Monographs* 22 (1955): 266–83.

41. *PPA 1940*, pp. 663–72.

42. Dallek, *Franklin D. Roosevelt and American Foreign Policy, 1932–1945*, pp. 258–60; Cantril, ed., *Public Opinion 1935–1946*, pp. 969–75.

43. Ralph Louis Towne, Jr., "Roosevelt and the Coming of World War II: An Analysis of War Issues Treated by Franklin D. Roosevelt in Selected Speeches, October 5, 1937 to December 7, 1941" (Ph.D. diss., Michigan State University, 1961), p. 144.

44. Theodore Windt, "The Presidency and Speeches on International Crises: Repeating the Rhetorical Past," in *Essays in Presidential Rhetoric*, ed. Theodore Windt, with Beth Ingold (Dubuque: Kendall/Hunt Publishing Co., 1983), pp. 61–70.

45. *PPA 1941*, pp. 384–92.

46. For an analysis of the *Greer* episode, see Joseph P. Lash, *Roosevelt and Churchill, 1939–1941* (New York: W. W. Norton and Company, 1976), pp. 417–21, Fullbright quoted p. 421; see also Dallek, *Franklin D. Roosevelt and American Foreign Policy, 1932–1945*, p. 289.

47. Hermann G. Stelzner, " 'War Message,' December 8, 1941: An Approach to Language," *Speech Monographs* 33 (1966): 420.

48. Proposed Message to Congress, draft 1, December 7, 1941, pp. 1–3; draft 2, December 7, 1941, pp. 1–3; Message to Congress, third draft, December 8, 1941, pp. 1–4; PPF 1820, Box 1400, FDRL.

49. For Hopkins's draft, see Memorandum, December 8, 1941, pp. 1–6, PPF 1820, Box 1400, FDRL; Sherwood, *Roosevelt and Hopkins*, p. 436; Stelzner, " 'War Message,' December 8, 1941: An Approach to Language," p. 433.

50. Stelzner, " 'War Message,' December 8, 1941: An Approach to Language," pp. 432–33.

51. Windt, "The Presidency and Speeches on International Crises: Repeating the Rhetorical Past," p. 61.

52. Stelzner, " 'War Message,' December 8, 1941: An Approach to Language," p. 433; see especially third draft, p. 4, PPF 1820, Box 1400, FDRL.

53. PPF 200-B, Box 222.

54. *PPA 1941*, pp. 529, 530.

CHAPTER 8

1. David Halberstam, *The Powers That Be* (New York: Alfred A. Knopf, 1979), p. 15. For a discussion of Fosdick's rhetorical career, see Halford R. Ryan, "Harry Emerson Fosdick," in *American Orators of the Twentieth Century: Critical Studies and Sources*, ed. Bernard K. Duffy and Halford R. Ryan (Westport: Greenwood Press, 1987), pp. 145–52.

2. Reading Copy, Syracuse, New York, September 29, 1936, PPF 1820, Box 924, p. 2, FDRL; Harold P. Zelko, "Franklin D. Roosevelt's Rhythm in Rhetorical Style," *Quarterly Journal of Speech* 28 (1942): 138–41.

3. *PPA 1939*, p. 464; Fireside Radio Address, May 26, 1940, PPF 1820, Box 1283, draft 1, p. 1 and Reading Copy, p. 1, draft 2, p. 1, FDRL; *PPA 1940*, pp. 634, 635, 638; *PPA 1941*, p. 389; see also Waldo W. Braden, "The Roosevelt Wartime Fireside Chats: A Rhetorical Study of Strategy and Tactics," The Presidency and National Security Policy, *Proceedings* 5 (1984): 131–53.

4. Declaration of War, December 8, 1941, PPF 1820, Box 1400, draft 1, 2, 3, stenographic copy, FDRL; Halford Ross Ryan, "Roosevelt's Fourth Inaugural: A Study of Its Composition," *Quarterly Journal of Speech* 67 (1981): 165.

5. Robert E. Sherwood, *Roosevelt and Hopkins: An Intimate History* (New York: Harper and Brothers, 1948), pp. 874–75; Samuel I. Rosenman, *Working with Roosevelt* (New York: Harper and Brothers, 1952), pp. 527–28.

6. *PPA 1934*, p. 314; *PPA 1937*, p. 406; *PPA 1939*, 181.

7. Handwritten draft, Annual Message, January 4, 1935, PPF 1820, Box 759, pp. 1–3, FDRL.

8. Kenneth S. Davis, "FDR as a Biographer's Problem," *American Scholar* 53 (Winter 1983/84): 102. See also chapter 5 for a review of the drafts for the First Inaugural Address.

9. For a synopsis of the positions regarding speech writers of presidential rhetoric, see Lois J. Einhorn, "The Ghosts Unmasked: A Review of Literature on Speechwriting," *Communication Quarterly* 30 (1981): 41–47.

10. Samuel I. Rosenman, COHO, pp. 137–38, 138, 128, FDRL.

11. Samuel Rosenman, quoted in "A Presidential Ghost Story," *Newsweek*, January 11, 1971, pp. 22; Earnest Brandenburg, "The Preparation of Franklin D. Roosevelt's Speeches," *Quarterly Journal of Speech* 35 (1949): 214; *PPA 1936*, pp. 391–92.

12. Ernest G. Bormann, "Ghostwriting and the Rhetorical Critic," *Quarterly Journal of Speech* 46 (1960): 288.

13. "Roosevelt on the Presidency," *New York Times*, November 13, 1932, sec. 8, p. 1; *PPA 1944–45*, p. 616, see also the following photographic plate for his handwriting; for a discussion of this speech, see Thomas W. Benson, "Inaugurating Peace: Franklin D. Roosevelt's Last Speech," *Speech Monographs* 36 (1969): 138–47.

Bibliography

MANUSCRIPTS

The most important sources for the study of Franklin D. Roosevelt's presidential rhetoric are in the Franklin D. Roosevelt Library, Hyde Park, New York (FDRL). The President's Personal Files (PPF 1820) contain individual boxes of drafts and Final Reading Copy, as available, for his major speeches, addresses, and Fireside Chats. Occasionally, drafts can be located in the Papers of Samuel I. Rosenman, FDR's chief speech writer; the Papers of Adolph A. Berle; and the Papers of Harry L. Hopkins. The letters and telegrams that Americans sent the president, indexed by speech, can be found in the public reaction file (PPF 200-B).

Audio-visual materials, consisting of clips from newsreels, voice recordings, a few home movies, and an extensive photographic file that is indexed by subject matter, are useful for gauging FDR's delivery.

Some oral history projects reflect Roosevelt's rhetorical practices. The best one is The Reminiscences of Samuel I. Rosenman (1959) in the Oral History Collection of Columbia University, which summarizes the whole range of Rosenman's activities as a speech writer. The Rexford Tugwell Oral History sheds some light on Roosevelt's speech practices, in passing.

The Diaries, 1919–1956, of Homer Stillé Cummings are invaluable sources for the study of the Supreme Court fight in 1937.

SPEECH TEXTS

The Public Papers and Addresses of Franklin D. Roosevelt (*PPA*) edited by Samuel I. Rosenman (13 vol.; New York: Random House, 1938–1950) have been collected in thirteen volumes under Samuel Rosenman's editorship. The texts are more or less accurate, depending on how much FDR ad-libbed in his speeches. Rosenman included most press conferences but not all, and he often edited the ones he included. For the definitive collection of the press conferences, see *Complete Presidential Press Conferences of Franklin D. Roosevelt*, introd. by Jonathan Daniels (25 vol.; New York: De Capo Press, 1972).

THE RHETORICAL PRESIDENCY

Bailey, Harry. "Neustadt's Thesis Revisited: Toward the Two Faces of Presidential Power." *Presidential Studies Quarterly* 11 (1981): 351–57.

Ceaser, James W., Glen E. Thurow, Jeffrey Tulis, and Joseph Bessette. "The Rise of the Rhetorical Presidency." *Presidential Studies Quarterly* 11 (1981): 158–71.

Germino, Dante. *The Inaugural Addresses of American Presidents*. Lanham: University Press of America, 1984.

Neustadt, Richard E. *Presidential Power: The Politics of Leadership*. New York: John Wiley and Sons, 1960.

Smith, Craig Allen. "The Audiences of the 'Rhetorical Presidency': An Analysis of President-Constituent Interactions, 1963–81." *Presidential Studies Quarterly* 13 (1983): 613–22.

————, and Kathy B. Smith. *The President and the Public: Rhetoric and National Leadership*. Lanham: University Press of America, 1985.

Underhill, Robert. *The Truman Persuasions*. Ames: Iowa State University Press, 1981.

Windt, Theodore. *Presidential Rhetoric (1961–1980)*. 2nd ed. Dubuque: Kendall/Hunt Publishing Co., 1980.

————, with Beth Ingold. *Essays in Presidential Rhetoric*. Dubuque: Kendall/Hunt Publishing Co., 1983.

ROOSEVELT'S DELIVERY

Brandenburg, Earnest, and Waldo W. Braden. "Franklin Delano Roosevelt." In *History and Criticism of American Public Address*. Ed. Marie Kathryn Hochmuth. 3 vols. New York: Russell and Russell, 1955.

————. "Franklin D. Roosevelt's Voice and Pronunciation." *Quarterly Journal of Speech* 38 (1952): 23–30.

Compton, Gail W. "Franklin D. Roosevelt: An Annotated Bibliography of His Speaking." Ph.D. diss., University of Wisconsin, 1966.

Greer, Thomas H. *What Roosevelt Thought*. East Lansing: Michigan State University Press, 1958.

Ryan, Halford R. "Franklin Delano Roosevelt." In *American Orators of the Twentieth Century: Critical Studies and Sources*. Ed. Bernard K. Duffy and Halford R. Ryan. Westport: Greenwood Press, 1987.

Sharon, John H. "Roosevelt and Truman: The Fireside Technique." *Daily Princetonian*, March 22, 1950, p. 4.

The FDRL has an indexed photographic file for many of Roosevelt's important speeches and Fireside Chats, as well as impromptu and whistle-stop talks. It also has Roosevelt's delivery on clips from the motion-picture newsreels, as well as a few of the "home movies" that the Secret Service did not confiscate because they showed FDR walking in his braces. The Library also has an extensive collection of recordings of FDR's major addresses and Chats.

THE MEDIA: RADIO, NEWSREELS, AND PRESS CONFERENCES

Braden, Waldo W., and Earnest Brandenburg. "Roosevelt's Fireside Chats." *Speech Monographs* 22 (1955): 290–302.

Furhammar, Leif, and Folke Isaksson. *Politics and Film*. Trans. Kersti French. New York: Praeger Publishers, 1971.

Halberstam, David. *The Powers That Be*. New York: Alfred A. Knopf, 1979.

Jacobs, Lewis. *The Rise of the American Film*. New York: Harcourt, Brace, and Co., 1939.

Littell, Robert. "A Glance at the Newsreels." *The American Mercury* 30 (1933): 263–71.

McMillan, Jill, and Sandra Ragan. "The Presidential Press Conference: A Study in Escalating Institutionalization." *Presidential Studies Quarterly* 13 (1983): 231–41.

Maverick, Maury. "The Next Four Years." *New Republic*, November 25, 1936, pp. 99–102.

Molella, Arthur P. *FDR The Intimate Presidency*. Washington, D. C.: Smithsonian Institution, 1982.

Naylor, David. *American Picture Palaces*. New York: Van Nostrand Reinhold Co., 1981.

Pollard, James E. *The Presidents and the Press*. New York: Macmillan Co., 1947.

Roosevelt, Franklin D. *Complete Presidential Press Conferences of Franklin D. Roosevelt*. 25 vols. New York: De Capo Press, 1972.

Rosenman, Samuel I. The Reminiscences of Samuel I. Rosenman. Oral History Collection of Columbia University (1959).

Sharon, John H. "The Fireside Chat." *Franklin D. Roosevelt Collector* 2 (November 1949): 3–20.

Strout, Richard Lee. "The President and the Press." In *The Making of the New Deal: The Insiders Speak*, ed. Katie Loucheim. Cambridge: Harvard University Press, 1983.

Sugrue, Thomas. "The Newsreels." *Scribners'* 101 (April 1937): 9–18.

Thorp, Margaret Farrand. *America at the Movies*. New Haven: Yale University Press, 1939.

White, Graham J. *FDR and the Press*. Chicago: University of Chicago Press, 1979.

Winfield, B. H. "Franklin D. Roosevelt's Efforts to Influence the News During His First Term Press Conferences." *Presidential Studies Quarterly* 11 (1981): 189–99.

Wolfskill, George, and John A. Hudson. *All But the People: Franklin D. Roosevelt and His Critics 1933–39*. Toronto: Collier-Macmillan Canada, 1969.

Newsreel clips for FDR's addresses and Fireside Chats, indexed by title and date, are available in the FDRL.

For the portraiture of Roosevelt from his youth to death, see David Meschutt, "Portraits of Franklin Delano Roosevelt," *American Journal of Art* 18 (1986); 2–50.

THE FOUR CAMPAIGNS

"Back in the Groove," *New Republic*, October 2, 1944, p. 429.

Bender, Dr. James F. "The Two Men: A Radio Analysis." *New York Times Magazine*, September 17, 1944, pp. 11, 36.

"The 'Bottom' Man," *New York Times*, April 9, 1932, p. 14.

"The Campaign," *Time*, October 30, 1944, p. 11.

"The Campaign in Essence," *New Republic*, November 4, 1940, p. 614.

"Campaign Sidelights." *New Republic*, October 30, 1944, p. 567.

Cantril, Hadley, ed. *Public Opinion, 1935–46*. Princeton: Princeton University Press, 1951.

Cole, Wayne S. *Roosevelt and the Isolationists 1932–45*. Lincoln: University of Nebraska Press, 1983.

Dallek, Robert. *Franklin D. Roosevelt and American Foreign Policy 1932–1945*. New York: Oxford University Press, 1979.

Davis, Kenneth S. *FDR, The New Deal Years, 1933–37: A History*. New York: Random House, 1986.

———. *FDR: The New York Years 1928–1933*. New York: Random House, 1985.

"Demagogues and Plutogogues." *New Republic*, April 27, 1932, pp. 285–87.

Divine, Robert. *Foreign Policy and U. S. Presidential Elections 1940–1948*. New York: New Viewpoints, 1974.

Donahoe, Bernard F. *Private Plans and Public Dangers: The Story of FDR's Third Nomination*. Notre Dame: University of Notre Dame Press, 1965.

Ferrell, Robert H., ed. *Dear Bess: The Letters from Harry Truman to BessTruman 1910–1959*. New York: W. W. Norton, 1983.

Flynn, John T. "Other People's Money." *New Republic*, September 16, 1936, pp. 155–56.

"God Willing." *Time*, November 4, 1940, p. 12.

"I Accept." *Time*, July 6, 1936, p. 9.

Mackenzie, Compton. *Mr. Roosevelt*. New York: E. P. Dutton, 1944.

Martel, Myles. *Political Campaign Debates: Images, Strategies, and Tactics*. New York: Longman, 1983.

"Mr. Roosevelt Speaks from the Heart." *Christian Century*, July 26, 1944, p. 870.

Moscow, Warren. *Roosevelt and Willkie*. Englewood Cliffs, N. J.: Prentice-Hall, 1968.

"Non-Political Campaign." *Time*, September 9, 1940, p. 11.

"The Old Magic." *Time*, October 2, 1944, p. 21.

"President Assails 'Falsifications.' " *New York Times*, October 24, 1940, p. 15.

Rollins, Alfred B., Jr. *Roosevelt and Howe*. New York: Knopf, 1962.

"Roosevelt's Soft Answer to Smith's Wrath." *Literary Digest*, April 30, 1932, pp. 3–4.

"Roosevelt Takes Oath in Crisis." *News-Week*, March 11, 1933, p. 9.

Rosenman, Samuel I. *Working with Roosevelt*. New York: Harper and Brothers, 1952.

"Say Dewey Rivals President on Radio," *New York Times*, June 29, 1944, p. 14.

Sherwood, Robert E. *Roosevelt and Hopkins: An Intimate History*. New York: Harper and Brothers, 1948.

Smith, Craig Allen. "The Audiences of the 'Rhetorical Presidency': An Analysis of President-Constituent Interaction, 1963–81." *Presidential Studies Quarterly* 13 (1983): 613–22.

Stone, I. F. "The Press Loses the Election." *Nation*, November 16, 1940, pp. 467–68.

Villard, Oswald Garrison. "Issues and Men." *Nation*, August 29, 1936, p. 242.

"*Viva la Democracia!*" *Time*, October 21, 1940, p. 16.

"The Waikiki Conference." *Time*, August 21, 1944, p. 21.

Weir, E. T. "I am What Mr. Roosevelt Calls an Economic Royalist." *Fortune*, October 1936, pp. 118–23.

"Why F. D. R." *Nation*, October 28, 1944, p. 504.

"Why Roosevelt Won." *Nation*, November 9, 1940, p. 435.

THE FOUR INAUGURAL ADDRESSES

"Address is Praised," *New York Times*, January 22, 1937, p. 1.

Brogan, Denis W. *The Era of Franklin D. Roosevelt*. In *The Chronicles of America Series*. Ed. Allan Nevins. New York: Yale University Press, 1950.

Campbell, Karlyn Kohrs, and Kathleen Hall Jamieson. "Inaugurating the Presidency." *Presidential Studies Quarterly* 15 (1985): 394–411. Reprinted in *Form, Genre, and the Study of Political Discourse*. Ed. Herbert W. Simons and Aram A. Aghazarian. Columbia: University of South Carolina Press, 1986.

Cantril, Hadley, ed. *Public Opinion, 1935–46*. Princeton: Princeton University Press, 1951.

Chandler, Lester W. *America's Greatest Depression*. New York: Harper and Row, 1970.

"Comment of Press on Roosevelt's Inaugural Address." *New York Times*, March 5, 1933, p. 6.

Crowell, Laura. "Roosevelt the Grotonian." *Quarterly Journal of Speech* 38 (1952): 31–36.

"The Faith of Roosevelt." *Nation*, March 15, 1933, p. 278.

Farr, Finis. *FDR*. New Rochelle: Arlington House, 1972.

"For the Fourth Time." *Time*, January 29, 1945, pp. 18–19.

Freidel, Frank. *Franklin D. Roosevelt Launching the New Deal*. Boston: Little Brown, 1973.

Gunther, John. *Roosevelt in Retrospect*. New York: Harper, 1950.

Hagerty, James A. "Roosevelt Address Stirs Great Crowd." *New York Times*, March 5, 1933, p. 2.

"Hail to the Chief." *Newsweek*, January 29, 1945, p. 40.

Hassett, William D. *Off the Record with F. D. R. 1942–1945*. New Brunswick: Rutgers University Press, 1958.

Hopkins, Harry. Foreword to *Nothing to Fear*, ed. B. D. Zevin. Boston: Houghton Mifflin, 1946.

"The Inaugural Address." *Christian Century*, March 15, 1933, p. 351.

"Inaugural Strides Away from Past." *New York Times*, January 21, 1941, p. 2.

Krock, Arthur. "The Fourth Inaugural." *New York Times*, January 21, 1945, sec. 4, p. 8.

Lash, Joseph P. *Eleanor and Franklin*. New York: Norton, 1971.

"Leaders Here Praise Address as 'Strong.' " *New York Times*, March 5, 1933, p. 6.

Leuchtenburg, William E. *Franklin D. Roosevelt and the New Deal: 1932–1940*. New York: Harper and Row, 1963.

———. "The New Deal and the Analogue of War." In *Change and Continuity in*

Twentieth-Century America. Ed. John Braeman, Robert Bremmer, and Everett Walters. Columbus: Ohio State University Press, 1964.

Miller, Nathan. *FDR: An Intimate History.* Garden City: Doubleday, 1983.

Moley, Raymond. *After Seven Years.* New York: Harper, 1939.

———. *The First New Deal.* New York: Harcourt, Brace & World, 1966.

"No Retreat Here." *New York Times,* January 21, 1941, p. 1.

Patterson, James T. *Congressional Conservatism and the New Deal.* Lexington: University of Kentucky Press, 1967.

Perkins, Frances. *The Roosevelt I Knew.* New York: Viking Press, 1946.

Phillips, Cabell. *From the Crash to the Blitz: 1929–1939.* London: Macmillan, 1969.

"The President's Speech." *The Times* (London), March 6, 1933, p. 13.

Rauch, Basil. *The History of the New Deal: 1933–1938.* New York: Creative Age Press, 1944.

Richberg, Donald. *My Hero.* New York: G. P. Putnam's Sons, 1954.

Robinson, Edgar Eugene. *The Roosevelt Leadership 1933–1945.* Philadelphia: J. B. Lippincott, 1955.

Rodgers, Cleveland. *The Roosevelt Program.* New York: Putnam, 1933.

Rollins, Alfred B., Jr. *Roosevelt and Howe.* New York: Knopf, 1962.

"Roosevelt Again President of the U. S." *New York Times,* January 21, 1941, p. 3.

"Roosevelt Asks Simple Inaugural." *New York Times,* November 15, 1944, p. 18.

"Roosevelt Calls Upon America to Defend Faith in Democracy." *Newsweek,* January 27, 1941, p. 13.

"Roosevelt Takes Fourth-Term Oath." *New York Times,* January 21, 1945, p. 26.

Rosenman, Samuel I. *Working with Roosevelt.* New York: Harper and Brothers, 1952.

Ryan, Halford Ross. "Franklin Delano Roosevelt." In *American Orators of the Twentieth Century: Critical Studies and Sources.* Ed. Bernard K. Duffy and Halford R. Ryan. Westport: Greenwood Press, 1987.

———. "Roosevelt's First Inaugural: A Study of Technique." *Quarterly Journal of Speech* 65 (1979): 137–49.

———. "Roosevelt's Fourth Inaugural Address: A Study of Its Composition." *Quarterly Journal of Speech* 67 (1981): 157–66.

———. "Roosevelt's Second Inaugural Address." Paper presented at the annual meeting of the Speech Communication Association, Washington, D. C., 1983.

———. "Roosevelt's Third Inaugural Address." Paper presented at the annual meeting of the Speech Communication Association, Chicago, 1986.

"The Second Inaugural." *New York Times,* January 22, 1937, p. 22.

"Seven of 9 Justices Hear Roosevelt." *New York Times,* January 22, 1937, p. 15.

Sherwood, Robert E. *Roosevelt and Hopkins: An Intimate History.* New York: Harper and Brothers, 1948.

"Swearing in the Rain." *Time,* February 1, 1937, p. 10.

Tugwell, Rexford G. *In Search of Roosevelt.* Cambridge: Harvard University Press, 1972.

———. *Roosevelt's Revolution.* New York: Macmillan, 1977.

Tully, Grace. *F. D. R. My Boss.* New York: Charles Scribner's Sons, 1949.

Zelko, Harold P. "Franklin D. Roosevelt's Rhythm in Rhetorical Style." *Quarterly Journal of Speech* 28 (1942): 138–41.

For the drafts and final reading copies of the inaugurals, see PPF 1820, FDRL:

First Inaugural Address, Box 610

Second Inaugural Address, Box 1030

Third Inaugural Address, Box 1355
Fourth Inaugural Address, Box 1570

FDR VS. THE SUPREME COURT

"Address is Praised," *New York Times*, January 21, 1937, p. 1.

Allen, Robert S. "Hughes Checkmates the President." *Nation*, May 29, 1937, p. 610.

Alsop, Joseph. *FDR 1882–1945*. New York: Viking Press, 1982.

————, and Turner Catledge. *The 168 Days*. Garden City: Doubleday, Doran, and Co., 1938.

Baker, Leonard. *Back to Back*. New York: Macmillan, 1967.

Burns, James MacGregor. *Roosevelt: The Lion and the Fox*. New York: Harcourt, Brace, and Co., 1956.

Chandler, Lester W. *America's Greatest Depression*. New York: Harper and Row, 1970.

Cummings, Homer S. Papers (#9973). Manuscripts Department, University of Virginia Library.

Farley, James A. *Jim Farley's Story*. New York: McGraw-Hill, 1948.

Filler, Louis, ed. *The President Speaks*. New York: Capricorn Books, 1964.

Frisch, Morton J. *Franklin D. Roosevelt: The Contribution of the New Deal to American Political Thought and Practice*. Boston: Twayne Publishers, 1975.

Gunther, John. *Roosevelt in Retrospect*. New York: Harper, 1950.

Halasz, Nicholas. *Roosevelt Through Foreign Eyes*. Princeton: D. Van Nostrand, 1961.

Leuchtenburg, William E. *Franklin D. Roosevelt and the New Deal*. New York: Harper Torchbooks, 1963.

————. "Franklin D. Roosevelt's Court 'Packing' Plan." In *Essays on the New Deal*. Ed. Harold M. Hollingsworth and William F. Holmes. Austin: University of Texas Press, 1969.

Lorant, Stefan. *The Glorious Burden*. New York: Harper and Row, 1968.

Manchester, William. *The Glory and the Dream*. Boston: Little, Brown and Co., 1973.

Martel, Myles. *Political Campaign Debates: Images, Strategies, and Tactics*. New York: Longman, 1983.

Miller, Nathan. *FDR An Intimate History*. Garden City: Doubleday, 1983.

"Mr. Roosevelt's Four Years." *New York Times*, March 5, 1937, p. 20.

Moley, Raymond. *After Seven Years*. New York: Harper, 1939.

————. "Today in America." *Newsweek*, March 20, 1937, p. 5.

"Party Foes Score Roosevelt Speech; Go to the Country." *New York Times*, March 6, 1937, p. 2.

Patterson, James T. *Congressional Conservatism and the New Deal*. Lexington: University of Kentucky Press, 1967.

Phelps, Bernard Fred. "A Rhetorical Analysis of the 1937 Addresses of Franklin D. Roosevelt in Support of Court Reform." Ph.D. diss., Ohio State University, 1957.

"Press Comment on Roosevelt Court Speech." *New York Times*, March 6, 1937, p. 2.

Pritchett, C. Herman. *The American Constitution*. 2nd ed. New York: McGraw-Hill, 1968.

————. *The Roosevelt Court*. New York: Macmillan, 1948.

Pusey, Merlo J. *The Supreme Court Crisis*. New York: Macmillan, 1937.

Rauch, Basil. *The History of the New Deal: 1933–1938*. New York: Creative Age Press, 1944.

Richberg, Donald. *My Hero*. New York: G. P. Putnam's Sons, 1954.

Robinson, Edgar Eugene. *The Roosevelt Leadership 1933–45*. Philadelphia: J. B. Lippincott, 1955.

Rosenman, Samuel I. *Working with Roosevelt*. New York: Harper and Brothers, 1952.

———, and Dorothy Rosenman. *Presidential Style: Some Giants and a Pygmy in the White House*. New York: Harper and Row, 1976.

Ryan, Halford Ross. "*Kategoria* and *Apologia*: On Their Rhetorical Criticism as a Speech Set." *Quarterly Journal of Speech* 68 (1982): 254–61.

"The Second Inaugural." *New York Times*, January 21, 1937, p. 22.

"Seven of 9 Justices Hear Roosevelt." *New York Times*, January 21, 1937, p. 15.

"Swearing in the Rain." *Time*, February 1, 1937, p. 10.

"Text of Hughes Letter." *New York Times*, March 23, 1937, pp. 1, 19.

Tugwell, Rexford G. *The Democratic Roosevelt*. Garden City: Doubleday, 1957.

———. *FDR: Architect of an Era*. New York: Macmillan, 1967.

Tully, Grace. *F. D. R. My Boss*. New York: Charles Scribner's Sons, 1949.

Wecter, Dixon. *The Age of the Great Depression*. New York: Macmillan, 1948.

Wheeler, Burton K. "My Years with Roosevelt." In *As We Saw the Thirties*. Ed. Rita James Simon. Urbana: University of Illinois Press, 1967.

———, with Paul F. Healy. *Yankee from the West*. Garden City: Doubleday, 1962.

For the drafts of the Court speeches, see PPF 1820, FDRL:

Message to Judiciary, Rosenman Papers, Box 20

Victory Dinner speech, March 4, 1937, Box 1040

Fireside Chat on the Judiciary, March 9, 1937, Rosenman Papers, Box 20

THE PURGE OF 1938

"And Now Georgia," *New York Times*, September 16, 1938, p. 22.

Childs, Marquis W. "They Still Hate Roosevelt." *New Republic*, September 14, 1938, pp. 147–49.

Clapper, Raymond. "Roosevelt Tries the Primaries." *Current History* 49 (October 1938): 16–19.

"Failure of the Purge Portends New Independence in Congress," *Newsweek*, September 26, 1938, p. 10.

"George Asks Fight on 'One-Man' Rule," *New York Times*, August 16, 1938, pp. 1–2.

Gravlee, G. Jack. "President Franklin D. Roosevelt and the 'Purge.' " In *Oratorical Encounters: Selected Studies and Sources of Twentieth-Century Political Accusations and Apologies*. Ed. Halford Ross Ryan. Westport: Greenwood Press, 1988.

Hall, Alvin L. "Politics and Patronage: Virginia Senators and the Roosevelt Purge of 1938." *Virginia Magazine of History and Biography* 82 (1974): 331–50.

High, Stanley. "Party Purge." *Saturday Evening Post*, August 21, 1937, pp. 16–17, 79–82.

Krock, Arthur. "To Many Voters Washington Still Foreign." *New York Times*, September 1, 1938, p. 22.

"Mild Shocks." *Newsweek*, September 12, 1938, pp. 11–12.

Moley, Raymond. "He Did, and They Did." *Newsweek*, September 26, 1938, p. 40.

————. "Why the Purge Petered Out." *Newsweek*, July 25, 1938, p. 40.

Polenberg, Richard. "Franklin Roosevelt and the Purge of John O'Connor: The Impact of Urban Change on Political Parties." *New York History* 49 (1968): 306–26.

"The President Reports." *New Republic*, July 6, 1938, pp. 237–38.

"The President's Purge." *Christian Century*, July 13, 1938, pp. 861–62.

Roosevelt, Franklin D. *Complete Presidential Press Conferences of Franklin D. Roosevelt.* 25 vols. New York: Da Capo Press, 1972.

"Roosevelt Now Seeks to 'Pack' the Senate with 'Yes Men,' Says Atlanta Constitution." *New York Times*, August 12, 1938, p. 1.

"Roosevelt Tightening on Reins after Aides' Bungling in Iowa." *Newsweek*, June 20, 1938, pp. 7–8.

Rosenman, Samuel I. The Reminiscences of Samuel I. Rosenman. Oral History Collection of Columbia University (1959).

"Sees Purge as Step to Dictatorship." *New York Times*, August 19, 1938, pp. 1, 5.

"Senator Tydings' Appeal to the People of Maryland Against Roosevelt." *New York Times*, August 22, 1938, p. 2.

Shannon, J. B. "Presidential Politics in the South: 1938, I." *Journal of Politics* 1 (1939): 146–70.

————. "Presidential Politics in the South: 1938, II." *Journal of Politics* 1 (1939): 278–300.

Wolfskill, George, and John A. Hudson. *All But the People: Franklin D. Roosevelt and His Critics 1933–39*. Toronto: Collier-Macmillan Canada, 1969.

Zeigler, Luther Harmon, Jr. "Senator Walter George's 1938 Campaign." *Georgia Historical Quarterly* 43 (1959): 333–52.

THE WAR RHETORIC

"America Condemns Japan as an Aggressor." *Newsweek*, October 18, 1937, p. 10.

Borg, Dorothy. "Notes on Roosevelt's 'Quarantine' Speech." *Political Science Quarterly* 72 (1957): 405–33.

Burns, James MacGregor. *Roosevelt: The Lion and the Fox*. New York: Harcourt, Brace, 1956.

Cantril, Hadley, ed. *Public Opinion 1935–1946*. Princeton: Princeton University Press, 1951.

Cole, Wayne S. *Roosevelt and the Isolationists 1932–45*. Lincoln: University of Nebraska Press, 1983.

Commager, Henry Steele. "Twelve Years of Roosevelt." *American Mercury* 55 (1945): 391–401.

Crowell, Laura. "Building the 'Four Freedoms' Speech." *Speech Monographs* 22 (1955): 266–83.

Dallek, Robert. *Franklin D. Roosevelt and American Foreign Policy, 1932–1945*. New York: Oxford University Press, 1979.

Divine, Robert A. *The Illusion of Neutrality*. Chicago: University of Chicago Press, 1962.

Hull, Cordell. *Memoirs of Cordell Hull*. New York: Macmillan Co., 1948.

Ivie, Robert L. "The Metaphor of Force in Prowar Discourse: The Case of 1812." *Quarterly Journal of Speech* 68 (1982): 240–53.

Krock, Arthur. "The 'Quarantine' Policy Must Await Definition." *New York Times*, October 6, 1937, p. 24.

Lash, Joseph P. *Roosevelt and Churchill, 1939–1941*. New York: W. W. Norton and Company, 1976.

"London and Paris Quickly Approve the President's Message to Dictators." *New York Times*, April 16, 1939, p. 40.

"Nation-Wide Press Comment on President Roosevelt's Address." *New York Times*, October 6, 1937, p. 24.

Payne, Robert. *The Life and Death of Adolph Hitler*. New York: Praeger Publishers, 1973.

"The Presidency." *Time*, October 18, 1937, p. 19.

"The President's Address." *New York Times*, October 6, 1937, p. 24.

"Quarantine." *Newsweek*, December 20, 1937, p. 11.

"Roosevelt's Plea Hailed in Congress." *New York Times*, April 16, 1939, p. 41.

Rosenman, Samuel I. *Working with Roosevelt*. New York: Harper and Brothers, 1952.

Ryan, Halford R. "Franklin Delano Roosevelt." In *American Orators of the Twentieth Century: Critical Studies and Sources*. Ed. Bernard K. Duffy and Halford R. Ryan. Westport: Greenwood Press, 1987.

Sherwood, Robert E. *Roosevelt and Hopkins: An Intimate History*. New York: Harper and Brothers, 1948.

Stelzner, Hermann G. " 'War Message,' December 8, 1941: An Approach to Language." *Speech Monographs* 33 (1966): 419–37.

Toland, John. *Adolph Hitler*. Garden City: Doubleday and Co., 1976.

Towne, Ralph Louis Jr. "Roosevelt and the Coming of World War II: An Analysis of War Issues Treated by Franklin D. Roosevelt in Selected Speeches, October 5, 1937 to December 7, 1941." Ph.D. diss., Michigan State University, 1961.

"What Comes Next?" *Christian Century*, June 19, 1940, p. 790.

"Whom the Shoe Fits." *New York Times*, October 7, 1937, p. 26.

Wiltz, John E. *From Isolationism to War, 1931–1941*. New York: Thomas Y. Crowell, 1968.

Windt, Theodore. "The Presidency and Speeches on International Crises: Repeating the Rhetorical Past." In *Essays in Presidential Rhetoric*. Ed. Theodore Windt with Beth Ingold. Dubuque: Kendall/Hunt Publishing Co., 1983.

WRITING THE RHETORIC

Benson, Thomas W. "Inaugurating Peace: Franklin D. Roosevelt's Last Speech." *Speech Monographs* 36 (1969): 138–47.

Bormann, Ernest G. "Ghostwriting and the Rhetorical Critic." *Quarterly Journal of Speech* 46 (1960): 284–88.

Braden, Waldo W. "The Roosevelt Wartime Fireside Chats: A Rhetorical Study of Strategy and Tactics." The Presidency and National Security Policy, *Proceedings* 5 (1984): 131–53.

Brandenburg, Earnest. "The Preparation of Franklin D. Roosevelt's Speeches." *Quarterly Journal of Speech* 35 (1949): 214–21.

Davis, Kenneth S. "FDR as a Biographer's Problem." *American Scholar* 53 (Winter 1983/84): 100–108.

Einhorn, Lois J. "The Ghosts Unmasked: A Review of Literature on Speechwriting." *Communication Quarterly* 30 (1981): 41–47.

Halberstam, David. *The Powers That Be*. New York: Alfred A. Knopf, 1979.

"A Presidential Ghost Story." *Newsweek*, January 11, 1971, pp. 21–22.
"Roosevelt on the Presidency." *New York Times*, November 13, 1932, sec. 8, p. 1.
Rosenman, Samuel I. The Reminiscences of Samuel I. Rosenman. Oral History Collection
    of Columbia University (1959).
————. *Working with Roosevelt*. New York: Harper and Brothers, 1952.
Ryan, Halford Ross. "Roosevelt's Fourth Inaugural: A Study of Its Composition."
    Quarterly Journal of Speech 67 (1981): 157–66.
Sherwood, Robert E. *Roosevelt and Hopkins: An Intimate History*. New York: Harper
    and Brothers, 1948.
Zelko, Harold P. "Franklin D. Roosevelt's Rhythm in Rhetorical Style." *Quarterly
    Journal of Speech* 28 (1942): 138–41.

SOURCES IN PRE-PRESIDENTIAL RHETORIC

Braden, Waldo W., and Earnest Brandenburg. "The Early Speaking of Franklin D.
    Roosevelt." *Franklin D. Roosevelt Collector* 3 (1951): 3–23.
Brandenburg, Earnest, and Waldo W. Braden. "Franklin Delano Roosevelt." In *History
    and Criticism of American Public Address*. Ed. Marie Kathryn Hochmuth. 3 vols.
    New York: Russell and Russell, 1955.
Cowperthwaite, L. LeRoy. "Franklin D. Roosevelt at Harvard." *Quarterly Journal of
    Speech* 38 (1952): 37–41.
Crowell, Laura. "Roosevelt the Grotonian." *Quarterly Journal of Speech* 38 (1952):
    31–36.
Davis, Kenneth S. *FDR: The Beckoning of Destiny 1882–1928*. New York: G. P. Put-
    nam's Sons, 1971.
————. *FDR: The New York Years 1928–1933*. New York: Random House, 1985.
Freidel, Frank. *Franklin D. Roosevelt: The Apprenticeship*. Boston: Little, Brown and
    Company, 1952.
————. *Franklin D. Roosevelt: The Ordeal*. Boston: Little, Brown and Company, 1954.
————. *Franklin D. Roosevelt: The Triumph*. Boston: Little, Brown and Company,
    1956.
Gertz, Elmer. "Roosevelt and Stevenson: Their First Campaigns." *Franklin D. Roosevelt
    Collector* 5 (1953): 18–27.
Gies, Joseph. *Franklin D. Roosevelt: Portrait of a President*. Garden City: Doubleday
    and Company, 1971.
Gravlee, G. Jack. "Franklin D. Roosevelt's Speech Preparation During His First National
    Campaign." *Speech Monographs* 31 (1964): 437–60.
————. "A Rhetorical Study of Franklin Delano Roosevelt's 1920 Campaign." Ph.D.
    diss., Louisiana State University, 1963.
Hoyt, Morgan H. "Roosevelt Enters Politics." *Franklin D. Roosevelt Collector* 1 (1949):
    3–8.
Kybal, Vlastimil. "Senator Franklin D. Roosevelt, 1910–1913." *Franklin D. Roosevelt
    Collector* 3 (1951): 3–23.
Lorant, Stefan. *FDR: A Portrait Biography*. New York: Simon and Schuster, 1950.
Miller, Nathan. *FDR: An Intimate History*. Garden City: Doubleday, 1983.
Morgan, Ted. *FDR: A Biography*. New York: Simon and Schuster, 1985.
Oliver, Robert T. "The Speech That Established Roosevelt's Reputation." *Quarterly
    Journal of Speech* 21 (1945): 274–82.

Rollins, Alfred B., Jr. *Roosevelt and Howe*. New York: Alfred A. Knopf, 1962.
Rosenman, Samuel I. *Working with Roosevelt*. New York: Harper and Brothers, 1952.
Ryan, Halford R. "Franklin D. Roosevelt." In *American Orators of the Twentieth Century: Critical Studies and Sources*. Ed. Bernard K. Duffy and Halford R. Ryan. Westport: Greenwood Press, 1987.

Speech Index

(Generic addresses, such as acceptance speeches, are listed chronologically; named speeches are listed by their familiar titles; otherwise, speeches are listed by place of delivery.

Subject Index

(Addresses, Fireside Chats, and press conferences are listed in the *Speech Index*.)

ABOUT THE AUTHOR

HALFORD R. RYAN received an A. B. degree in speech from Wabash College in 1966, and an M. A. in 1968 and a Ph.D. in 1972 in speech communication from the University of Illinois. He is professor of public speaking and director of forensics at Washington and Lee University. He edited and contributed to *American Rhetoric From Roosevelt to Reagan: A Collection of Speeches and Critical Essays*, authored *Persuasive Advocacy: Cases for Argumentation and Debate*, coedited with Bernard K. Duffy, *American Orators Before 1900: Critical Studies and Sources* (Greenwood, 1987) and *American Orators of the Twentieth Century: Critical Studies and Sources* (Greenwood, 1987), and edited and contributed to *Oratorical Encounters: Selected Studies and Sources of Twentieth-Century Political Accusations and Apologies* (Greenwood, 1988). He is preparing a book on the Reverend Harry Emerson Fosdick's significant sermons and speeches.